GOLDEN
EARTH

D0369854

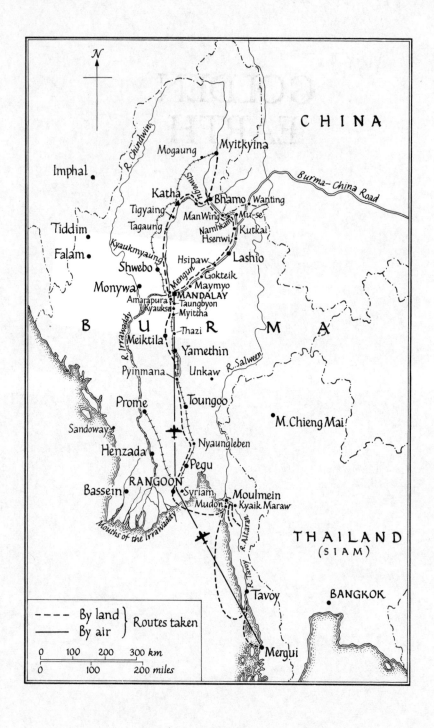

N

CHINA

Mogaung   Myitkyina

Imphal

Katha   Bhamo   Wanting

Tigyaing   ManWing   Mu-se
Tagaung   Namhkam   Kutkai
Hsenwi

Tiddim

Falam   Kyaukmyaung   Hsipaw   Lashio

Shwebo   Mengun   Gokteik
Maymyo
Monywa   MANDALAY
Amarapura   Taungbyon
Kyaukse   Myittha

B   U   Thazi   R   M   A

Meiktila

Yamethin

Pyinmana   Unkaw

Toungoo

Prome   M. Chieng Mai

Sandoway

Henzada   Nyaungleben

Pegu

Bassein   RANGOON
Syriam   Moulmein
Mudon   Kyaik Maraw

Mouths of the Irrawaddy

THAILAND
(SIAM)

Tavoy

BANGKOK

Mergui

Burma-China Road

R. Chindwin

Shweguli

R. Irrawaddy

R. Salween

R. Attaran

R. Tavoy

- - - By land ⎱
————— By air   ⎰ Routes taken

0   100   200   300 km
0   100   200 miles

GOLDEN EARTH

Travels in Burma

NORMAN LEWIS

ELAND
London
HIPPOCRENE
New York

Published by
ELAND
53 Eland Road, London SW11 5JX

First issued in this paperback edition 1983
Reprinted 1984, 1991

First published by Jonathan Cape 1952

Printed in Great Britian by
Redwood Press Limited, Melksham, Wiltshire SN12 6TR

Cover design © Patrick Frean
Map © Reginald Piggott

BIOGRAPHY

Norman Lewis was born in Essex in 1908, and since then most of his life has been spent travelling or writing. He regards his life's major achievement as the world reaction to his article, *Genocide in Brazil*, published in the Sunday Times in 1968 (reprinted in *A View of the World*).

Among his novels, *The Volcanoes Above Us*, based on personal experience in Central America, sold six million copies in Russia – enormously to his surprise, he says, as the book expressed no political point of view. *The Sicilian Specialist*, incorporating at that time undisclosed facts about the Kennedy assassination, was withdrawn from sale in some American cities following a Mafia ban.

His first major non-fiction work was *A Dragon Apparent*, an account of Indo-China, before the tragedies of the Vietnam war. This, along with *Golden Earth* and *Naples '44*, are considered three of the great post-war classics of travel. Eric Newby has described him as "one of the great travel wrriters of our time", and Graham Greene has written that he is "one of the best writers, not of any particular decade, but of our century".

Norman Lewis lives a quiet life with his wife in Essex, tending a garden of rare and beautiful plants. He still likes to travel, ideally in a remote country with an especially malignant strain of malaria.

FICTION

SAMARA

WITHIN THE LABYRINTH

A SINGLE PILGRIM

THE DAY OF THE FOX

THE VOLCANOES ABOVE US

DARKNESS VISIBLE

THE TENTH YEAR OF THE SHIP

A SMALL WAR MADE TO ORDER

FLIGHT FROM A DARK EQUATOR

EVERY MAN'S BROTHER

THE SICILIAN SPECIALIST

CUBAN PASSAGE

A SUITABLE CASE FOR CORRUPTION

MARCH OF THE LONG SHADOWS

NON FICTION

A DRAGON APPARENT

NAPLES '44

THE HONOURED SOCIETY

VOICES OF THE OLD SEA

JACKDAW CAKE

A VIEW OF THE WORLD

THE MISSIONARIES

CONTENTS

ILLUSTRATIONS

FOREWORD

IN 1949, with the creation of the People's Republic of China, that country became as remote and inaccessible as Thibet had been of old. I believed that this policy of self-isolation might spread to neighbouring countries and, having determined to see before I died something of the Far East, I went in 1950 to Indo-China, and covered a little of the area still open to travel in that fabulous country. In that year there was no slackening in the rate at which the Far Eastern lands were passing beyond the reach of the literary sightseer. Korea was scorched off the map, and if we were embroiled with China, said the observers, the flames of this conflagration might spread to Burma where Communist guerrillas were already firmly entrenched. One of two things would then happen: either the country would pass with China behind what had been called the Bamboo Curtain, or it would be defended by the West, as Korea had been defended, and with similar results. In either case the traditional Burma, with its archaic and charming way of life, would have vanished.

In a rational plan for seeing a little of the Eastern world these grave considerations seemed to me to entitle Burma to priority. Accordingly I flew there at the beginning of 1951.

GOLDEN EARTH

CHAPTER I

RANGOON

BURMA spread as a dark stain into the midnight sea. Soon the inert grey of water lifted to the horizon, but the darkness that followed it was sprinkled with points of light. There was a bleared reflection from broad waterways of the wasting moon; the blinking of lamps strung out in lines, leading web-like to the centre of some unseen city; then the banal reality of that accepted wonder of the air-traveller's world, the Shwedagon Pagoda by night. The moonlight was too weak to reveal the pagoda's golden surfaces, and as it was late most of the artificial illumination had been switched off. What remained was a deserted fair-ground at midnight — a few trivial pendants of lights which sketched in, without revealing, the august shape.

At the airport, the bleak, palely lit buildings, where lines of passengers awaited their interrogation by innumerable officials, were decorated, as if by design, by groups of tiny, silk-clad, elfin creatures — unmistakably adult, since some nursed at the breast exquisite miniatures of themselves. And while the dreary procession of sleep-walkers dragged by from official to official, from bureau to bureau, the little silken groups sat comfortably apart, faces impeccably powdered, hair garlanded, hands in lap, watching us with unblinking eyes, no evidence of relish, and only the occasional ejaculation of a stream of betel. There seemed no answer to the riddle of their presence. They were there when first we staggered into the building and still there, squatting silent and motionless in unchanged positions, when, hours later, as it seemed, the bus took us away. Of Mingaladon Airport it could at least be said that it did not suffer from the cosmopolitan insipidity natural to airports. Here one was bathed in the essence of the country while waiting to pass through the formalities.

I awoke next morning feeling dazed and queasy. There had been an earthquake in the small hours — the first of any importance, the papers said, since that of 1931 — but although half awakened I had put the sensation down to a mild heart attack, or some manifestation of over-tiredness, and immediately dropped off again. Now I was aroused once more by an unfamiliar clamour. Outside the window was a courtyard, and mynas were using it for their exercises, giving out shrill, bubbling cries, indistinguishable from the gurglings of those pipes which are filled with water and used to imitate bird-sounds. There were crows as well; fine, glossy, Asiatic specimens, not very large, but very sprightly, their shoulders splashed with a blue iridescence. They were extremely noisy in their affable crow-like way. Above their endless cawings could sometimes be heard a shrill kitten-like mew. This came from a kite perched on a wireless aerial. It was useless to hope for more sleep.

In any case, there was a knock on the door and a smart young Indian page appeared and handed me a card on which was printed, 'U Maung Lat, Ex-Head Master'. Further inquiries from the boy produced nothing better than nods and smiles, so reluctantly I dressed and went down. U Maung Lat, who was sitting in the lounge, rose to greet me. He had the manner of a savant and was dressed conserva-tively, wearing a hand-tied turban, and the frayed jacket of the impe-cunious man of letters. Smiling gently, he produced a newspaper cutting which said that among the passengers to arrive on that morn-ing's plane had been the author Lewis Morgan. The police, he said, had been able, from their records, to direct him to my hotel. It is one of the accepted humiliations of the writer that, however simple his name, no one can ever get it right. In my travels in Indo-China I had been given an identification paper describing me as Louis Norman, writer, commissioned by Jonathan Cape Ltd. of Thirty Bedford Square. By a slow process of compression and corruption I finished this journey as Monsieur Thirsty Bedford; which, as the name and description had been recopied about twenty times, I did not think unreasonable. But on the present occasion, having written out my name in full perhaps a dozen times within the past few hours, I found the distortion less pardonable.

However, U Maung Lat's smile was irresistible. 'Mr. Morgan,' he said, coming straight to the point, 'I have decided my wish to place upon your shoulders the responsibility of publishing my treatise, amounting to ninety-four thousand words, on those three things for which Burma is of all countries the most famous.' The three things, said my visitor, were snake charming, the playing of rattan football, and the destruction of the invading forces sent by a Ming Emperor of China. This, his lifetime's work he said, had been accepted, during the Japanese occupation, by the Domei Agency, but, alas, through subsequent events beyond their control, they had been unable to fulfil their contract.

Many other new arrivals in Rangoon, I have no doubt, must have met this charming eccentric, but on me this delightful piece of oriental dottiness, gleaned from my first non-official contact in Burma, had a tonic effect. Immediately the irritations of the night before vanished. I was full of hope for the future.

Rangoon, even in temporary decline, is imperial and rectilinear. It was built by a people who refused compromise with the East, and has wide, straight, shadeless streets, with much solid bank-architecture of vaguely Grecian inspiration. In the town one is constantly being taken back to Leadenhall Street; while down on the Rangoon river-front the style is that of the London Customs House. Within these edifices, there is something ecclesiastical in the gleaming of dark woods and brass. In passing over these thresholds the voice is instinctively hushed. There is much façade and presence, little pretence at comfort, and no surrender to the climate. This was the Victorian colonizer's response to the unsubstantial glories of Mandalay.

These massive columns now rise with shabby dignity from the tangle of scavenging dogs and sprawling, ragged bodies at their base. In recent years, the main thoroughfares, with such resolutely English names as Commissioner's Road, have acquired a squalid incrustation of stalls and barracks, and through these European arteries now courses pure oriental blood. Down by the port it is an Indian settlement. Over to the west the Chinese have moved in with their outdoor theatres and joss-houses. The Burmese, in their own capital city, content themselves with the suburbs. Little has been done by the new authority to check the encroaching squalor. Side lanes are piled with stinking refuse which mounts up quicker than the dogs and crows can dispose of it. The covers have been taken off most of the drains and not replaced. Half-starved Indians lie dying in the sunshine. Occasionally insurgents cut off the town's water supply. There are small annual epidemics of cholera and smallpox, and the incidence of bubonic plague is unlikely to decrease because the sewers of Rangoon swarm with rats, which it is irreligious, according to all Burmese and most Indians, to kill. Even when the rats have been caught alive in traps, to what end it is not clear, they have actually been released by the pious, who were ready to rise earlier than the rat-catchers, if spiritual merit could thereby be earned. Wherever there is a vacant space the authorities have allowed refugees to put up pestiferous shacks, which now flank in unbroken lines the country roads leading into Rangoon, the railway tracks, and the shores of the Royal Lake.

Amidst this fetor the Burmese masses live their festal and contemplative existences. Untouched by the decaying middens in which they live, they emerge into the sunshine immaculate and serene. The Burmese must be the best-dressed people in the world. There is no misery of the kind that manifests itself in rags and sores. In Buddhism there is a positive, tangible advantage — the acquisition of merit — to be obtained by works of charity. These are chalked up to the credit of the soul in subsequent existences. Unfortunately for the Indian immigrants this purchase of merit seems to apply somewhat less in the case of not-altogether-human foreigners.

It was Burma Union Day, one of the many public holidays when the Burmese are able to practise their aptitude for leisure in the many ingenious ways they have developed through the centuries. The streets of Rangoon, wallowing in sun, flashed and scintillated with strolling crowds, skirted in their best silk longyis. All places of public entertainment had been open since early morning. A cinema showing a Burmese film was advertising this by a full-scale orchestra, with

[*facing:* THE SHWEDAGON PAGODA

drums, gongs and a squealing flute, set up outside on the pavement. But the Burmese were not exacting in the matter of entertainment and the products of Filmistan – the Indian Hollywood – were being patronized with equal enthusiasm. A production called 'Ekthi-Larki' had attracted long queues. It was a comedy; the posters said in English that 'when you come out you cry, because so roaring is this film'. On the whole the Orient prefers straight drama in its films, and that as sensational and horrific as possible. Such productions are known here as *se-ta*, a Burmanization of the word stunt. I later discovered that, of twenty-two films showing in Rangoon at that moment, eighteen were *se-tas*.

The Burmese cinema was, by the way, showing a South Sea Island affair; a Polynesian epic *à la* Hollywood; but orientalized to local taste. In the advertising stills the hero, a Burmese Johnny Weis-muller, wore check shorts, a satin shirt and pearl-handled pistols. For some obscure reason he carried in one hand an *Industry Year Book and Directory* for 1934. The heroine wore a sarong, of the type Miss Dorothy Lamour has described as her contribution to culture, and a brassière. She was definitely Anglo-Burman with marked Aryan characteristics, thus strengthening my theory formed by previous observation in the Far East that standards of beauty eventually accommodate themselves to the ideals set by the real possessors of power. In other words: unless and until the balance of world power swings from West to East, urban Easterners will go on trying to look like American film actors and actresses; and, in the course of centuries, the process will probably be more or less completed by natural selection. I first formed this theory when I heard that (before recent events) Pekinese young ladies of fashion were building up a modish aquilinity of feature by having an ivory wedge inserted by plastic surgery along the bridge of the nose. A further operation was practised, according to my information, upon the upper eyelids, to abolish for the very wealthy the reproach of almond-shaped eyes.

The chief Western contribution of the moment to the entertainment of Rangoon film-goers, was 'Anna and the King of Siam', 'enshrouding all the Glamour and Mystery of the East'. Glamour and Mystery! Can

B   G.E.   17

facing: NIGHT AT THE SHWEDAGON PAGODA]

it be that only now, when for us Cathay and the Indies have been stripped of those shadowy attributes, orientals themselves are beginning to be persuaded of their existence . . . just as the natives of the Isle of Capri and Old Monterrey have accepted with enthusiasm the songs composed in their honour in Brooklyn. In the case of Anna and the King, the film had not yet started, and a tight, neck-craning circle had formed round someone who was entertaining them. A picturesque mountebank demonstrating some traditional Eastern legerdemain? Not at all. Merely a machine which for eight annas engraved your name, while you waited, on the barrel of your fountain pen.

And so with all the rest of it. What was trashiest in the only half-understood West had been found most acceptable. The Russian Bala-laika night club, where respectable Burmese business men submitted uneasily, for good form's sake, to the fondling of Chinese hostesses and listened without appreciation to Jock d'Souza's Super Hep Swingtette; the Impatient Virgins and Hard-Boiled Virgins on the bookstalls; the useless, illegally imported American cars, which it was unsafe to drive outside the town. These were no more than the greedily snatched-at symbols of prestige.

This undigested Westernism was much in evidence, too, in the national celebrations. For several hundred years orientals have kept the West under close observation, hoping ultimately to extract the secret, to uncover the mechanism behind that mysterious supremacy in such matters as accurate clocks and automatic weapons. How was it that not even the benign interest of the Heavens, as shown by the most splendid of horoscopes, could protect a man against a Western bullet? The reason clearly lay in the effectiveness of the barbarians' semi-magic rites and ceremonies; one of which, and a spectacular one, consisted of gathering in groups to practise stertorous, rhythmic breathing accompanied by the shamanistic jerking of arms and legs. Here then, in the public gardens of Bogyoke Square, was a deputation of ladies from the Karenni States, marching and counter-marching, bending and stretching, holding their breath for enormous lengths of time, before, when on the verge of asphyxiation, expelling it in geyser-like erup-tions. Having come under Burmese civilizing influence, the Karen ladies had left at home their own splendid national costumes and appeared in Burmese blouses and longyis; the limit of Westernization they could decently permit themselves.

The Chinese, stamped with the uniformity of national renaissance, had gone further and donned P.T. kit for the celebration. Lorry after lorry roared by filled with the young adherents of Mao Tse-tung, looking very purposeful in their blue outfits, and carefully graded, lorry by lorry, according to size.

Further down the street an open-air film show reproduced scenes from the previous year's rejoicings. The Prime Minister of Burma, the honourable Thakin Nu, was shown feeding a large concourse of Buddhist monks. A Burmese prime minister feeds monks on public occasions in much the same way as the heads of other states, or their representatives, inspect troops. The procedure is intended to emphasize the spiritual and renunciatory basis of Burmese civilization, and ortho-dox Burmese were as much shocked by the omission by the British Viceroy of this ancient and regal custom as by any other aspect of their loss of independence.

No effort is spared by the Burmese government to underline its devotion to non-materialistic ideals. A further scene showed the Prime Minister at the head of a solemn procession and carrying a tooth of the Buddha, which was being taken in state to a shrine in the Chin country. The tooth was probably a miraculous self-reproduction of one of the originals and duly authenticated as such by the Buddhist priesthood. Such miracles are extremely rare and thus the existing teeth continue to be valued by Buddhists beyond all price. In 1560 the Burmese king offered the modern equivalent of about a million pounds to the Portuguese for one they had looted from Ceylon, but the Portuguese turned down the offer, and destroyed the tooth as an idol.

The film show ended with secular light relief in the form of a selection of dances and ceremonies by remote tribespeople. They included an amiable drinking rite carried out by some Chins which involved the transfer, in a kind of Valentino kiss, of mouthfuls of rice-liquor from the men to the women of the tribe. The original supply of liquor was contained in beer-bottles, on which the labels had been carefully preserved. When all the participants had been warmed up by these preliminaries, they linked arms and broke into what looked like — and perhaps was — the Lambeth Walk.

Across the gardens where the well-conducted oriental revels were taking place, gleamed softly the inverted golden bell of the Sule Pagoda. The erection of this monument in the eighteenth century was a religious gesture on the part of Alaungpaya, one of the last great Burmese kings. Always an amateur of the grand manner, Alaungpaya's human sacrifices were the best that could be procured; so that at the foundation of this pious institution the victim was a Talaing prince-ling, who was buried alive with extraordinary pomp. In this way he became the spirit-guardian of Rangoon, a minor god, who is shown in effigy simpering upon a golden throne, apparently unresentful of the process by which his divinity was acquired. The spire of the Sule Pagoda is plated with gold, furnished by the devout. It is approached by four covered stairways, with a minor temple, well constructed in corrugated iron, built over each entrance. These additions have been given at various times by leading merchants of the city, who have thereby acquired great merit and probably avoided numerous re-incarnations. Some, according to the inscriptions, were Hindus, at least by origin, and may, as good business men, have considered the expense no more than a reasonable insurance risk.

The sanctity inherent in the pagoda begins at the first step leading from the street pavement up to the platform under which the sacred relics are buried. It also extends to the various shops built into the pagoda's surrounding wall, some of them — including a lottery-ticket seller's — being of a remarkably secular character. Before entering any of them, as well as before ascending the pagoda steps, the shoes must be removed. One of the shops was the publishing centre of a Buddhist mission and several short sermons in English were stuck on the window. These dealt with the technique of suppressing the lusts of the flesh. I was about to go in when I caught sight of the notice — familiar in Burma — 'no foot-wearing'. Elsewhere about the pagoda (the Burmese have an affection for manufactured participles) umbrella-ing was forbidden. As I was struggling with my shoes a young man came from the back of the shop and asked me, in an Oxford accent and with the mild, well-bred manner of the dilettante shop-keeper, what he could do for me. I told him I should like to have some of his tracts and he said, 'Why, of course,' supposing, by the way, that I must be Mr. Morgan. Admitting this, I said that it seemed odd to me that he should have guessed it and the young man replied that he knew all of the resident white population by sight, adding, with resignation, that he supposed his shop would have a curiosity value for a literary visitor. He was a well-known English Buddhist, and subsequently — Buddhist homilies being a noteworthy feature of Burmese journalism — I read and enjoyed several of his sermons in the Rangoon press.

CHAPTER II

PREPARATIONS

I WANTED to leave Rangoon as soon as possible and to travel in the interior, covering before the arrival of the wet season, at the end of April, as much of the country as I could. My ignorance of conditions in Burma was quite extraordinary. This was partly due to an efficient censorship and the fact that foreign journalists do not usually leave Rangoon. The last occasion when Burmese affairs had been strongly featured in the British press had been in 1948, when the Karen insurgents had taken Mandalay and seemed to be about to overthrow the Burmese government. Since then interest had died down, and communiqués from the country had become more and more infrequent. In July 1949, the Prime Minister had announced that peace was attainable within one year. Having heard no more I assumed that it had been attained. At all events I imagined that Burma would be as peaceful as a Friesian dairy farm by comparison with Malaya, Indonesia or Indo-China.

When in December 1950 I saw the Burmese Ambassador to Britain to ask for permission to visit the country, my lack of information was such that I actually suggested that I might be allowed to enter Burma from Manipur in the north. With visions of a leisurely progression, in the Victorian manner, from the northern frontier to Tenasserim in the extreme south, I was prepared for austerities rather than hazards. The transport would be slow and primitive; in crowded, rickety buses and antique, but incredibly picturesque, river-steamers. Food and lodging would be no more than adequate, but always interesting. There would be many delays and minor miseries, but from these a retrospective pleasure could be distilled. This was the Burmese journey for which I was prepared in the imagination and it was for this that I had built up a reserve of philosophic tolerance. His Excellency U Ohn listened with indulgence to my suggested itinerary, and then suggested that it might be better to go to Rangoon first and make my further arrangements from there. This seemed to me a great waste of time as well as bad geographical organization. However, I found the conversation deftly changed to poetry and art, from which, while lunch lasted, it was never allowed to deviate. Never was an ambassadorial decision conveyed with more diplomatic finesse.

My delusions about the possibilities and character of travel in Burma were stripped away, in regular stages, within thirty-six hours of my arrival. On the first morning I bought a newspaper and noted with slight surprise that a ferry-boat crossing the river to a suburb of Rangoon had been held up by pirates and three members of the crew killed. Mention was made of a village, some twenty miles away, where the whole population had been carried off by insurgents. Serious fighting seemed to be going on, too, in various parts of the country as there were a few extremely vague reports about government troops capturing towns. Sometimes the towns were 're-captured', which suggested a certain aggressive capacity on the part of whoever it was the troops were fighting. In this newspaper I made my first acquaintance with that familiar Anglo-Burmese verb, to dacoit. At ten o'clock on the previous night a private car had been dacoited in the outskirts of Rangoon itself.

Further doubts about the stability of the country were aroused by an account of the experiences of a Canadian friend, employed as a specialist by the Burmese government, who had just returned from a visit to Syriam. Syriam, five miles away, across the Rangoon river, was the scene of an ambitious and revolutionary governmental experiment in land reform and was obviously chosen because it was at Rangoon's back-door and therefore accessible at all times to the forces of law and order. My friend, however, had been accompanied by a formidable escort of infantry and had felt more like a Caribbean dictator than an adviser on statistical problems.

My final awakening to the true state of affairs came as a result of an interest in ornithology. A Burmese was squatting at the entrance to the Strand Hotel with a wicker cage containing half a dozen fine specimens of the Asiatic variety of the purple moorhen. They would eventually provide, he assured me, the basis of a curry. I asked where they had come from, and the man said that he had netted them in the swamps, not two miles away, across the river. The possibility of a refreshing spell of early-morning bird-watching immediately occurred to me. There would be other waders; certainly bitterns – perhaps ibises. Could he take me with him? The shake of the head was emphatic. An onlooker enlightened me. 'Across the river, they will shoot you, and no one will hesitate to consider your fate. Be sure that on sighting your near approach they will shoot at you without delaying.' It was a piece of sensationalism, a gross exaggeration, but it gave at least a hint of the sad condition of human security outside Rangoon.

Later that day I presented my letter of introduction to U Thant at the Secretariat. U Thant, the Permanent Secretary at the Ministry of Information, saw no reason why I should not go wherever I wished. Later I found that as this was his first experience of a request to travel about the country, he was not quite sure of the official procedure to be followed. However, any doubts were veiled beneath more than even the normal measure of Burmese charm. There were regular air-services to all the larger towns, he said hopefully. I replied that if I travelled by air, I should not see Burma. U Thant said that the railway service from Rangoon to Mandalay was working. It was perhaps a little inconvenient because of a break in the line. Proper arrangements were made to carry passengers across the gap in rail communications, either in lorries or bullock-carts, and if they were sometimes held up it was only to extract a kind of toll. That was to say, no violence was ever done. Where would I like to go first? Down to Mergui, I said. A coastal ship was leaving Rangoon in two days, and as such ships sailed at rather long intervals it seemed an opportunity which ought not to be missed. U Thant agreed: perhaps with relief. As long as you stayed on a ship you were out of harm's way. And now, he said, he would pass me on to U Ba San, chief of the Special Branch police, dealing with foreigners, who would handle the mere formality of issuing a travel permit.

U Ba San's cordiality, naturally enough in view of his office, was on a more limited scale. The permit for Mergui was made out, together with permission to go ashore when the ship put in at Moulmein on the way. Tavoy, he said, was quite out of the question, because the military situation there was uncertain. And at Mergui and Moulmein I must report immediately upon arrival to the District Commissioner and the Deputy Superintendent of Police. In the interests of my own safety, he said, I should not attempt to go outside the limits of either town. I then brought up the matter of my proposed visit to Mandalay and the Shan and Kachin States. To save any further call upon his time, could any permits required be issued there and then? U Ba San shook his head. The question of any further journeys could be gone into on my return from Mergui. But would such permits be forthcoming? I asked. U Ba San said he could promise nothing. I must understand that there were security problems involved. The authorities in the various districts would have to be warned of an impending visit to allow them sufficient time, of course, to facilitate my journey in every possible way.

After leaving U Ba San I visited the British Consulate where it was suggested that more might be discovered about travelling conditions in Burma by applying to one or two of the old English residents, particularly the executives of the big companies.

Following this advice I presented myself at the headquarters of the Burmah Oil Company. There was about this palatial building a mortuary stillness, in which might have echoed the lamentations of Hebrew prophets over mighty empires and enterprises doomed to decay. In this potential habitation of dragons and abode of owls I was received by an officer who told me that although he had been in Burma a number of years he had never managed to get to Mergui. He hoped to go one day, when he could find time. Meanwhile, he suggested, speaking as an ex-journalist, that if I wanted some journalistic copy — and sensational copy at that — I might try going up to Mandalay on one of the river-steamers that went there occasionally. As far as he knew, no European had done the trip since 1947. It might be a bit uncomfortable. Probably have to kip on deck and look after yourself for food. And then of course the boats were mortared and machine-gunned, but they kept too far from the shore for it to do much damage. On the whole, a pretty interesting trip, he thought. Lots of half-sunken craft all over the place, and always the chance of a hot reception when you tried to put in at a village which had changed hands since you called there last time.

In answer to my polite inquiries after the company's fortunes and prospects, I was told that so far as their Burma interests went, they couldn't be bleaker. The refineries had been destroyed in the war, and as for the pipe-line, they once went to the trouble of counting the holes in a mile length of the pipe and found over a thousand of them. Couldn't get a new pipe-line because of the steel shortage and even if they could the insurgents would knock thousands of holes through it, as, if and when installed. Nowadays all they did was to extract just as much oil as they could sell in the area round the wells themselves. It was cheaper to bring it from Abadan to Rangoon than to ship it down the river. My informant mentioned that the Burmese government now demanded a half share in the enterprise, but as they hadn't any money, the British government was being approached for a loan to finance the transaction. The cruellest cut of all, he said, was that they weren't allowed to discharge any of their thousands of surplus employees.

CHAPTER III

DRAMATIC ENTERTAINMENT

THERE was a clear day to spare before the ship left for Mergui, and having heard that at this time of the year traditional Burmese pwès were to be seen in the outer suburb of Kemmendine, I went up there next afternoon. Pwès are the dramatic entertainments inseparable from the many Burmese festivals, which to the Burmese are the most important things in life. No charge is made to watch these open- air performances. They are paid for by public subscription, or out of the generosity of some citizen who feels himself temporarily in funds and in this way acquires social prestige. The streets of Kemmendine seem to have been designed with public celebrations in mind. They are enormously wide and well shaded by trees. Usually two or more pwès, with their attendant side-shows of all kinds, are going on at a time.

I happened to arrive in Kemmendine just before the necessary religious preliminaries to the rejoicings which would begin that evening. Prominent families of the district had built pavilions along both sides of the streets; small garish pagodas, bedizened with a fair-ground decoration of gilded cardboard, spangles and mirror-glass. Here on carpets and at low tables friends would be entertained by feasting and music – chiefly from portable gramophones. The more pretentious pavilions contained potted trees laden with almond or peach blossom. At least, so it appeared until this inflorescence was submitted to close inspection, when the several thousand delicate blossoms proved to be made of paper. Such art, such ingenuity had gone into these creations that it was hard to believe that they were not, indeed, the vulgar and quite unacceptable real thing. There was another tree, too, a larger one, from which the unrefined foliage had been removed, and from the branches were suspended the gifts destined for the hundred and ten Buddhist monks who were the district's spiritual advisers. All the presents — mostly aluminium cooking utensils — were contained in white paper bags which had been supplied, without charge, I was told, by a local firm in exchange for permission to print upon them the firm's name, together with an appropriate text in somewhat smaller lettering.

At three o'clock precisely, the ceremonial march of the holy men was due to take place. For this moment — the culmination of the year's activities — the whole population was lined up, having that morning observed solemn fast. Not until their venerated guests had eaten would they break bread. Matrons, who had done their hair for the occasion in the most elaborate and matriarchal fashion, looked as if they were balancing shining cauldrons upon their heads. The faces of the young girls and children were faultless masks of white, complexion-protecting powdered bark. From each adult mouth protruded a ceremonial cheroot of enormous length, its barrel swathed in white or scarlet paper. There was a smart tattoo of gongs, a general hiss of excitement and respect, and the leader of the saintly procession came into view. A proud Burmese citizen at my elbow told me that enough had been collected in the neighbourhood to give each of the hundred and ten pongyis a present of fifty rupees. To the gong's thudding the procession continued towards the Christmas tree with its burden of cooking pots. The distribution was made, the faces of both donors and recipients frozen by the solemnity of the occasion. After that the great moment had come when the possessors of pavilions could supplicate their spiritual lords to permit them to acquire merit by partaking of the food which had been prepared. Only when the unworldly stomachs had been filled would the family be entitled to clear up what was left.

At nine o'clock in the evening the secular celebrations began. On a raised platform two clowns were giving a slapstick performance, which was funny enough — even when not a word of the dialogue could be understood. At regular intervals an actress came in and sang and danced. She was a tiny, doll-like creature with a face that was plain and even sullen in repose. But as soon as she began to dance she became transfigured. She had all the poise and fire of a Spanish flamenco dancer, plus the snake-like head and eye movements of an Indian. To this she added the Burmese speciality of thrusting out her arms in such extraordinary positions that they appeared to be dislocated at the elbows. As she leaped and cavorted she repeatedly kicked away from her prancing but invisible feet the long skirt and train of the ancient Burmese court-dress she wore — a difficult feat which has been incorporated into the formal movements of the dance. Sometimes the clowns joined in, dancing in mimicry of the actress, who, as soon as she had finished her piece, would suddenly relapse into a set pose, turn her back on the public, and squatting on her heels, make up her face or drink tea.

This performance would go on until one-thirty in the morning, when straight theatrical shows, lasting until dawn, would begin in other parts of the pwè-ground. For over four hours these clowns would pour out a stream of extempore wit and topical allusion, while the two or three actresses of the company would wriggle and leap. Only then would this typical pantomime audience have had their temporary fill of knockabout farce and be ready to face situation and plot.

The Burmese adore comedy and although the strait-laced classical plays of neighbouring countries have been introduced in the past, they are soon so completely transformed by buffoonery as to become unrecognizable. Thus the Ramayana, the play of Sanskrit origin, which runs to some sixty thousand verses and takes three days to present in an abbreviated form, could never survive in Burma. There is no action, and gesture is all-important; so much so that elaborate treatises have been written on the various gestures and their meaning. When the Burmese conquered Siam they may have felt some rankling sense of inferiority, as conquerors sometimes do, in the face of what they suspect to be the more polished culture of the defeated. Something of this kind, perhaps, led to an attempted transplantation of this elephantine divertissement. But it was quite unable to survive Burmese comic genius. Burmese parodists went eagerly to work on the Sanskrit gods and goddesses, who soon appeared as pie-slinging comedians. The ancient Burmese miracle plays suffered a similar fate, degenerating into pure farce. Actors had to be threatened with magical sanctions, in the form of death from supernaturally induced diarrhoea, to restrain them from actually introducing skits on religion into their performances.

Unlike their neighbours, the Siamese, the Javanese and the Cambodians, the Burmese have never had shadow plays. On the other hand, they have possessed since earliest times a well-developed and highly interesting puppet show. This, according to Dr. Maung Htin Aung, the authority on Burmese drama, began to decay immediately after royal patronage was lost with the dethronement of the last Burmese king. In his work upon the Burmese theatre this authority says that when in 1921 a puppet performance was given at Pegu, English officials asked to be his father's guests, for although they had been some years in Burma, they had never been able to find a puppet show. In those days there were only two companies left, and in 1936, says Dr. Maung Htin Aung, the puppet show definitely ceased to exist.

In view of these findings by an expert I must count myself as exceptionally lucky — particularly after missing by a hair's breadth in Cambodia, the year before, the last of the Cambodian ballets and shadow plays — to have stumbled quite accidentally on a full-scale puppet show of the type supposed to be extinct. The puppet show was being presented a few yards along the street from the clowns and dancers; that is to say about three miles from the centre of Rangoon.

During the day a large stage had been put up with a proper drop-curtain, and for about an hour before the show started a full-scale orchestra had set to work to attract an audience. The instruments consisted of a heavily carved and gilded circular frame containing seventeen gongs of various diameters and another housing as many drums. There was a large and very decorative, boat-shaped xylophone, several big drums and several pairs of cymbals. The air was sketched in by a player upon a hnè — the Burmese flute terminating in a horn, which produces notes of a singularly penetrative quality. With goodwill and fair perseverance one can acquire a taste for this music, the keynote of which is unabashed vivacity.

Through the wide cracks in the makeshift stage-carpentry, the puppet-masters could be seen, engaged in prayer for some time before the show began. Presumably these prayers are to the thirty-seven nats, the gods of the ancient Burmese, to whom, Dr. Maung Htin Aung says, they also make offerings of food — although I did not see this. When the curtain rose the senior puppet-master leaned over the low back-drop and sang to the audience a lengthy description of the drama to be presented. The curtain was then lowered, and when it was again raised, the stage was occupied by a puppet dressed as a peasant carrying a large sword, and a dragon of the Burmese or serpentine variety. After solo dances, followed by a vigorous combat, the dragon was defeated and, since to show the taking of life — even that of a mytho-logical monster — would have been an impropriety, the Burmese St. George mounted the dragon's back and rode away. This curtain raiser was followed by a dance by two genial-looking giants and then a series of dances by various birds, a white horse and a monkey. Each of these performers had its signature tune which was crashed out by the orchestra whenever it made its appearance. The dances were extremely funny, the puppets being handled with amazing skill. In particular there was a kind of Disney stork, an animal of grotesque benevolence which opened and shut its bill and flapped its eyelids in time to the music. Everything that was essentially stork-like had been captured in this caricature. On the other hand, human puppets, when the intention was not comic, were manipulated with such fidelity to observed human postures and movements that spectators far back in the audience could easily have had the illusion that they were watching flesh-and-blood players.

After these animal interludes the main performance began, a tradi-tional 'royal play' with the king himself, princes and princesses, the ministers and, of course, clowns. It is interesting that the semi-divine Burmese kings did not object to these stage representations of them-selves, insisting only that the court dress, manners and customs shown should be correct in every detail. On the legitimate stage royal im-personations could not be carried to the length of wearing the golden shoes — supreme symbol of kingly authority — and breaches of this ordinance were, once again, supposed to be followed by supernatural retribution in the form of a mortal attack of diarrhoea.

Oriental crowds in a festive mood are remarkably docile. Nothing seems to disturb their poise, to unsettle their capacity for relaxation. They are prepared to compose themselves at short notice, to watch with utter absorption whatever is offered in the way of entertainment. They never find it necessary to convince themselves or others, by boisterous display, that they are having a good time. Movement is slow and languorous, the crowd's internal currents intertwining with processional solemnity. Like that of some other Far Easterners, the training of the Burmese, however great their curiosity, does not permit them to stare at the extraordinary sight of a foreigner, or to betray any interest other than the discreetest of passing glances. There is no nudging, no muffled giggle, no turning of the head. No other Westerner was to be seen in this gay but decorous concourse; nor did I ever see one on the many subsequent occasions that I visited the pwès at Kemmendine. This seeming indifference was Burmese good-breeding. If I happened to be standing at the back of a crowd I could shortly expect a discreet tap on the arm and then an invitation by nods and gestures to make my way to the front. Once in a good position there would be no further overtures; but it was always possible, simply by looking puzzled, to get a description, in halting English, of what was going on. This, since the cross-talk of Burmese comedians is usually bawdy, would be bowdlerized in an attempt to befit it for Western ears. Accompanying actions sometimes made it difficult to impose this censorship. 'See, the lady and the gentleman have gone away to the wood together. Beyond the stage you shall imagine a wood . . . now they are disturbed . . . suddenly they return.' (A scream of laughter from the crowd.) 'They think this is funny behaving because the lady and the gentleman wear now, without realization, each other's skirts. These jokes are to please the country people who are not serious. For us, too, they are vulgar.'

The Burman's ready kindliness towards the stranger is remarkable, when it is remembered that through failure to spend a token period as a novice in a Buddhist monastery, the foreigner has never quite qualified as a human being. In the old days, indeed, the same auxiliary was applied to visitors from the non-Buddhist world as to pigs or

32

[*facing:* CLOWN ACTRESS AT A PWÈ

buffaloes. Referring, for instance, to two foreigners, the Burman said, 'two (animals) foreigners'. The contemporary attitude is one of secret compassion. The alien's present incarnation has fallen only just short of success. Many acts of merit in previous existences have rescued him from re-birth as a cockroach or a pariah dog, and all that is now required to attain complete humanity is that final spark of enlightenment provided by the acceptance of the noble eight-fold path. This may be accomplished in the very next existence.

The attitude of the Burmese Buddhist is, then, less exclusive and more encouraging than that of certain Christian sects, with their final damnation through lack of faith. All living things are perfectible in this muted, archaic Darwinism. Even that symbol of all the excellences, the white elephant, had probably passed in previous existences through the condition of an intestinal worm or a sewer rat, and could still return to them — as King Mindon ruled in a specific instance — through loss of accumulated merit, as a consequence of the trampling of a groom.

Clearly the Burmese recognized the virtue which had raised me from the protozoan slime. Observing my interest in the puppet show, one of the stage hands appeared and invited me back stage. There the puppet-masters took snacks with their families, or slept between acts. They had the grave, dedicated faces of a monkish order and were dressed with elaborate conservatism; turbans wrapped round the old-style bun of hair; longyis tied in front with a great, billowing prodigality of cloth. Their solemn and sacerdotal manner was in no way diminished by the horn-rimmed spectacles they wore. Puppets hung, in bunches like carrots, from the roof. Some of the more extravagantly decked-out specimens were detached and dangled for my admiration. One, stiff with gold thread and brocade, and with an acutely introspective expression, was introduced as 'the Princess of Wales'.

I was allowed to stand and watch over the shoulders of the showmen at their business, noting that effective control of the puppets was not the only consideration. Their hands could be seen by the audience, and these as well as each separate finger had to be moved with prescribed rhythm and exact gesture, like those of a Sanskrit dancer.

facing: THE LAST OF THE BURMESE PUPPET SHOWS]

As they were by far the best of the few poor examples of Burmese art I had yet seen, I wanted to buy a collection of puppets; but inquiries were met with evasion. The puppets were not to be bought anywhere. They were made specially to the order of the troupe. Where were they made? — Mandalay. (It was always the inaccessible Mandalay to which one was directed, in response to this kind of inquiry.) A few more feelers on the subject and I realized that I had been attempting to trespass in guild preserves, and that puppets were not to be had by outsiders.

When I left I was accompanied by the senior puppet-master to the most fanciful of the nearby pavilions, a pleasure-dome of glittering unsubstantiality, in which a party of upper-class Burmese sat on chairs, thus separated by distinguished discomfort from the mass of their mat-squatting countrymen. On a wicker table — an expensive and rickety European importation — in the pavilion's centre had been placed a bowlful of sinister-looking liquid, its surface broken by lumps of black jelly. Seizing a glass, the senior puppet-master expertly wiped the rim with his fingers, plunged it into the bowl, and removing a gobbet which stuck to the outside edge, handed it to me. With severe hospitality he raised his glass in my direction before putting it to his lips. There was no avoiding this rite. Holding back the black frogspawn with my teeth I drank deeply of the warm, sweetish, iron-tasting liquid.

CHAPTER IV

EXCURSION TO THE DEEP SOUTH

T H E prospect of a sea trip to Mergui by coastal steamer was something to exercise the imagination. I had memories of such rovings, vagrant and obscure of purpose, along the Arabian and Red Sea coasts. The ships had been wonderful, battered, old relics, full of nautical mannerisms and impregnated with the musk of exotic cargoes. They had been laid down in ports like Gdynia, with cabins built round the boiler-room in sensible preparation for arctic voyagings; and at the end of their lives, when long overdue for the scrap-heap, they had been picked up for a song by Arabs with sharp trading practices, renamed after one of the attributes of the Almighty, *The Righteous* or *The Upright* and relaunched upon Arabian seas. Such ships were usually skippered by empirical navigators, captains who lost themselves when out of sight of familiar coastal landmarks. They were as nearly useless as the vessels they sailed in; drank like fishes; went in for religious mania, or for spells of mild insanity in which they were liable to stalk the bridge in the nude. The passengers, too, fitted into the general picture; sword-bearing rulers of a corner of a desert, half-crazed lighthouse keepers, broken-down adventurers scraping a living in any dubious enterprise they could smell out. There was no better way to get to know the seamy side of the seafaring life.

From first impressions down by the landing stage, nothing could have looked more hopeful. The Rangoon river-shore was encrusted with deserted junks, showing a fine tangle of masts and archaic, demoded rigging, patched and variegated sails, defaced figure-heads. At the water's edge there was a desultory skirmishing of pariah dogs. A few ancient gharries were grouped for hire in the shade of the riverine trees, and as their drivers, white-bearded patriarchs, dreamed, bulbuls warbled softly in the branches above them. Somewhere a gong was being tapped intermittently, in the way that pianos are tinkled upon in

35

English suburbs on fading Sunday afternoons. There was a lassitude in the air propitious to the embarkation upon a voyage to decaying southern ports.

I looked forward to days of enforced meditation, punctuated by meals taken with some garrulous old salt, delighted to have found so appreciative an audience for his fables. It was taken for granted that with the possible exception of a missionary, I should be the only European aboard, but I expected that at the Captain's table I should meet a Chinese merchant on his way to the Mergui archipelago to negotiate for a cargo of edible birds' nests.

From the first glimpse, however, the *Menam* discouraged further indulgence in dreams. It was larger and trimmer, I thought, than the Southern Burmese coastal trade justified. At the moment of my going aboard, a certain amount of fussy re-painting was being done, but the smell of turpentine could not entirely overlay a boarding-house whiff of cooking greens. In the cabins there were notices about boat-drills, and others asking passengers to be punctual for 'tiffin'. Dinner was due to be served immediately we sailed, and to nothing less than my dismay this was heralded by one of those tinkling shipboard airs, those witless Alpine glockenspiels, that are heard on transatlantic liners as a prelude to the mealtime interruption of boredom.

On reaching the dining saloon, I made, in the absence of a steward, for the nearest table, at which, although several very obviously English people were already seated, there were a number of vacant places. Before sitting down, I asked as a matter of courtesy, if the vacant places were not reserved. To this question there was no reply although I received several embarrassed looks. I therefore left this table and went and sat down at the next, which appeared to be occupied by, what I imagined from their dress to be, Anglo-Burmese. Apparently some allocation of places had already been made — and evidently on a basis of colour and race. The *Menam* was, in fact, a little enclave of diehard Englishry. It had been years since I visited a British colony, and I had forgotten what it was like. When Burma had gained its independence it had reasonably been made illegal to attempt to exclude Burmese on racial grounds from hotels and clubs in Rangoon. In the few days I had spent there I had come to take for granted, to accept without question or thought, the mingling of English, Burmese, Anglo-Burmese, and Chinese in the hotel bars, lounges and dining-rooms. And here, in the port of Rangoon was this floating redoubt of the old system. About the *Menam* there was none of the seedy, globe-trotting fellowship I had hoped for. When the dining saloon was full I saw that the English were seated — with internal social grading carefully maintained, no doubt — at several separate tables. Another had been reserved for a group of Australian Catholic missionaries. At another the pure Burmese had been isolated; while at mine the Anglo-Burmese were gathered together. Soon the ship's wireless operator, an Anglo-Burman, joined us, being evidently excluded from the company of the white ship's officers at meal times. Shortly after I had taken my seat, a steward appeared and came over to ask me if I would like to change my place; but as the Anglo-Burmese seemed not to object to my presence, I decided to stay where I was.

At the shipping office I had inquired hopefully about the cooking, remembering that on very small ships you can sometimes eat the adventurous food cooked in the crew's galley. All the cooks, said the shipping clerk, were Chinese. But now I knew that my relief had been premature and the meaning of that whiff of greens was explained. Chinese cooks there were; but they had been compelled to adapt themselves to a new and strange culinary art — one in which specific gravity could matter more than flavour. 'Thick or clear soup, sir?' the steward murmured in my ear. After that came stewed meat with the boiled vegetables; then college pudding.

Fortunately we were too few and too divided for the traditional frolics to be arranged; but there were deck-quoits, and a library with a fair assortment of such titles as 'Lay Her Among the Lilies'. The key was found and the volumes, bright with their dust-jacket promise of rape and murder, distributed against signature in the book. Meanwhile the flat-lands of the delta slipped past in the darkness, broken only by the wallowing passage of a junk, with lamps at its mast-head, or a twinkle of illumination outlining the shape of a pagoda on the land.

I had come to be thankful for the social exclusiveness through which I found myself among the Anglo-Burmese. Hearing, with some surprise, that I was really interested in Burma, one of my fellow-diners asked if I would like to meet a Burman of some renown who was travelling in the ship, a fellow citizen of his who was returning to Moulmein after spending some time in hospital in Rangoon. This proved to be one of the most happy contacts I made in Burma.

I was presented to U Tun Win next morning, and found him seated at table, separating the flakes of his breakfast cereal as if they had been the leaves of an incunabulum. His small, frail, aged body was animated by an extraordinary alertness, and when I or anyone else produced some piece of politely empty small-talk, he would stop with upraised spoon or fork, intent and smiling dreamily as if in appreciation of good music. Whenever he put a question he would await the answer with the nervous impatience of a terrier on guard at a rabbit hole. Then he would repeat it aloud, very slowly, dissecting it clause by clause, as if subjecting it to the arguments of learned counsel, before passing with nods of approval, the verdict, 'Good — yes, very good.' He was prone to a materialistic over-simplification of human motives, which led him into a mistaken estimation of the reasons for the Anglo-Saxon passengers' habit of arriving for their meals up to an hour later than the advertised time. 'It is their habit to do this because they judge that in this way they can be served with superior food without arousing our unfavourable comment.'

U Tun Win was, indeed, a most delightful old man, an ex-barrister who possessed inexhaustible information about his country, and had also acquired the ability, rather uncommon in the Orient, to arrange his facts and conclusions in a logical, organized manner.

It was U Tun Win who went to the trouble of explaining the Land Nationalization Act to me, a radical piece of land-reform, comparable with that carried out in China by Mao Tse-tung. Under this enactment any bona-fide landless cultivator will be given ten acres of land, which is the maximum it is believed that he can work efficiently by his own labour and with one yoke of oxen. Landowners are to be compensated by receiving an amount in cash equal to twelve times the annual tax they pay on the land relinquished. This measure, said U Tun Win, was really outright confiscation, because the amount of compensation was very small and would only be paid when the government was in a position to do so — and you knew what that meant. The maximum amount of land any bona-fide cultivator could hold — and he must work it himself, or with his family — was fifty acres (as compared with three hundred acres allowed in their land reforms by the government of Pakistan).

U Tun Win hastened to say that he could not approve of this measure which he regarded as little less than robbery. In defence of his opinion he quoted certain utterances of the Buddha which he interpreted, although I could not agree with him, as condoning the accumulation of property, and the capitalist order in general. U Tun Win was a Mon (as the Talaings of old are now called) and many of his people in the Tavoy, Moulmein and Mergui districts are in revolt against the government. They would be willing to unite with the Karens in the formation of an independent Mon-Karen State, he said. It was evident from what he told me that this State, if ever it came into being, would be reactionary by comparison with the Union of Burma, and that the land nationalization measures would be abolished in Mon-Karen areas.

It is remarkable how intimate a part religion plays in the life and thought of the Burmese, when there is no attempt to canalize it into public observances restricted to one day in the week. U Tun Win attacked the Land Nationalization Act because, quite sincerely, I believe, he considered it contrary to Buddhist teaching. Thakin Nu, the Prime Minister, found it necessary to invoke precisely the same religious authority when the bill was submitted to parliament. His speech on this occasion was nothing less than a lengthy sermon, with immense quotations from the Buddhist scriptures and a searching analysis from the religious point of view of the illusion of wealth. One can imagine the consternation, the exchange of embarrassed glances, if the present Prime Minister of Great Britain took it into his head to engage in a fervent advocation of primitive Christianity, including the quotation *in extenso* of the Sermon on the Mount, during, say, the debate on the Steel Nationalization Act.

However, much as U Tun Win could not agree with the action that had been taken, he agreed that something drastic had to be done. Following in the footsteps of the English, a horde of hereditary Indian money-lenders — the Chettyars — came to Burma. With centuries of money-lending technique behind them, they found the Burmese an easy prey. Agents were sent into villages to induce Burmese farmers to accept loans. Enchanted at the prospect of being able to give parties and pay for pwès out of harvests they had yet to reap, the farmers rushed to take the money at two per cent *per month*. By 1945 sixty per cent of the petty rice lands of Southern Burma had fallen by fore-closure into the hands of the Chettyars, who had increased their capital ten times since their arrival in the country. The Indian community, as a whole, owned two-thirds of Burmese agricultural land. The interests of the Chettyars were purely financial, and as the weight of custom prevented them from leaving their traditional avocation and becoming farmers, they let the lands to the highest bidder, but without security of lease. This rack-renting brought about a steady decline in the fertility of the soil, because the tenant farmer, who could not be sure of keeping his land for more than a season, took no pains to im-prove it, and did not even trouble to keep the bunds (water-retaining dykes) in repair. Land at Moulmein, said U Tun Win, which in the time of their forefathers had yielded sixty bags of paddy per acre, was now down to a yield of twenty-five. What was worse, free and com-paratively prosperous Burmese farmers had been turned into a landless agricultural proletariat, from whose ranks the bandit and insurgent forces were readily recruited. 'Thus, if property is not given to those without property much misery is caused,' said the Buddha, in the Ċakkravatti Sermon.

Still, U Tun Win would not go so far as confiscation. What should be done, he said, was to compel landowners by law to improve their land, and only if they failed to do this should the land be resumed by the government. You would get the land all the same, he said (with the suspicion of a wink), because nothing would ever make the Chettyars work, and they would have to go. But there would be no outright injustice, no flagrant conflict with religious principle.

The morning was lustrous. We were about half a mile off shore, approaching Moulmein, and the sun gleamed on a landscape brilliant with the fresh greens of marshy vegetation. There was a narrow coastal plain, with oxen feeding in the grass down by the many creeks that intersected it. Gondola-like sampans were moored at the mouths of inlets, their double sterns painted in red, white and orange geometrical shapes. Inland four junks in line, showing only the burnt-umber triangular fins of their sails, passed shark-like along some unseen waterway. An occasional tall tree among the luminous serration of water palms by the shore was silhouetted against a soft, water-colour smear of hills. From each hill's summit protruded the white nipple of a pagoda. Butterflies came floating out to the ship; the sombrely splendid ones of the South-East Asian forests. Blown up against the deck-houses and derricks they were held there for an instant, flattened as if for exhibition, before fluttering away.

We passed a headland tipped with sand, on which egrets swarmed like white maggots. A junk reeled by in the glassy billows; a black, raffish silhouette, with delicately tapering bows, and a tiered poop with the passengers in their coloured silks crowding to the balustrade. Its great, blood-red sail was carried like a banner. Had I known it, I could have had a stylish passage down to Mergui in one of these craft, and thus have avoided the stifling bourgeois atmosphere of the *Menam*.

My favourite descriptive writer on Burma, the Reverend Mr. Malcolm, an American Baptist missionary, was much impressed with this prospect when, in 1835, he visited Moulmein. 'The scenery is rendered romantic and peculiar', he notes, 'by small mountains, arising abruptly from the level fields to the height of four, five and six hundred feet; the base scarcely exceeding the size of the summit.' The worthy man's aesthetic satisfaction is blighted, however, by another feature (which I have already mentioned) of this otherwise peerless landscape. '. . . On the summits of many of them, apparently inaccessible to human feet, Boodhist zeal has erected pagodas, whose white forms, conspicuous far and near, remind the traveller every moment that he surveys a region covered with the shadows of spiritual death. Some of the smaller hills I ascended. My heart sickened as I stood beside the dumb gods of this deluded people . . . nothing is left to prove they have been, but their decayed pagodas, misshapen gods, and unblessed graves.'

I find books by early Victorian missionaries extremely readable. These vigorous men showed an unquenchable curiosity about every aspect of the countries in which they struggled for the salvation of souls. As a result they are full of exact information about the geology, the natural history, products, commerce and customs of the people. Their pages are naturally salted with quotations from the more ferocious books of the Old Testament and they are scandalized by almost everything they see; but the main thing is that, whether they disapprove or not, they write it all down. With all their arrogant fanaticism, their stupid condemnation of all they do not understand, how much more one can learn about the country from them than from so many modern collections of impressions, with their amused tolerance, their tepid, well-mannered sympathy.

Malcolm went to Moulmein to combat polygamy, establish a native seminary, and — rather remarkably — to put into practice a plan for giving English names to the native children. Although he never ceases to insist that the people of Moulmein are 'perishing in their sins' for 'Boodhists have no idea of the remission of sins in any way. Their only hope is to balance them with merit' — he seems to have come off rather well at the hands of the benighted heathen. 'Wherever we stopped to eat, we entered a house freely and were immediately offered clean mats, and treated with the utmost hospitality . . . they sometimes expostulated with the servant, as he was cooking our meals, that he had brought rice and fowls, instead of allowing them to furnish our table. They [the missionaries] are bountifully supplied, even where their message meets only with opposition.' On the whole the reverend gentleman seems to find this display of apparent virtue in the heathen a source of irritation. It is an imposture, he decides. 'Though, in this world, hypocrites mingle with God's people, and resemble them,' he moralizes, 'the Great Shepherd instantly detects them, and, at the appointed time, will unerringly divide them.' This comforting thought expressed, the author feels entitled to call a truce to sermonizing and launches into a most exact description of brahminy cattle.

Moulmein came into sight beyond a headland; the twin Mogul towers of a mosque rising above a spinney of masts, the receding planes of corrugated iron roofs, palms brandished like feather-dusters held at many angles, the tarnished gold of pagodas on the sky-line.

As the ship approached the shore the details took recognizable shape. There were the decaying houses of vanished commercial dynasties, perhaps more noble in their decline than in their heyday. An old warehouse with a baroque, eau-de-nil façade had become a cinema. On a ribbon of sand at the water's edge a few vultures spread their wings furtively over what the sea had surrendered to them. The colours of this town were old and faded, degraded and washed out: the red of rust, the greens and greys of patinas and stains. A stench of mud and decomposing vegetation lowered itself like a blanket over the ship.

It was still early morning when we tied up alongside the wharf, and about an hour later I was just about to sit down to breakfast when an exceedingly handsome young Burman came to my table and introduced himself as U Tun Win's son. U Tun Win had mentioned vaguely that he expected me to be his guest as long as the ship stayed at Moulmein, but I had taken this no more seriously than a European invitation of the 'do look in and see us any time you happen to be round our way' variety. Since the old man had gone ashore without saying goodbye, I did not expect to see him again. I now learned from his son — who told me to call him by his familiar name of Oh-oh — that the invitation had been seriously meant indeed. In fact an intensive programme of sightseeing had been arranged in the hour U Tun Win had been ashore. Beyond the wharf-gate a canary-coloured jeep awaited us. In this, said Oh-oh, we would first see the sights of the town. At eleven o'clock we were invited to a party given by a family whose son had just entered the Buddhist novitiate. Then we would breakfast, after which he proposed an excursion into the surrounding countryside, since I should naturally want to visit the principal pagodas of the Moulmein district. The suggestion of breakfasting at about mid-day was my first introduction to the Burmese custom of taking one's first meal of the day — universally known as breakfast — at any time between dawn and three-thirty in the afternoon. Somewhat alarmed at this suggestion — although otherwise, of course, enchanted — I insisted on Oh-oh's joining me there and then at the bacon and eggs.

Moulmein was a town of strong baroque flavour. It was as if the essence of the Renaissance had finally reached it via Portugal, and after careful straining through an Indian mesh. There was a spaciousness of planning; an evidence of studied proportion about the old stone houses. Doors and windows were often flanked with heavy double columns. Much crudely stained glass was to be seen. Balconies were of wrought iron and from the eaves depended stalactites of fretted woodwork. The original roofs had been replaced by corrugated iron. It was as if an Indian architect had been responsible for this style, after spending perhaps a week in Goa. Crows alighted and perched swaying on the potted sunflowers put out on balconies. Rows of coconuts had been suspended from the eaves for the tutelary spirits' accommodation.

The Indians were here in strength and had brought with them their sacred cows, their 'medical halls', their 'select recommended gents' oriental tailors'. Business was done beneath fascia boards painted with ferocious tigers, firing howitzers and bombing planes. The cinema with the fine old façade was showing 'The Good Earth' and had distributed its advertising boards in various parts of the town. One leaned against one of the multiple trunks of a huge banyan tree, which was the home of one or more nats, for shrines were attached to it, and votive wooden horses hung from its boughs. Girls sat in a streamer-decorated shop and sewed shirts while a musician played to them on a mandoline. In the town lock-up, a little further down the street, a single prisoner balanced on one leg in a bamboo cage. At the other end of the town there had been an attempt at road repairs, but this had clearly been abandoned several years ago. Now the steamroller, which had been left where it stood, was already sunken to its axles. In a few more years it would probably have disappeared from sight, a rich find for the archaeologist of future centuries.

There was, of course, a festival going on, with booths and pavilions filling all the side streets and open spaces. Some of the citizens, anticipating the distractions of the evening, already carried hydrogen-filled balloons as they went about their business. The main street was jammed with bullock-carts and jeeps. All the latter had been vividly repainted and carried such names as 'Hep-Cat' and 'Lady for a Night'. Oh-oh's was called 'Cupid'.

Above the cheerful animation of this scene rose in majestic aloofness, the fabulous, almost unearthly, golden shape of the Old Moulmein Pagoda; so hateful to Malcolm, so nostalgically romantic to Kipling. It was all that remained without change of the magnificence of the East.

The novitiate party was held over U Sein's pawnshop. Although the Burmese are less interested in money than most other races, it is usual to announce the cost of such celebrations. In honour of their son's coming of age and his automatically entering a monastery for a short period, the U Sein family had spent five thousand rupees — say four hundred pounds. The reception would last three days, and, in the biblical manner, guests were to be brought in from the highways and byways. The U Seins had also paid for an open-air theatrical show for the three nights.

It called for a high order of organizing ability to deal with the crush of guests, but when the Burmese felt like it they could be very efficient. You went in by one door and left by another, passed in the interim through the successive stages of the U Sein hospitality. Just by the entrance, the members of the family, in gorgeous turn-out, awaited new arrivals. Only the son, the *raison d'être* of the party, was not present, for he had already, with shaven head and in yellow robes, made his token renunciation of the world. In the background lurked a pair of young ladies, as bejewelled as Eastern queens, whose office it was to collect the shoes. It was at this point that the organization was so noticeable, because in exchange for the shoes you received a numbered fan, and a slip bearing a corresponding number was put in the shoes themselves. There was a room full of them, all arranged in numerical order.

The first part of the reception took place on the first floor. Here, in a room which was as big as a small dance-hall, about two hundred guests were seated on mats on the polished floor. As each new party appeared at the top of the staircase, hostesses floated towards them and shepherded them across the room to the patches of vacant floor space. These girls had developed a kind of cinema-usherette technique, signalling to each other with their hands as usherettes do with torches. Once the party was seated other lady-helps materialized, gliding up with silver trays set with the impedimenta of betel-chewing (clearly a convention, since no one chewed), and others containing saucers heaped with such Burmese hors d'oeuvres as pickled tea-leaves, salted ginger, fried garlic, sesamum seeds, roasted peas and dried, shredded prawns. It was the accepted thing to sit round this refection for about an hour, by which time 'breakfast' would be ready.

Fortunately, orientals are not obsessed by the necessity of keeping up polite conversation. It is sufficient to contribute an occasional remark; to produce for the benefit of those sitting opposite, a smile, which, indeed, tends after a time to stiffen into the kind of grimace produced at the demand of the old-fashioned photographer. It seems, even, that the European capacity for sustained conversation is found rather wearisome in the Far East. There we sat with unexerted sociability, nibbling occasionally at the tea-leaves or prawns, speculating on the fee the principal actor would demand that evening, and admiring the furnishings of the room. One of these was a three-dimensional picture, a grotto bespangled with fragments of mirror-glass and adorned with artificial flowers in which cut-out figures knelt in adoration of the Virgin Mary. There was a coronation of King George V, charged with the flat detail and oppressive colours of such works of art, and a collection of portraits of American film-stars, about a hundred of them, all stuck side by side in a frame. In the corner a Buddhist shrine had been fixed up on a platform. It was a standard commercial product put out by a Burmese manufacturing firm, and available in several sizes — of which this was the largest — all in identical style and furnishings. In addition to concealed lighting supplied by the makers, the pawnshop had added, as befitted a successful enterprise, fluorescent tubes of alternate pink and green.

Representatives of all the races of Moulmein had come to the party; Indians, Malays and, of course, Anglo-Burmese, who wore European clothes, and with a certain difficulty forced their thoughts into an English linguistic mould. The Burmese women were resplendent as brides, with their halos of white blossoms. I wondered how many pledges the pawnshop had temporarily relinquished to decorate for an hour those much braceleted arms, those pearl-adorned throats.

Music had been provided, so a notice said, by the New Electric Photographic Studio, which evidently sold gramophones and radio sets as well. They blasted us from several loudspeakers, playing without pause or remission a resounding medley of swing and the national music of which Malcolm said, 'it is keen and shrill ... although I never heard pleasant tunes from it'.

After the customary hour had passed, our group became a little fidgety. Oh-oh leaned across to tell me, in his hesitant English, that by this time breakfast should have been ready. It seemed that the great influx of guests had strained the organization. The sign that food was prepared for us would be given by the arrival of one of the young lady helpers, who would present each of us with a flower. Soon after, in fact, she arrived; cool, correctly aloof and imperturbable, despite the heat and the enforced speeding up of her normal pace. As promised, we received our flowers; white orchids — artificial, of course, since it would have been demeaning to the house to have offered anything so ordinary as a genuine blossom.

Trooping downstairs we presented our flowers for inspection to more helpers, who, after a glance at them, led us to our table. In a matter of seconds we were served plain and fancy cake, ice-cream and sago pudding flavoured with coconut and various seeds. Following the example of the others I added these ingredients together, stirred them up and swallowed the result with a spoon. Eating took perhaps ten minutes. After that it was in order to leave. We passed out, after showing our fans and collecting our shoes, by the exit door. On one side a maiden waited holding out foot-long cheroots. On the other stood a large tub filled with paper bags containing gifts for each departing guest. Mine was an aluminium basin.

What was left of the morning was spent in routine visits to Oh-oh's relations and friends. Such calls involved no tiresome exchange of platitudes. You just sat down, explained what you were doing there, smiled a little, waited a little. Unexplained persons drifted in from the street, or appeared from inner rooms, looked at you and went away. Usually a bottle of branded mineral water — occasionally from a precious reserve of Coca-Cola — was produced in your honour. These were the unceremonial visitings of honest country people the world over.

At the very hottest time of the early afternoon, when for a moment I thought regretfully of the naps the sahibs on the *Menam* would just be about to take under the electric fans in their cabins, I learned that we were going for a drive outside the town. Seven of us — the oriental minimum of passengers — squeezed into the jeep, and we were off to visit a pagoda at a village called Mudon, a Sunday afternoon jaunt which seemed to be an institution. It now occurred to me to mention that a member of the Special Branch of the Burmese Police who had visited the ship had emphasized that on no account should I leave the town, and that to attempt to do so was to risk kidnapping or assassination. Oh-oh, replying with his calm Burmese smile said there was no danger. We would all go to Mudon. And how far away was Mudon? Eighteen miles, Oh-oh said. Slightly alarmed by now, as I had imagined that this village was an outer suburb of Moulmein, I asked again, were there any Karen rebels in the neighbourhood? Oh-oh said there were. And did they ambush cars? He shook his head. Attack them? . . . An emphatic nod. So that was it. He had not understood. The word ambush had been too much. And there the difficulty lay in our communication with each other. So much of what was not understood was passed over with a smile and a nod. It was better to say yes, and let it go at that, than to admit that one hadn't understood the question.

All our party spoke English, and one, a garlanded Burmese lady with the name of Amelia Williams, actually taught it. But it was a special brand of English, based on the Old Testament and the Sankey and Moody of the Baptist missions. Those whose knowledge of the language had been gained in this way had a queer, archaic flavour about their speech. One took food, rather than ate; strove to attain rather than tried to get. People were stricken with divers sicknesses rather than became ill; from which they did not die, but succumbed, or rendered up the spirit. Into this sonorous idiom many raucous notes had been introduced, the jargon from technical books, American cinema-slang. Thus, removed from its fresh, native sources, English, still the lingua-franca of much of Southern Asia, was degenerating into a kind of Creole. Already, in such a simple matter as inquiring about the situation outside Moulmein, I could not quite make myself understood. There seemed to be no way of finding out just what risks were involved. Oh-oh, smiling continually, said that it was dangerous, and yet somehow not dangerous. People got shot sometimes; but this fate, mysteriously, could not happen to us. There was a tight ring of insurgents round Moulmein, but in some unexplained way we could pass unscathed through this cordon and reach Mudon.

Our road was through country which had once been jungle and would soon be jungle again. The paddy-fields had been deserted and were grown over with scrub-bush. Where villages, now vanished, had once existed, a few thinning garden flowers grew, and bougain-villaea raced like purple lightning through the thickets. A few hamlets remained, with shacks made of great, dried leaves stuck over frames. Girls were strolling about wearing parakeet-crests of flowers, and in this part of Burma — I never saw them again — the bullock-carts were decorated with carvings as intricate as the figure-heads on old Maori war-canoes. I tried to buy some carving and Oh-oh, who went off to make inquiries, returned with a small ivory medallion produced for the tourist trade in Mergui. There were a few of the hills which Malcolm had admired so much, geological curiosities with precipitous sides, and virgin jungle growing on the top.

At the end of our pilgrimage we found a lake, pleasantly surrounded by sparsely wooded hillocks. Here our party got down from the jeep, immediately, by way of a holiday convention, donning tinted spectacles. A few more picnicking jeeps were parked on what had been agreed upon as a beauty spot. Soldiers of the Union of Burma army strolled about with rifles slung and parasols opened. The crew of an armoured car were asleep in the shade of their vehicle and were not roused by a distant exchange of shots. The pagoda was built entirely of corrugated iron, but seen across the water the composition of striated greys and silvers was not out of harmony with its surroundings.

After dutifully viewing the pagoda of Mudon we now set off again at full speed, with the intention, it seemed, of pushing as far eastwards as we could without running into a battle. The limit was reached at the village of Kyaik Maraw, on the Altaran river, which had been the scene of a sharp fight a few days previously. From the sight of serene groups of Burmese girls in the streets it was hard to imagine that this was an outpost, with Mon-Karen insurgents on the other bank of the river. While we stood on the bank and looked across the stream to where, half a mile away, a pair of insurgent soldiers were doing something to a sampan, a fisherman came past, paddling his canoe after his net which was floating downstream at a fair speed. Sticks protruded from various points in the net, and just as it passed us one of the sticks dipped, in indication that a fish had been caught. At a cry from Oh-oh, the fisherman shot over to this place, extracted the catch, paddled back to us, and handed it to Oh-oh, in exchange for a few small coins. Then he was off again like a streak, paddling furiously to overtake his fast-disappearing net. The fish, a fine, large, regularly shaped specimen, was laid tenderly in the shade, and eyes were averted while it leaped and quivered in mortal convulsion. Fishermen, as takers of life, are much despised by the orthodox Burmese who, occasionally, as part of a celebration, or in a moment of religious fervour, buy the contents of a net and throw them back into the river. The fishermen have always claimed in self-defence that they do not kill the fish or even damage them by the use of a hook. All they do is to put them out on the bank to dry after their long soaking in the water. If in this process they should happen to die, there can be no harm in eating them.

It proved that the bond which, with the exception of Mrs. Williams, united my friends, was a common membership, or ex-membership of the local boy-scouts' troop, of which Oh-oh was scout-master. Back in Moulmein, we visited each home in turn, to view the trophies accorded for scout-lore, and groups photographed at annual jamborees.

Easterners have an ostrich digestion for all that promises, however obscurely, to benefit their souls. Any association with a profession of ideals is eagerly embraced. Whether gained as scouts, rotarians, masons, rosicrucians or Oxford groupers, a contribution of virtue is eagerly accepted and added to the jackdaw store. When my friends spoke of camping they did so with reverence. It ranked as a kind of yoga exercise helping to quicken one's step on the road to salvation.

They had all been to the Baptist school, where, in pursuance of the policy instituted in Malcolm's time they had been given such names as John, Michael or Peter, which the missionaries had believed would help them in their struggle with the devil. These names had been taken, and in most cases added to those already possessed. Sometimes a surprising amalgam resulted. Amongst the members of the Moulmein scout troop were a Sunny Jim Than Myint, an Abraham Ba Nyunt Dashwood, and an Edwin Saung Chin Stephen Min. Not all of these had become Baptists, but many of those who had, had then gone one step further and, without racial justification described themselves as Anglo-Burmese.

At five o'clock I dined with U Tun Win. Dinner was on the enormous balcony of his wooden house, and the old man asked if I had any objection to his sitting cross-legged on the seat of his chair, as he could never really relax in any other position. While we toyed with the usual Burmese hors d'oeuvres, a servant swarmed up a palm in the garden and hacked off coconuts to be used in the curry. Among the dishes served was some dried fish, which attracted a handsome Siamese cat. Springing on the table, where its presence was tolerated, it waited until its master's head was turned, and then seized the tail. This, it seemed, was a morsel of exceptional succulence, which U Tun Win was not prepared to give up, and, recovering it after a short struggle, he ate it hastily.

Although U Tun Win claimed that Burmese women enjoyed absolute equality with men, and quoted long extracts from the ancient Laws of Manu, in support of this contention, none of his several daughters was to be seen. According to custom they would eat in one of the inner rooms, after their father had finished his meal. The mother had been dead some years and the old man said that he relished his new freedom too keenly to contemplate re-marriage. From his account the Burmese were exceedingly liberal in matrimonial matters — though slightly less so down in the conservative South. Marriage is considered to exist, without further ceremony, when a couple are seen to eat together; although there is nothing particularly compromising about people of different sexes sleeping in the same room. Divorce takes place by mutual consent, without going to court; and if a man enters a monastery, his wife can remarry at the end of seven days. Wives and husbands retain their separate property, but infinite legal complications are introduced in divorce cases, over the matter of the children's maintenance. A Christian cannot marry a Buddhist in the informal manner which is customary when both parties are Buddhists. In this case a legal ceremony is required; and if a foreigner shows preference for the custom of the country by simply living with a Burmese woman, she has the right to go before the court and demand that he be legally declared her husband.

Many Westerners, despite the evidence of the Old Testament, cling to a smug belief that romantic love is a Western invention, dating vaguely from the era of chivalry. With this goes the equally fallacious opinion that Easterners are coolly matter-of-fact in their relations between the sexes. This view is reflected in the novelist's stock portrait of the white-man-in-exile's dusky mistress; an acquiescent shadow, who comes to life only if thrown aside, when, sinister and vindictive, she is ready with the wasting poison. This matter-of-factness does not exist. Although much sexual freedom before marriage is the rule in most Eastern races, courtship is often very prolonged and subjected to all kinds of self-imposed restrictions. In many parts eliminative contests are arranged between suitors, and there is much serenading and creation of simple poetry. An old-style Moulmein courtship took about three years, said U Tun Win, to develop through all its stages. He did not, however, mention a curious custom of the district—a Mon one — which was described to me later by a European who had married a local girl — although he denied having taken part in this ceremony himself.

All the Mon houses are built on piles, with floors about four feet above ground. On the floor of a certain room of each house there is a small hole, through which a hand can pass. About dusk each day, the admirers of a girl of marriageable age will start to collect near her residence, and as soon as it is dark, each youth will, in the order of his arrival, take his turn to go under the house and pass his hand up through the hole in the floor. The girl sits on the floor near the hole, and as the hand appears, she holds it in one of hers. Etiquette demands that she must clasp each hand, but as soon as she releases it the admirer must depart, allowing the next man in turn to take his place. Although the girl cannot see the man, and neither is allowed to speak, she is supposed to be able to recognize the various hands, and shows her favour by holding one hand longer than the rest.

In view of the extraordinary freedom existing in matrimonial affairs, it is remarkable that the law should interfere more in matters relating to property than it does in the West. The Burmese Buddhist has no testamentary powers. Upon his death his property is divided among his family in proportions laid down by the ancient Indian legal code which the country adopted in remote times. When I asked what happened if there were families by more than one wife, U Tun Win said that every contingency was provided for, but that the law was so complex on such points that an exposition of it would occupy what remained of the evening.

Although U Tun Win kindly invited me to spend the night in his house, there was some doubt about the time the ship would be sailing next morning so, rather than be stranded in Moulmein for a week, I felt it safer to return. On the way to the quay I passed the procession with which the pwè would be inaugurated. First came one of the glittering manufactured Buddhist shrines, carried on a pedicab. It was lit by festoons of coloured electric bulbs, supplied from an accumulator carried on another pedicab just behind. After that came an ex-American army G.M.T. truck which had been painted — tyres included — bright scarlet, and on which a harp had been mounted. The music plucked from the strings of this was broadcast through an amplifying system, so that every corner of Moulmein, the cabins of the *Menam* included, was penetrated by a powerful twanging.

We were later than had been expected in finishing the loading of our cargo of rubber next day. In the morning the Karen Bishop of Tennasserim came aboard and preached a sermon on moral re-armament, devoutly listened to by the Burmese and Anglo-Burmese, whether Christian or not. Meanwhile the radio had been left on, tuned into London, though the reception was weak and distorted. Sometimes it faded out altogether and the crisp voice of the overseas announcer was replaced by the wavering semitones of a vina played by someone in Colombo. The English, none of whom seemed to have bothered to go ashore, sat relaxed before their beers in comfortable boredom. One was making a rug.

We had been joined by a party of young Anglo-Burmese women who had convinced their doctors that they were in need of a bracing sea voyage; and now, released from the pressure of the suburban English life they had inherited along with their names, they exploded in an effervescence of girlish high-spirits. Led by a Mrs. Forbes-Russell, a strapping sixth-former in a longyi, they romped about, discharging gushes of long-stored emotion on appropriate objects: awe at the vision of the engine-room, consternation at the notices relating to alarm signals given in emergency, delight at the huge fans, set in frantic motion at the pressing of a button. Like many provincial travellers they had been afraid of starving on the voyage and had brought with them pots filled with delicious messes of kyaw-swe — vermicelli fried in the Burmese style. Soon platefuls were being distributed to passengers in the first-class saloon — offered even, to their obvious embarrassment, to the sahibs. Fortunately, further excesses of attempted fraternization were prevented by the ship's anchors being raised, when, despite the sea's being as flat as the surface of a frozen lake, the newcomers, snatching up their bottles of eau-de-cologne, retired to be ill. At tea-time they appeared again, only to be shaken by the sight of honey on the table. In Burma this is used principally to preserve the corpses of holy men for the decent period of a year or so which must elapse before they are cremated, and even when offered for consumption is suspected of having been put to this use.

All along the river from Moulmein the banks were covered with rich, velvety turf, with clumps of water-palms kindled by the sun into glowing green fire. As soon as we reached the sea, jungle closed in over the land, tumbling down the low cliff-sides to within a few feet of the water. There were a few small islands, carrying helmets of vegetation, pierced with caves and slashed with white sand where their bases entered the sea. White cranes flew majestically in the tree-tops, and swifts came out to meet us, ringed the ship and flew back. Pagodas had been placed like follies or Hohenstaufen castles, on the sheerest, the most inaccessible spurs.

Further south the coast receded; we passed range after range of pale mountains, seen as a reflection in dark water. Here we saw shoals of flying fish and occasionally a slim, streamlined shape broke surface and skimmed away from us, propelling itself forward in a leap of twenty yards or so by violent oscillations of the tail whenever it touched the water. Finally, in the late afternoon we anchored in the Tavoy river, about twenty miles from the town. It was reported that conditions were so bad there that it was not safe to take the ship in. Lighters were waiting for passengers and cargo, and after an hour we steamed on.

That night I found I had a cabin companion; a Burmese official who had joined the ship at Moulmein. He carried a suit-case filled entirely with copies of *Tit-Bits* and *Reader's Digest*, which he read, lying in his bunk, late into the night. Reading maketh a full man, and I have no doubt that he was full of the concentrated information purveyed by his favourite journals. He was content however to remain as he was, without adding the attributes of the conversationalist to those of the reader. During the rest of the voyage, although he smiled when our eyes met, he never spoke. He possessed the knack of manipulating his knife and fork with great efficiency, although he held them as if they had been a chopstick held in each hand. It was evident that he was a man of some consequence, because next day, at Mergui, there was a deputation of notables to meet him. Before going ashore he dressed himself carefully in a flowered shirt and Tyrolean *lederhosen*.

CHAPTER V

MERGUI

WHEN I came up on deck, soon after dawn, we were a few miles short of Mergui and the ship was full of the heavy perfume of the liliaceous flowers of which floral tributes are so often composed. This fragrance of the embalming parlour reached us from jungles which were still a mile or two away. All round the ship were wonderfully complicated fish-traps; elaborate marine corrals fashioned from plaited osiers, with arched openings to permit the entrance of small junks, and narrow footways built all round them to facilitate inspection. Attached to them were rafts with sleeping quarters and the Burmese equivalent of 'mod. con.' Once these floating mazes had been constructed — and no doubt they were capitalist enterprises — there was nothing more to be done than keep up fish-collecting patrols.

Mergui emerged from behind a foreshore of shining slime, from which the ribs of ancient wrecks protruded. A few grey, Dutch-shaped roofs thrust up through the mud, with a strip of mist lying along them. There was a gilded pagoda, with causeways up its artificial mound, making it look like a Mayan truncated pyramid. King Island broke off from the mainland, and slipped past on our right, with landslides of swarthy earth showing through the webbing of green. The trees growing on it were so tall that their doubtlessly stout trunks were like long spindly wireless masts. We passed, in midstream, an antique oil tanker, completely coated with rust, called *The Golden Dragon*.

If you had been set on retirement from the world in the traditional South Seas manner of the 'nineties, you need have gone no further than Mergui. Or at least, so it seemed at first sight. It was immediately clear that this place had been purged of the vulgar agitations common to most ports. The jetty had fallen into the harbour and no one had bothered to recover it. Ships anchored a hundred yards off shore, and sampans — when there were any about — unloaded passengers. They were dumped on a sloping wasteland of slime-covered boulders, up which they scrambled and slithered to reach the quay-side. Semi-wrecks lay about the harbour with vitals bursting through their rotting planks. The wharves — mostly empty — were pleasantly styled go-downs. A civil-supplies building — a place of most eerie dilapidation — had convolvulus and flowering bean plants crawling over its façade, and through the paneless upper windows you could see bats hanging from the rafters. On the quay-side a large iron tank bore the notice 'to drink', and a honey and white fishing eagle balanced on its edge, peering wistfully into the inner depths. The junks anchored along the front had small platforms built into their sterns where their guardian spirits could conveniently perch. Well-dressed young men came up and said 'Where are you going?' then walked on, without awaiting an answer.

What, too, could have been more romantic than the traditional pro-ducts of this island — esculent birds' nests and pearls? True there was also a bit of rubber and some tin; but not enough of either to bring about any rise in the commercial temperature of the place. But, alas, one outstanding characteristic of Mergui eclipsed all others, and would certainly have broken the resolve of the most tenacious escapist. This was the smell. In Eastern travels one becomes so familiar with the smell of open drains that in the end it loses its power to offend. A selective mechanism comes into action. One can sniff appreciatively at the fragrances of drying tobacco leaves, aromatic resins and incenses while ignoring that of excrement. In Mergui such a discrimination was not possible. The whole of an otherwise charming promenade down by the sea befouled with a carpet of fish, spread out to decay sufficiently to be regarded as edible in the form of gnapi. 'Most malodorous', as the old Portuguese Father put it, with understatement. 'The common people use a variety . . . which neither dogs nor cats will touch. This obviates the necessity of putting a watch over it. This class stinks so badly that people unaccustomed to such a bad smell have to hold their noses when they pass the place where it lies.' Father Manrique's observation was exact. The packs of ill-starred pariahs

which infest Mergui's streets, hunting continually for the wherewithal
to keep life in their hideous bodies, salute the gnapi beds continually in
the usual canine way, but make no attempt to eat it.

Mergui's dog population might prove a further deterrent to the
would-be South Seas recluse. There are more dogs than humans; they
are a slinking, evil breed, cursed with every conceivable affliction.
Their suppurating wounds, their goitres, their tumours are hideously
evident on their hairless bodies. Bitches suffering from some ghastly
elephantiasis go trailing morbidly swollen paps in the dust. Many
were earless, partially blind and had paralysed or dislocated limbs.
There had been couplings with horrid pathological results it was
impossible not to see. One dog's hindquarters were completely out
of action. It could only drag itself along by its front legs and whenever
it stopped, being unable to sit down, it turned round several times and
then collapsed. When the final twilight of decrepitude is reached, a
ring of dogs forms and closing in upon the snapping, snarling victim,
they devour it. In Upper Burma the only service the Japanese did the
people was to eat most of the pariah dogs; which the Burmese will in
no circumstances bring himself to kill. Perhaps even the Japanese
stomach was turned by the dogs of Mergui.

The main street was Moulmein all over again. English had retained
its prestige as the advertising medium. The Oriental Gents Smartman
Tailors were there. You could buy an Ideal Leisure-time hat, or
observe a cobbler at work under a tiger-flanked 'Shoe to repair
invisible'. The pharmaceutical trade was shared by Messrs. May and
Baker, and Maclean, and the anonymous house responsible for that
familiar Burmese specific composed of newly-hatched crocodiles in a
black unguent. Misguided effort had gone into the manufacture of
quaint miniatures, bullock-carts and peacocks, from the mother-of-
pearl obtained from the giant conches which litter local beaches.

There was one product of Mergui, famous in the old days, which I
could not locate. 'There is a village called Mirgim,' said Caesar
Fredericke, 'in whose harbour every yeere there lade some ships with
Verzina . . . which is an excellent wine . . . whose liquor they distill,

and so make an excellent drinke cleare as christall, good to the mouth, and better to the stomake, and it hath an excellent gentle virtue, that if one were rotten with the french pockes, drinking good store of this, he shall be whole againe, and I have seene it proved, because that when I was in Cochin, there was a friend of mine, whose nose beganne to drop away with that disease, and he was counselled of the doctors of phisicke, that he should go to Tanasary at the time of the new wines, and that he should drinke of the nyper wine, night and day . . . This man went thither, and did so, and I have seene him after with good colour and sound.'

In those days Mergui was a port of Siam, as it was a hundred years later when it was the scene of the activities of the English pirate Samuel White, who got himself appointed harbour-master by the Siamese government. White was a latter-day De Brito, but a man of lesser calibre since whilst De Brito set out to turn Lower Burma into a Portuguese possession, all White hoped to do was to fill his pockets as quickly as possible and get back to England. The difference between common piracy and empire-building is a matter of scale and success. If White could have held on to Mergui and facilitated its ultimate annexation to the British crown he would have been an empire-builder but, as it was, his enterprise failed; although, by robbing all who fell into his clutches he put by enough to enable himself to set up as a squire when he finally reached home.

The massacre by the Siamese that put an end to White's dictatorship at Mergui resulted in the declaration of war upon Siam by the East India Company. This was a period when the interests of a commercial faction could be openly identified with those of the nation, and a declaration of war upon a friendly foreign power need be no more than a matter of resolution taken at a board meeting of directors. Fortunately for both nations, the company had another war on its hands at the time — with Aurungzeb — and could not spare men or ships to avenge the White debacle. The thing was allowed to fizzle out.

As the *Menam* would be continuing its voyage from Mergui down to Penang and Singapore, I had arranged to fly back from Mergui. In Rangoon the importance had been stressed of organizing the return trip so as to avoid staying a night in Mergui. Outside Rangoon, hotels as Europeans understand them do not exist. Before the war, most towns had 'Dak' bungalows, or Circuit Houses for the accommodation of officials on tour. Although equipped with monastic simplicity, they were kept clean by a caretaker, and the traveller's servant could cook him the kind of food he was used to. In this way the white man was able to maintain himself in hygienic isolation. Now, for one reason or another, the bungalows were not available; they had been bombed, had fallen derelict, or had been taken over by the military, or they were located outside the town in situations once desirable, but now undefended from dacoits.

At all events there were no lodgings to be had in Mergui, apart from Chinese doss-houses, at the thought of which even the Burmese shook their heads. In case an unexpected breakdown in arrangements compelled me to spend a night or more in Mergui, I was recommended to present myself at a Buddhist monastery, where I could always be sure of a well-swept corner, a clean mat, and a simple meal.

There was a club-room atmosphere in the office of the airline which was reached by a rickety outside staircase, at the top of which a man lay in a hammock picking at the strings of a guitar. A highly efficient-looking radio set occupied most of one side of the room. It looked like ex-army equipment and although it had probably been installed for some technical reason, passers-by dropped in frequently to twiddle the many dials, producing, with cries of admiration, a vociferous cross-section of the radio programmes of Eastern Asia. A beautiful woman with golden safety-pins in her ears stood thumbing the pages of a Burmese ladies' journal dealing with romance, fashions and the home, and called (in Burmese) *The Bloodsucker*. A further attraction was a fine, large tank of tropical fish, fitted with devices for maintaining an even temperature and aerating the water. An official, seeing my interest in this came over and described the various types of fish, and their peculiarities. There was one specimen of the most refined and fragile ugliness which, he claimed with pride, had never before been kept alive, in Mergui. That he had been able to do so he put down to the continual noise and light.

When the matter of the plane was raised, he sighed. In the first place he had received no telegram, so no seat had been reserved. Anyway all the planes were booked for several trips ahead. He went away to confer with a colleague. There was a rattle of Burmese monosyllables in which such words as time-schedule, over-booked and Sunday-plane, continually occurred; fitful beams of comprehension that in some way contrived only to deepen the murk of future prospects. The Burmese language, as now spoken, is studded with English words which the Burmese find not easily translatable. All the sinister euphemisms like 'liberation' are there, and such verbs as 'to neutralize' are appropriated with joy. The official told me that it took six words to say Sunday-plane in Burmese, and the same number, of course, to say Thursday-plane. This also was 'over-booked'. With knotted brow he re-checked his list. On Sunday a delegation was off to stick gold-leaf on the Shwedagon Pagoda. Thursday's plane was monopolized by Rotarians. The Burmese people enjoyed travel. To be on the safe side he suggested that I should contact the shipping company. The *Menam* would be calling on its return journey in two weeks' time. Or I could more easily get a plane from Moulmein – if only there were any way of getting to Moulmein.

I went down to the police station to inquire for lodgings. Outside, a great crowd had collected to examine a travelling exhibit of photographs of traffic accidents. When fatal accidents happen in Burma the grim composition is left undisturbed until the police photographer arrives with his equipment, deftly composes the face – if any remains – of the victim, and sets to work. From these grisly tableaux I learned, by the way, that when a body is bisected by a train, the normal disposition of the parts can remain unaltered, top and bottom sections still tenuously united by the clothing.

The station-sergeant was cheerful. There was no accommodation problem in Mergui. A constable was sent along to conduct me to a reeling shack, plastered with Chinese ideographs, with a notice in English which said 'Yok Seng. Licensed under the hotel and restaurant tax act'. Yok Seng's was on the edge of the residential quarter, and surrounding buildings were made entirely from the perforated steel used by the Americans on their air-field landing strips. This, in Mergui, being airy and dacoit-proof, is regarded as choice building material. But the quality of the material is offset by a serious disadvantage. The construction of a normal wooden Burmese house is a matter of skill and connoisseurship, called for on account of the invisible thread of fortune connecting the building with its inhabitants. The building posts, according to shape, are masculine, feminine, or neuter; and the feminine ones, which swell out at the base, are — provided that all other things are equal — fortunate and honourable. A fat Burmese manual exists, giving a great number of rules for the construction of the lucky house. It goes carefully into such questions as the number of and position of the knots in the wood, and the effect on the occupiers' fortunes of the shape of the side pieces of the steps leading up to the veranda. Finally, the house-guardian, when it does not live in a coconut — as at Moulmein — occupies the south post of the house, which is adorned with leaves. There is no doubt that the terrible simplification introduced by the use of airstrip perforated-steel will produce new problems. There's no luck — and no ill-luck — about the house. Its occupants must pay for their convenience by surrendering themselves to an atmosphere of ghastly spiritual neutrality.

The ground-floor of Yok Seng's place, which was open to the street, contained a few tables and chairs, and beneath them, on the beaten earth, pariah dogs and a stunted breed of Rhode Island Red chickens twitched and scuffled as vermin troubled their siesta.

After the policeman had banged his rifle a few times on a table top, a Chinese came down some stairs in the rear, wiping his hands, as he approached us, on his only garment, a bloodstained pair of white slacks. There would be no trouble in putting me up, he said amiably and in excellent English. I could sleep anywhere I liked, on the floor downstairs — the shutters were pulled down at night — and this had the advantage of privacy. Or, if I liked company, he could find space on a comfortably boarded floor upstairs, where a few of his friends — all respectable merchants — were sleeping. Downstairs, of course, I could pick my own position, relax and have the place to myself. Better still, he said, as soon as the customers were gone he would put a couple of tables together and I could sleep on those.

It was becoming clear to me that on my projected journey through the interior of Burma — if it became reality — I should not be able to look forward to anything in the matter of lodgings much better than Yok Seng's establishment. Indeed the time might soon come when I should remember its appointments with nostalgia. I therefore settled there and then for the two tables, clinching the deal with the proprietor over a formal cup of tea.

Much to my delight I found that besides running his hotel Yok Seng was in the export business, and that among the products he shipped to Hong Kong were as many edible birds' nests as he could buy, although as they were at that time out of season, he was unable to show me any. From what he told me of his own experiences of this precious merchandise, together with the information given in a printed leaflet with which he presented me, I was able to form a clearer idea than ever before of the harassed existence of my favourite bird the *Collocalia francica*, or Grey-Rumped Swift.

The *Collocalia francica* which breeds in caves on islands of the Mergui archipelago is famed in the Far East for the immaculacy by which all its acts are characterized. In the leaflet — it was published in 1907 and had scientific pretensions — I read that this excellent bird was believed to obtain its nutriment from the air. Its name in Siamese means 'wind-eating bird', and it is stated never to have been observed in the act of taking solid food of any kind. The nest, which is fixed to the most inaccessible parts of high caves, is half the size of a small saucer. It is transparent and takes, in the first place, three months to make from the fine, web-like threads of saliva secreted by the bird. Its first nests are collected as soon as complete. The bird then hastily produces a second, which is regarded as an inferior *cru*; and when this is taken, a third, of which it is sometimes left in possession. These are 'white' nests, unsullied by any foreign material. A related species of bird, of less ethereal habits, produces 'black' nests, containing feathers, flies and even droppings. These are not acceptable in Hong Kong, the chief birds, nest market; but find buyers among the less exacting Chinese of the Straits Settlements. The Grey-Rumped Swift not only does not foul its nests, but does not permit its young to do so, although perhaps in view of its reputed feeding habits, the impulse is slight. At all events nests are as spotless and saleable after incubation as before.

It was inevitable that so remarkable a performance should have attracted the attention of those dauntless empiricists, the Chinese. In about 1750 a Chinese called Hao Yieng presented his wife, children and slaves, together with fifty cases of tobacco to the Siamese king, asking in return to be allowed to collect birds' nests on the islands. He soon became immensely rich and was made Governor of a province. Realizing the value of the monopoly, the Crown then took over. A corps of hereditary collectors was created; officers of the crown who were not allowed to change their employment, and who were permitted to carry firearms to guard the caves. Nest poachers were heavily fined. After an analysis conducted in the manner of their day a body of early Chinese scientists unanimously declared that the nest was composed of solidified sea-foam. It was a short step to regarding it as an essential ingredient of the elixir of life. Although the elixir remained elusive, a combination of birds' nests and ginseng is still considered by the Chinese to be the nearest thing to it ever discovered, and capable in nine cases out of ten of restoring to life a patient on the point of death.

Unfortunately, said Yok Seng, many unscrupulous practices had crept into the trade. One was the manufacture by unprincipled persons of spurious nests. Such nests were made of jellies extracted from various seaweeds, and sometimes most artfully flavoured by the addition of a trifling percentage of the real thing. And just as in the intensive agriculture of Tonkin, where human excrement is the most valuable commodity after rice itself, there are assayers able to detect fraudulent adulteration with inferior substitutes, so the merchants of Mergui employed experts to nibble judiciously at samples of nests. 'But be sure,' said Yok Seng, 'that when you order bird's nest soup in a restaurant, it is the fake you will be served.' It took a nest-eater of many years' experience to tell the difference between the genuine article and the succulent imitation which would fail to double your span of years.

It came almost as a disappointment when the necessity for submitting to the experience of the Yok Seng hospitality was removed. Unexpectedly, the *Menam* was to stay another night at Mergui, and that evening a message came from the Air Company's office to say that there had been a cancellation on the Sunday-plane and they had booked the seat for me.

There was something of a party on the *Menam* that night. A couple of tin-miners came aboard and were entertained by friends. The Captain made his first appearance, and later came over to my table. He had heard that I was a writer, and would like to know what I proposed to write about. Burma, I told him, knowing infallibly what was to come. And what were my qualifications? . . . How long had I lived, or would live in the country? I had arrived a week before, and might stay a few months.

The Captain found it hard to conceal his exasperation. For twenty-eight years he had knocked about these coasts, and he seemed to feel that anyone who had spent less time in the Far East than he, had no right to write about it. The things he had seen in his days! The stories he could tell if he felt like it! And what did this rare information amount to, when finally after a few more double whiskies the process of unburdening began? A little smuggling; a little gun running; repetitive descriptions of homeric drinking bouts in which the Captain had justified his manhood and his race against all comers; fun with Burmese 'bits of stuff'. Of this material were his Burmese memories composed.

And this was the common, almost the invariable attitude. The old hands seem to feel that they possess a kind of reluctant, vested interest in the place of their exile. Without having suffered with them the long, boring years of expatriation, it was an impertinence to have an opinion. And yet when questioned they would often boastfully display their ignorance, their contempt and distaste for everything about the country. As soon as the central streets of Rangoon were left behind there was never another European to be seen.

It has always been the same. Of all the Europeans who visited

Burma, from earliest times down to the days of Symes' Embassy at the beginning of the last century, only eight troubled to give any account of the country, however brief. Hundreds of factors of the East India Company resided in Syriam, Pegu or at Ava, yet none of them in his letters shows any evidence of curiosity about the strange life that went on around them, or that he ever thought of Burma other than in terms of 'Ellephants teeth, Pegue Plancks, Tynn, Oyle, and Mortavan jars'.

Early next morning I put my bag into a sampan which lay alongside the ship, heaving in the tide's pulse, and then, with a thrust of the oars, we were carried away, swept with the current downstream. Shorewards rose magic mountains of shining garbage, and on the beach at their base, the sea peeled off its layers of indolent water. Beyond, over the curve of the earth, rose the town's silhouette; the roofs, the mysterious towers, the minarets of abandoned factories. On a black rock a group of Burmese children, with top-knots and fringed hair, threw stones into the water, and laughed seawards. We skimmed through a marsh to land, and as the incoming tide rippled before us it lifted the flat, green leaves, and the water glistened round their rims. This was the last I saw of Mergui.

The airport jeep was waiting at the appointed place and, as we went up through the woods, through the patchy scarlets of flamboyant trees, and past the tarnished gilding of pagodas, the driver chatted amiably. He wanted to talk about the scandal of the Seventeen-Days festival that was just over in Mergui. It would be my good fortune to be travelling with one of the greatest of Burmese actors, who had been playing every night and in the course of the seventeen days had been paid half a lac of rupees — about four thousand pounds. On these celebrations the people of Mergui had spent a total of eight lacs, say sixty-five thousand pounds, and were now reduced to temporary penury. The pawnshop had been obliged to close down on the first day, after running out of cash.

This kind of thing, said the driver, eager as the Burmese always are to condemn their national vices, was the curse of Mergui. People spent all they had on the pwès, and then just scraped along as best they

could for the rest of the year. Tradition had a lot to do with it. Miser-
liness was one of the Burmese deadly sins, ranking in the hierarchy of
crime on a level with fratricide. That was why the Indians, who
regarded thrift as a cardinal virtue, were getting control of the country's wealth. The driver sighed and shook his head at such foolishness.
He was dressed with suspicious plainness for the possessor of such a
gadget-loaded car, and had probably gambled away most of his resources, including his silk longyis. For the next few weeks he would
live on plain rice and gnapi. After that he would dress in silk again,
continuing on plain fare, however, until he had redeemed his wrist-
watch and ruby ring. Then would follow another visit to the gambling
tables and the pawnshop; and the process of recovery would start all
over again.

The airport was a prairie of burnt grass surrounded by bush. Snacks
were being served in a palm-leaf shack, and an official who attached
himself in an informal, almost abstracted way, led me to this and
ordered cups of thick sweet tea, and hard-boiled eggs, for which he
would not allow me to pay. A few soldiers were hanging about, and
presently these scattered to various points of the perimeter, where they
took up position behind light machine-guns. An army lorry came
charging up, loaded with more troops, who tumbled out and formed
two ranks. They were smartly turned out in British uniforms, with
knife-edge creases in the right places. Eyes were turned skywards in
response to a faint throbbing and the Sunday-plane came into sight,
glinting distantly. Dropping down gently, as if lowered on a thread,
to land, it disappeared, absorbed in the heat-haze, from which it
suddenly burst forth when almost upon us. The plane, a Dakota,
stopped, with its idly slapping propellers raising squalls of dust. A door
opened and a military figure leaped down. Two officers ran forward,
saluted and shook hands. One raised a Leica to his eye. There was a
yelp of command, in traditionally unrecognizable English, followed by
a smacking of butts as arms were correctly presented. A Brigadier had
arrived to take over operations in the South.

The normal seating equipment of the Sunday-plane had been

removed to allow the carriage of more passengers and freight. We sat on what looked like theatre-queue stools, with backs. The airline had a reputation for keeping its planes in the air as much as possible and the floor was littered with the debris of several previous trips. The party on their way to gild the Shwedagon spire were seen off with garlands, in the Hawaiian manner. Sensibly, as the temperature in the plane must have approached a hundred and twenty degrees, the door was left open until the very last instant before the take-off, and then shut with some difficulty against the pressure of air. My neighbour, a sophisticate in European clothing, spent the first half-hour trying to take photographs with a new Japanese camera through the dirty window. He then settled down to a Penguin D. H. Lawrence, automatically fingering through his prayer-beads with his free hand. Burma's outstanding actor was travelling with his pearl-festooned wife and children. He was a dark, sullen-faced fellow, who dressed with costly indifference in the old-fashioned style, and wore his hair in a bun on top of his head. Although he made more money than most Hollywood film stars, he seemed to have no fans on the plane. No one took the slightest notice of him. Most of the passengers were too busy with their smelling-salts to care.

CHAPTER VI

CONDUCTED TOUR

B ACK in Rangoon, I set about the organization of the journey to the interior. Many difficulties suddenly appeared, some of which showed signs of hasty fabrication, and it was soon evident that the authorities preferred foreigners to remain quietly in the capital. The Burmese airline served about a dozen towns, of which only two or three could be visited without special authorization. Otherwise, travel so far as Westerners were concerned seemed to have come to an end since the outbreak of the insurrections, although the Indian and Burmese merchants I consulted told me that plenty of goods still went by road, and that it was easy enough to accompany them.

It was unfortunate for me that two Europeans — both journalists — had quietly left Rangoon without official blessing, in the last year or so. Their adventures had spoiled the going for future travellers. One, a Frenchman, had reached Kentung, a very troubled area, and had there hobnobbed with Shan dissidents. On his return he had experienced a short stay in Rangoon gaol, before being expelled from the country. The second journalistic venture had produced more lasting damage. A representative of a London newspaper had actually contacted Karen rebel leaders — a sensational scoop to a newspaper-man, and a piece of flagrant espionage to the Burmese. Although the classic English traveller is spurred on in almost all cases by nothing more sinister than an extravagant curiosity, it has been hard at the best of times for others to believe that he is not an agent of the Intelligence Service, especially after the occurrence of such an incident. In army circles there were many who still believed that the British had not renounced all ambition to return to Burma, and they thought it quite natural that attempts would be made to maintain contact with pro-British and anti-Burmese minority groups.

Until I made my application it had been possible simply to go down to the air company's office and buy a ticket for such towns as Lashio and Bhamó; but in my honour it seemed, new regulations were quickly slapped on. Suddenly no foreigners could be granted permission to visit these towns, even by air, without application being made on their behalf by their own embassy to the Burmese Foreign Office. The matter would then, it was explained to me, be referred by the Foreign Office to the War Office, and finally passed for sanction or rejection to the General Staff Department. It was clear that this formidable procedure offered the maximum scope for pigeon-holing, and I felt that the hidden intention might have been to break the applicant's spirit by manufactured delays. In any case, it turned out that the British Embassy could not agree to intervene, as this was the first they had heard of such a regulation. I was unofficially recommended to extract what comfort I could from the knowledge that others were, or had been, in the same case, including the United States Military Attaché, and the representatives of a celebrated American magazine, who had come to do a picture reportage, and had left after seeing little more of Burmese life than was to be observed in the uncharacteristic public rooms of the Strand Hotel.

After a few days of struggling, ever more feebly, in the tightening snares of red tape, I was told that even Mandalay had been put out of bounds. At the police headquarters, U Ba San also mentioned with deadly casualness that whenever I got my Burmese travel permit, I should have to apply again (through channels) for one issued by the Minister for the Shan States. The psychological effect of these blows was almost decisive, and I was on the point of packing up and going home. As a last resort, and because there was nothing to be lost, I decided to cut across channels, and go directly to the real seat of power. I therefore presented myself at the War Office, and asked to see a high-ranking staff-officer, whose name I had been given. To my surprise he received me. I found that he had a great sense of humour, and after we had laughed together uproariously about my predicament, the permit was typed out on the spot. I went straight to the air-office and booked a seat on the plane to Mandalay two days later. At this time my intention was to fly as far north as possible, and work my way back to Rangoon by road and river.

Next day was another public holiday. My Canadian friend, Dolland, released from official duties, suggested a jaunt across the river to Syriam. His previous visit had been a rapid and unsatisfactory conducted tour, and behind his screen of protective troops he had seen very little.

Dolland, a rare eccentric in matters of travel, was moved in all things by a single principle — a determination to get as close to the country as was possible in the course of his three months in Burma. With this creditable purpose steadfastly in view he frequently travelled about Rangoon, clinging to the platforms of crowded buses, and sometimes arrived at the Strand Hotel in a kind of springless pony-trap of the kind used by peasants to bring vegetables to market. It cost more than a taxi. He was also learning Burmese, wore the national costume whenever he could find an excuse, and finally moved out of the hotel and went to live with a Burmese couple he had persuaded to take him as a paying guest.

On this occasion, then, in accordance with his general line, Dolland wanted to travel second-class on the ferry. My attitude to this was that the presence of two foreigners squatting in agony on mats on the deck among the coolies, would be interpreted by the Burmese not so much as democratic interest, as meanness. Dolland squatted for a few moments and then joined me up on the first-class benches in the stern, which were, of course, equally patronized by Burmese.

Having landed at Syriam we were about to walk uphill to the town, about a mile away, when our attention was attracted by a great deal of activity down by the water. Female labourers were loading rice from one of the government depots, on to lighters. As they were paid by the basket-load, they worked at a tremendous, almost alarming, speed, in great contrast to the languorous movements of the Burmese female who is not doing anything in particular. We went over to the yard and the girls grimaced, and made witty remarks while we photographed them, going in short dashes from the piled-up rice to the boat, with their enormous loads on their heads. We were just moving off when we were accosted by a very polite, sad-faced young man who said he was the overseer, and what could he do for us. There was nothing much he could do, and our hearts sank when he mentioned that as he was just going off duty, he would show us the town. Outside the yard he hailed another young man, who came over and said, as he shook hands, 'What do you want, sir?' This was the township officer, principal citizen of Syriam. A Ford truck panted at the kerbside behind him. It was loaded with his henchmen. There was no escape. The conducted tour had begun.

I wanted to look for any traces that might remain here of the factories of the East India Company, where they had maintained themselves uneasily for a century, selling their hats and ribbons, and understandably failing to sell their English broadcloth; 'we haveing great quantetyes decaying by us'. From this stronghold, too, the seventeenth-century Portuguese adventurer De Brito had only just failed, from lack of Goa's support, to turn the delta area of Lower Burma into a Portuguese colony. Somewhere on the hill, after defeat by the Burmese king, he met his end by impalement. He failed to adopt the recommended posture – to sit quietly and permit the sharpened stake to penetrate the vital organs – and the point passed out through his side. He lingered three days.

Our hosts were determined that we should see their town in the proper fashion. There was no escaping the inspection of public monuments, the hospital, the town hall. Finally, making them understand the nature of our interests, we were taken to a tiny ruined chapel, in which a tombstone commemorated, in most elegant script, the death in 1732 of one Maria Dias. The township officer carefully noted my translation in his notebook.

On the way back to the ferry – we were still confined to the Ford truck – we asked in desperation if we might walk. It was clear that our Burmese friends were dumbfounded at such eccentricity. Further explanation of what we actually proposed was necessary before the driver was ordered to stop. Then the four of us got down and walked gravely downhill in the middle of the road, while the lorry followed, grinding along in bottom gear, about ten yards behind.

CHAPTER VII

BURMESE GAOL

THE morning of my departure for Mandalay was nicely filled in by a visit to the Rangoon gaol. U Thant arranged this at a moment's notice. Even if the Burmese were a little dubious about letting people see what was going on in the interior of their country, they clearly had no misgivings about the condition of their gaols. It was casually mentioned, with perhaps a touch of pride, that in England such a request would have to be made through the Home Office and was not lightly granted. Here all U Thant had to do was to get the Director General of Prisons on the phone, and the thing was fixed in a matter of minutes.

It was the Director General himself, U Ba Thein, who called for me at seven o'clock next morning. U Ba Thein was a small, dapper man, with that concentrated, almost ferocious, energy often found in men of destiny. He told me with some satisfaction that he was of humble origin, but I have no doubt that in traditional Burmese fashion he possessed a spectacular horoscope, and that in his youth vultures had been seen to perch on the houses of his enemies. He was also genial in the extreme, even for a Burman, having a sense of humour that was French rather than English, expansive and *spirituel*.

We shot off in a small English car driven by the Director himself, and soon entered the road leading to the prison entrance, which was guarded with barbed-wire entanglements. The atmosphere was a martial one. At the approach of our car there were warning cries, and a guard tumbled out rather too late to present arms. There was much leaping to attention and saluting as we went through the gate, and U Ba Thein, sighing, and quoting Chaucer, said 'God keep my body out of a foul prisoun'. The Director General had a great reputation as a disciplinarian. He also liked poetry, and the English way of life; in particular, he said, kippers and watercress for tea.

The Rangoon gaol was at first sight less forbidding and dolorous than

74

the average prison. During the recent war, I was unfortunately brought into contact with the repressive arrangements of several countries. At the bottom of the scale were the French in North Africa, where colonial dissidents were put in black holes in the ground — living tombs. Above these were the Italians and Germans with their heartless efficiency. There were no gyves or pinions; but solitary confinement, sound-proof cells, rows of steel doors which opened slowly at the throwing of a switch. In these all-electrically operated hells, food was a dosage with calories; a medical measure against death by starvation. A doctor stood by with a stethoscope while punishment was administered, and in the constant blue light bodies turned as white as if they had been drained by vampires.

Rangoon gaol, perhaps because there had been a merciful shortage of funds, had never been able to run to such refinements. It was no more than a great cage; a collection of barrack-like buildings, where no attempt had been made, as in most prisons, to prevent inmates from seeing even the sky. In these barrack-rooms the prisoners lived communally; each occupying an allotted amount of floor space. When U Ba Thein told me that each building was called a 'house' and that the head-warders were 'house-masters' I admit to a suspicion that this might be no more than another of those sinister euphemisms for which the Burmese have such a genius. Occupants of the various houses wore different coloured longyis, and while, I felt, this grim echo of the public-school system might have been wasted on them, it was at least something that they did not wear prison clothes.

They rose at dawn, U Ba Thein informed me, said prayers and then did P.T. for half an hour. I could have been sure of it. P.T. has become an oriental panacea for all the ills, both of body and mind. It would have been extraordinary not to have found it figuring largely in the reformative processes of an up-to-date prison. For up-to-date Rangoon was. The bars were made of wood, and, as the Director General cheerfully admitted, very easy to cut through. However they would not be replaced. Such grants of money as they received would be spent in a more positive way. He was aiming, eventually, at a prison without walls. 'That edifice over there,' he pointed to a blackened building, 'was accidentally devastated by fire. A fortuitous circumstance. We can do without same. Now there will be no excuse for the non-existence of a football pitch.' There was no problem here about making the prison too comfortable. He had heard of some place — Mexico, he thought — where this had been done. 'Why, do you know those fellows actually asked to come back when they were discharged!' It was enough to stop a Burman from gambling and dressing-up. Liberty was a precious thing.

The influx of prisoners — eighteen thousand passed through their hands in one year — was attributable to the unsettled times and the breakdown of monastic education, with nothing to fill the gap. The present custom, said U Ba Thein, of entering a monastery for a week was useless. In the old days a boy spent at least a year there. Now he got no schooling until he was ten years of age, if at all. Parents wouldn't send their children to boarding school, far from home. 'There but for the Grace of God . . .' he quoted. U Ba Thein had been a village boy himself, he told me; and had first gone to school when he was ten. 'For several years they caned me daily, because like uneducated Burmese people I pronounced f as p.' It had been the *pons asinorum* of the Director General's youth. Having in the end surmounted this obstacle he had taken to learning with a zest, and found what remained comparatively easy. He had gone about noting down all the new words he heard, committing them to memory and practising in conversation as soon as he could. Usually he got the meaning wrong. But no matter, it impressed most people. U Ba Thein said it was a habit he had never grown out of. 'You may have noticed that I still use long words in the wrong place? It is a habit I am noted for. People are still continually pulling my leg about it.'

At the end of the war U Ba Thein had visited England to enable him to study the British prison system on the spot. He had been impressed by the kindness he had received, the kippers and the water-cress of course, and by the favouritism of people behind the bars of public-houses, who had produced cigarettes for him from under the counter. No one had ever guessed that he was Burmese. It was at a time when all Far-Easterners were Japanese, although nobody had apparently bothered to inquire what a Japanese was doing in England at such a time. When, on one occasion, he addressed some Borstal boys, he invited questions at the conclusion of his remarks. He had mentioned Buddhism, and one of the boys asked if it was true that Buddhists could have more than one wife. 'I informed them that that was so,' U Ba Thein said, 'and I must say they all seemed to regard it as an excellent thing.'

As we paced solemnly down the passages, the prisoners stood to attention by their folded bedding. 'Look at those fellows,' U Ba Thein said. 'They are a product of the times. There is no inherent criminality in those faces.'

It was perfectly true. The convicts looked no more vicious than the young fellows to be seen in the streets outside. They were in for robbery, crimes of violence, murder. Fortunately, sexual crimes were very rare. There was no sexual repression in Burma, the Director General said, owing to the freedom practised between the sexes from the age of puberty. Bigamy was not an offence, and charges of rape were rarely brought because the offender in such cases was considered automatically to have married the girl.

In Burma, U Ba Thein said, robbery and violence had always been the problem. He was inclined to trace some of it back to the deliberate policy of the Burmese kings, who encouraged delinquency in a certain restricted area in Upper Burma in order to provide themselves with a reserve of suitable recruits for their armies. The old Burmese kings were, above all, well intentioned. They had none of the cynical disregard for human rights displayed by recent European aggressors. All men were brothers and equally entitled to the salvation which the Burmese kings — who had seen the light — knew that only they could bring. They wanted nothing better than to extend their enlightened benevolence to all humanity; to govern according to the five fundamental precepts, and the four kingly laws, which ordained that the king should content himself with the tithe, that he should pay his servants regularly, lend money without interest to the necessitous, and use courteous and fitting language according to the age and the degree of the person addressed.

It was unfortunate that only by totally non-Buddhistic measures could those nations which continued in ignorance of the Law be gathered into the fold of Buddhist felicity, so that the kingdom of Heaven on Earth might become a reality. But since all the king's subjects had received a monastic training in the course of which it had been emphasized that of the five precepts, the most important was to take no life at all, how could they be persuaded — even in pursuit of a sanctified end — to enslave, to ravish and to slaughter all those who persisted in their error. The solution was the delimitation of the area within which, for the kingdom of heaven's sake, the five precepts were ignored. From this the king's janissaries were obtained, and from this still come a disproportionate number of the students at this strange public school of Rangoon.

It was reasonable to expect, I thought, that the Director General would have organized this visit with a little window-dressing in mind. We passed, for instance, a block of solitary confinement cells, which, although 'the inheritance of inhumanity was rapidly being wiped out', were obviously still in use. There were three or four prisoners there who couldn't be put with the rest, but no offer was made to show me them. However, when, with a wave of dismissal, U Ba Thein indicated the women's block, saying that he didn't suppose I wanted to see it, I made it clear, as tactfully as I could, that I did. This seemed a good opportunity to visit a part of the prison where probably no preparations had been made. Before going any further we had to await the escort of the head wardress. This lady, a most chic custodian, arrived swinging her symbolical bunch of keys, her face larded with cosmetic. Bracing myself for a vision of screaming harridans in the manner of the women's prison at Naples, I was surprised to find an atmosphere of gentle domesticity.

With a trace of embarrassment, U Ba Thein excused the presence of the women's babies which, he said, while not in keeping with European practice, they tolerated here for the babies' sake. There were toys that had been made in the prison workshop strewn about the floor: wooden horses, lobsters, elephants. Each mother had a prison pushcart. This building was built of air-field metal landing-strip, and the kittens, which the children had been allowed to keep, wandered in and out of the perforations. The women were spruce in their ordinary clothes. They were importunate, too, and ignoring the wardress, came up to U Ba Thein to ask favours. Most of them were serving sentences for carrying fire-arms, and one, a delicate, almost ethereal creature, with the face of an Eastern madonna, had organized a huge diamond swindle.

There was one other class of prisoner. We came on a rather tall man, with an unusually gentle expression. He seemed more reflective and less animated than the average Burman, and although some difficulty is found at first in telling the Mongolian peoples apart, I at least realized that the man was not Burmese. He turned out to be a Japanese *kampé*, one of a number who were serving ten-year sentences for war crimes. U Ba Thein said he had no idea what this one had done, but he had heard that some of them were sentenced for burying prisoners alive. A few words had been exchanged in English. Was he short of anything? The Japanese nodded down at his ragged trousers and the Director General said that he would see to it that he got another pair. We turned away. 'Patience,' said U Ba Thein, in parting salutation, and the Japanese smiled with gentle resignation. 'There but for the Grace of God . . .' said U Ba Thein again as we moved on.

CHAPTER VIII

TO MANDALAY

I N the late afternoon, and several hours behind schedule because of the heat-haze, the plane bumped down on Mandalay airfield. The moment the plane door opened I knew that this was a different heat from the Rangoon kind. The horizon was ringed by scorched hills that wavered slightly as you moved your head, as if seen through bad, uneven window glass. The passengers clambered down and took refuge under the wings; sheltering as though from torrential rain. Waves of scorching air rippled from the plane's metal surfaces. Working very slowly, the airport staff dragged out the baggage.

Mr. Tok Galé, representative in Mandalay of the British Information Service, was to have met me. The problem of lodgings was supposed to be particularly bad, and it was hoped that this gentleman, who had been warned by telegram from Rangoon, might have been able to find me a room. Outside the airport huts one or two decayed taxis waited for passengers. These soon filled up and went lurching and bobbing away. The various officials prepared to close down for the day. Mr. Tok Galé had evidently given up hope of the plane's arrival.

Another half an hour passed and an outlandish vehicle came rumbling up out of the dust. It was, as I soon discovered, a typical Mandalay gharry. This once modish conveyance had a galvanized iron body, decorated with the British Royal Standard, and much fancy scroll-work in brass. Huge glass rubies were dotted about the coachwork, and there were several diamond-shaped insets of coloured glass. Enormous lamps were supported on fancy brackets, and the wheels turned unevenly under high, polished, metal mudguards. This piece of fantasy, which had clearly been created and maintained with tender pride of ownership, had something ghostly about it. It was like one of those fragile, immensely aged ladies who, clad in the height of Edwardian fashion, still haunt remote London squares. Nothing could have better typified Mandalay.

[*facing:* LAKE AND PAGODA AT MUDON

Seeing that he had a fare the ancient driver climbed down from his seat. He was gripping a bag, and his horse was allowed to mumble a few mouthfuls of the dried herbs it contained, to give it strength for the new journey. The piece of cord which did service as a handbrake was then untied from the wheel and we set off towards the thorny hedges, the stagnant pools, the ruined palaces of Mandalay.

Mandalay. In the name there was a euphony which beckoned to the imagination, yet this was the bitter, withered reality. Through the suburbs mile followed mile of miserable shacks; a squalid gipsy encampment, coated with a bone-white dust which floated everywhere, like a noxious condensation of the heat-haze itself. Pigmy pagodas sprouted like pustules. Hideous dogs snarled and scuffled in the streets, which were still rutted and broken from the pounding of war-time traffic.

Mr. Tok Galé, whom I found in his office, was a small, quiet-voiced Burman in well-pressed European clothes. He was just about to make another trip out to the airport, which temporarily could not be reached on the telephone. With relentless efficiency, Tok Galé had already worked out the details of a comprehensive sight-seeing programme to fill in my stay in Mandalay, which was to begin, it seemed, the moment I arrived. A jeep had been hired, and awaited us with the driver standing respectfully bare-headed in the terrific sunshine. While Tok Galé stood by I washed off a layer of dust. Within five minutes I was sitting in the jeep, lulled by the balm of my guide's gently imparted information, jerked into wakefulness as we crashed through pot-holes.

The most important of Tok Galé's many kindly services consisted of finding a room for me. The circuit-house, he said, was out of the question. It was a mile or two from the town's centre, well inside the dacoit zone. The room was owned by a Chinese merchant. It had been divided by partitions, and he and several tenants slept in beds that had been distributed as evenly as possible about the available space. It was reached by an outside staircase, at the top of which was a platform with a small table, an ancient, filthy but still beautiful pitcher, full of water, and an aluminium wash-basin. Here, at night, a lonely but brilliantly neon-illuminated figure, I performed my toilet, watched

facing: MON FISHERMAN IN THE ALTARAN RIVER, MOULMEIN]

incuriously by the Burmese seated at the tables of the tea-shops below. It seemed that Mandalay was without drains. When I asked my Chinese host what was to be done with the waste water, he pointed to the palm-thatched roof of the house below. When I had finally brought myself to accept his implied suggestion there was a sharp exclamation from within, as if the inmates had never been able entirely to accustom themselves to the procedure.

Night in Mandalay called for special qualities of endurance. As the evening wore on, both heat and noise increased. The large, modernistic windows with their westerly exposure had been a sun-trap since the early afternoon, and by the evening the heat was seeping through the walls themselves. At about six-thirty the sun went down redly in a glittering haze of dust particles. Immediately the lights of Mandalay came on. A fluorescent tube had been installed for decorative purposes across the façade of our building, providing a pale glare until the early morning hours. The cinema across the road was outlined with flickering fires of neon. Probably as an anti-dacoit measure, because it was left on all night, a large, naked electric bulb was suspended outside my window. This supplied, when other sources failed, a continuous, death-cell illumination.

At all times a cheerful hum of café gossip ascended to my window, mingled with the exuberant blowing of motor-horns. In the evening, the cinema came to life, advertising itself with trailer-music broadcast from powerful loudspeakers, and by the pertinacious note of an electrically struck gong, attached to the wall nearby. Above this background of confused noise several pagodas sometimes asserted themselves, signalling their religious offices by harmonious and long-echoing sounds struck from the huge triangles of brass suspended in their courtyards.

The windows were open wide in the hope of catching a current of air, and sparrows flew in, and in their fluttering set in brief motion an otherwise static frieze of lizards.

I took my meals at a Chinese restaurant across the way, called the

Excelsior. Whenever I went in the proprietor would come out of the kitchen and guide me firmly into the polite solitude of a private room. A moment or two later I would hear a preliminary scratching and the gramophone would begin to play 'Kathleen Mavourneen', followed by 'The Harp that Once . . .' The sides of the record were always played in this order. Always the proprietor asked with a hopeful uplift in his voice, 'Eggs and chips?' And always I shook my head, pointing without understanding to some Burmese or Chinese speciality on the wall menu. This was never available, and the dish finally served was fried soft noodles with mincemeat, although it was always given a fresh name. This was sometimes followed by a turnip-tasting fruit, called in Burmese, 'Ice from Russia'. Mandalay Pale Ale could be had here at the source for three rupees, or four and sixpence. You could also buy Fire-Tank Brand Mandalay Whisky at seven rupees a bottle, which was reasonable compared to genuine imported Scotch at the black-market figure of eighty.

Every night I sat in this sallow cubicle, trying to put off the time when I should have to face the oven of my room. Across the road a rank of small covered-wagons, decorated with brass cupids, would be drawn up. These had brought peasants to market and now their owners were sitting in teashops, gambling away the proceeds of their sales. Once a woman sat on the pavement outside, giving her baby alternate sucks of a nipple and a fat cheroot, and once while I sat there a silent, thickly-bearded Indian came in and handed me a slip of paper on which was printed, 'a conjurer will make your party a success'. On another occasion there was a Chinese private party in a booth opposite and, as the door was slightly ajar, I caught a glimpse of one of the ladies sitting on her escort's lap, washing his face after the meal.

There was no important reason for Mandalay's existence. It never possessed strategic or commercial importance, and the whole district had had a detestable climate since, centuries before, pious kings had cut down all the trees to be used as fuel in brick-making for pagodas. At some time in the remote past astrologers had declared the area to be astrally favoured, so Ava and Amarapura had been built. These had finally been deserted, as Burmese towns were, when it was decided that the efficacy of the human sacrifices made at the foundation was exhausted. And then, in Victorian times, the pious King Mindon had been tempted to try his luck again. On the advice of the Brahmin astrologers an exemplary mass-sacrifice was arranged, including that of a pregnant woman. According to the old Mongolian belief the spirits of mother and child would unite in death to form a composite demon of exceptional malignancy. This would be animated by an implacable desire for revenge, directed — with seemingly defective logic — against the king's enemies. As a Buddhist scholar of renown and the leading authority of his times on Pali texts, Mindon probably disapproved of this stone-age practice. If he permitted the woman to be buried alive, he did so in the same spirit as a socialist cabinet minister might dress for dinner — not because he agreed with the principle, but because these things were expected of him; and, after all, there was nothing to be lost one way or another.

These sacrifices probably established a Burmese record for short-lived efficacy. Twenty-nine years later Mandalay fell to the British without the slightest attempt at defence, either ghostly or human.

CHAPTER IX

KINGS AND A PRINCE

As far as the conventional sights went Mandalay was a town to be dealt with in summary fashion. Apart from a gaudy fantasy of a palace, a few monasteries and the Arakan Pagoda, it had never contained anything worth seeing; and now, after the passing of the bombers, the palace had vanished as completely as if it had never existed.

On the morning of the second day, Tok Galé took me to see the Arakan Pagoda. This was built to enshrine the great Mahamuni image which for so many centuries had been the palladium of the kingdom of Arakan, as well as the most important of the Buddhist sacred objects. The peculiar sanctity of this image lies in its acceptance by Buddhists as a contemporary likeness of the Master. It was cast in brass when the great teacher visited Arakan, at that time a remote Indian kingdom. The work was done supernaturally by none other than Sakra, the old Hindu Lord of Paradise, who had become converted to Buddhism. When completed, the portrait, which was indistinguishable from the original, was embraced by the Buddha, and thereafter emitted an unearthly refulgence, and actually spoke a few words. Naturally, its possession was coveted by many pious kings, in particular the greatest of Burmese historical figures, Anawrahta, who organized a large-scale raid into Arakan with the object of removing this along with sacred relics to his capital at Pagan. The king's purpose was frustrated by the size and weight of the image: the white elephant which accompanied his army, and was regarded as the only suitable means of transport, could not carry it.

It was finally obtained in 1784 by Bodawpaya, who is declared, in an inscription at the pagoda, to have drawn the image to its present resting place by the charm of his piety. In fact an expeditionary corps of thirty thousand men was involved, after elaborate precautions to deprive the image of its magic power had first been taken by Burmese wizards disguised as pilgrims.

I had been told that only in Mandalay would real Burmese works of art, wood-carvings, bronzes and ivories, be found; and that the colonnades of the Arakan Pagoda would be the most likely place in Mandalay itself. As in the Shwedagon at Rangoon, the roofed-over approaches were lined with stalls selling devotional objects; flowers, votive images and triangular gongs. Such carvings as there were among the trayfuls of toy jeeps and tanks and hideous Buddhas, seemed to me the crudest and most barbarously ugly objects I had ever seen. Burma is a land where art has never freed itself from the thraldom of religious or magic motives. The Burmese never grew up spiritually, as did the Chinese, nor allowed the philosophical content of their religion to free itself from its trappings of superstition. As a result their creative energy was diverted into the primitive and unrewarding channels of pagoda-building, from which they expected to derive not mere aesthetic pleasure, but a substantial spiritual reward. As a minor adjunct to this perpetual heaping up of piles of brickwork, there was some skill displayed in woodcarving and the application of lacquer; but when it came to the graphic arts no Burmese painter of monastery frescoes could approach the most primitive of the old Italians, just as no worker in ivory could compare with the least of China's anonymous masters.

Notwithstanding the impressive attribution of the Mahamuni image, the result, regarded as a work of art, is negligible; a mere seated idol, in the lifeless convention which is still adhered to in most parts of the Buddhist world. An attempt at portraiture would probably have been sacrilegious. What we have here is not a divine teacher but the stylization of a fat man, with heavy, inert features which have suffered further coarsening by the gold-leaf applied by the faithful.

The toleration of Buddhists — however debased their particular brand of the religion — is limitless. Anywhere in the Muslim world a *kafir* would have been chased by mouth-foaming fanatics from the precincts of so holy a place. But here, whatever the condition of one's soul, one spread no contamination. A permanent crowd was gathered before the railings of the shrine behind which the twelve feet high image brooded somnolently, but they were quite ready to make room for a not completely human foreigner to take a photograph. One sophisticate even questioned the feasibility of getting a result in so dim a religious light. Whatever one's creed or colour the shrine attendants would accept a bouquet of flowers which could be bought at a nearby stall for a rupee. Gold-leaf was sold for five rupees a packet and the purchaser was entitled to apply it himself, clambering as reverently as possible up the sacred stomach to reach the face. Pilgrims of many races waited their turn to perform this illustrious task. Outstanding were a contingent of Thibetans of the kind that wander about Burma selling gems and hideous medicinal concoctions. There they stood in grimy purple togas; their faces unwashed, gentle, set in masks of beatitude, packets of gold-leaf gripped tightly in their hands. Laboriously they had trudged the roads of Burma, selling their rubies, their bezoars, their serpents' tongues and bats' blood. Now they would squander their gains in one unforgettable devotional spree.

Out in the courtyard, stacked haphazardly against a wall, we found the six survivors of the thirty magic images of Ayuthia, captured by Bayinnaung when he went to Siam for white elephants, and took and sacked the Siamese capital. These potent bronze monsters, triple-headed elephants and snarling, armour-clad demons, were now, at least, put to a useful purpose by Burmese children who played hide-and-seek about their legs.

The brief, routine tour of the capital is incomplete without a visit to the leper asylum. We were received in a large, dim room in the ranch-like administrative building by one of the handful of Franciscan nuns who are left to conduct this work. The sister was a Maltese woman who one day, when she was a girl of eighteen, and living in her native village, had felt the vocation. The call to surrender her life to the hardest of all forms of service was no mere emotional whim. Her first step, on abandoning her family and the comfortable trivialities of her home existence, was to go to Italy to train as a nurse. After qualifying, she came, with resolve unabated, straight out to Mandalay where she had been ever since.

One by one the other sisters came silently into the room. They were all from the Mediterranean countries. All seemed to move in an aura of extraordinary simplicity, of other-worldliness, of embalmed youth. One, who came from Santander, was delighted to be able to speak a few words of Spanish for the first time for years. And then she seemed ashamed of having felt pleasure at this reminder of the world she had renounced and, excusing herself, she left the room. The sisters' lingua-franca was French. The oldest of them, a vigorous old lady, had been there for fifty-two years. None of them had ever been infected, although in Colombo two members of their order had died of leprosy. The years had passed quickly for them, filled with hard work. By dint of concentrated prayer their hospital had come unscathed through the war, although bombs had fallen all round. Even the Japanese had respected them, and given them what help they could. Now, of course, things were worse — worse than they had ever been. Dacoits had taken to breaking in, and stole their equipment and even the medicines.

Later we passed in sombre procession through the buildings where the patients were housed; the rooms, empty but for the row of cheerless beds; the leper faces, often contorted by the disease into apparent fury; the whispers of '*bonjour ma mère*' — or sometimes only a voiceless mouthing — as we passed each bed. The children's wards were inevitably the most pathetic. Sometimes the wistful faces were smooth and clean, sometimes frightfully ravaged. 'This one may recover,' said the Maltese sister, in her cool, even voice . . . 'this one will not.' Thus we passed along the ranks, hearing, as each pair of childish eyes was raised to ours, the dispassionate verdict, 'death very soon now', or 'here there is a small chance'. 'Before the end comes,' said the sister, 'we remove them to a separate building, where they will not upset the others. The sight is depressing to those who are not accustomed to it.' The disease seemed to progress in a series of leaps with intervals of quiescence, the sister explained, and it was only in the crisis that accom-

panied the entering upon a new stage that the patients really suffered ...
then, and in the final agony. Thirty-five years of contact with disease
and death in its most appalling form seemed to have raised the sister
above ordinary emotional sympathy. She had become what was
necessary, an efficiently working, charitable machine.

The hardest part of these lepers' condition seemed to me the cruel
boredom they must have suffered. All day long they lay still, sat up,
even walked a little, surrendering themselves without distraction to the
slow disintegration. There was nothing to take their mind off this
death meted out to them over the years, to be dreadfully consummated
in most cases only after the loss of all five senses. Once they had been
allowed to stage occasional plays, but these for some reason to do with
the unsuitability of the subjects, had been given up. The cinema, even
if possible from the point of view of cost, was unthinkable because of
the worldliness of the films.

It seemed that if the leper wished to surrender himself to the efficient
care of the Christians, with the accompanying faint hope of a cure, he
had also to be ready to submit to that adamantine virtue, that saint-like
abstraction from the world in which only duty and meditation were
permissible. If the lepers wanted to live like ordinary sinful humanity,
there was nothing to stop them from leaving the asylum; but then of
course that last tenuous hope of recovery had to be abandoned. Perhaps the sisters secretly believed that the disease had been a blessing in
disguise, the opportunity to save valuable souls at the expense of worth-
less bodies.

The Burmese, of course, are more human about such things — more
human, and less responsible. There are forty-two thousand registered
lepers in Burma, most of whom continue to live in their villages with
their families. Nothing is done for them except by foreign missionaries;
probably because at the bottom of the Burmese mind lies the conviction
that in this cruel state they are no more than righting an adverse balance
of merit accumulated in previous existences. In this attitude is to be
found, from the Western viewpoint, the main criticism of Buddhist
practice. The performance of acts of charity is praiseworthy, but not
nearly so much so as the building, or repair, of a pagoda. There were

no public funds available to supply essential medicines or amenities for Mandalay's lepers although seven hundred thousand rupees could be spent a month before on the cremation of a saintly individual called U Khanti whose work of merit had consisted of adding new pagodas to the already congested Mandalay Hill. But for all their deficiencies the Burmese do not in any way segregate or persecute the lepers. No medicines or treatment are forthcoming, but neither are the unfortunate creatures' last years made miserable by an enforced monastic way of life.

Before we left, the sister showed us a remarkable piece of religious architecture. It seemed that when the bombings were taking place the nuns vowed, if the hospital were spared, to construct a miniature Lourdes. Shortly afterwards the war ended. There had been a prisoner of war camp in the neighbourhood, and the commanding officer, when approached, had lent them a number of Japanese prisoners to carry out the project. The Japanese had set to work with traditional vigour and produced a miniature mountain of rocks and concrete, as steeply pinnacled as one in a Hiroshige woodcut. After that, with mounting enthusiasm, they had added a willow-pattern river with an appropriate bridge. The Japanese captain himself had undertaken to carve the statue of the Virgin, and it had been lovingly done, with just the faintest suggestion about it of a smiling, slant-eyed Kwannon, the Japanese goddess of mercy. From where we stood Mandalay Hill could be seen, frosted with its innumerable shrines. Few of them, surely, had been erected in more curious circumstances than this.

Of the citadel of Mandalay and its palace – the Centre of the Universe – nothing remained but the walls and moat. And it was here by the water's edge, before the heat of the day had gathered, that, of all places in Mandalay, it was most agreeable to saunter. The gilded royal barges had gone and the moat was grown over with lotuses, and spangled with flowering aquatic plants. Children fished with bent pins from ruined causeways and girls came down continually with their petrol cans for water. Hoopoes popped in and out of holes in the willows, and fishing-hawks made occasional sallies over the water.

Hundreds of small wading birds were emitting cheerful, chuckling cries as they stepped daintily from lotus leaf to lotus leaf. The deeply castellated red walls that formed the background to this genial scene, were no more forbidding than the barbican of a Highland hunting lodge; and the gate-houses and defence-towers, with their joss-house architecture and frantic profusion of carving, seemed hardly more serious in purpose than the battlemented Chinese bridge erected in St. James's Park in celebration of the Glorious Peace of 1814.

When in 1858 the foundations of the wall were laid, three carefully selected persons had been buried alive under each gate-house, and one at each corner of the wall. Four more were entombed under the Lion Throne, and yet others at strategic points, scattered throughout the fortress. The grand total was fifty-two, a figure considered by the Board of Astrologers to err on the side of parsimony. They were taken from all walks of life, and included the pregnant woman, indispensable to the composition of a satisfactory foundation-sacrifice. While this was happening, King Mindon, a kind of Burmese Edward the Confessor, was probably splitting hairs with his theologians over obscure scriptural passages. There was a comfortable dualism about the state religion as interpreted by the Burmese kings. The population was enjoined to follow the tenets of the purest form of Buddhism, which forbade the destruction of even the most noxious forms of life, but in matters of state policy the king fell back on his Court Brahmins, Indian specialists in statecraft and occult matters, who were always ready to agree that the means were justified by the end.

Why should it have been supposed that those who had died in such terrifying circumstances should be content, after death, to guard the city of their murderers? And did it ever occur to the victims to warn their executioners that they would refuse to accomplish what was expected of them? Every city in Burma and nearly every bridge and weir had its complaisant ghosts who, according to popular belief, were always ready to drive off intruders, human or otherwise. As in the Far Eastern countries the living and the dead are divided by the most diaphanous of veils; the guardian spirits sometimes took on human form, fought with the weapons of their day, and were even wounded.

A case in point was observed on the occasion of the annihilation of the Burmese army by the Mongols of Kublai Khan, when the guardian spirits of the Burmese cities, who had gone armed, presumably with spears and javelins, to the battlefield, were put out of action by the deadly archery of the Tartar horsemen. The Glass Palace Chronicle describes the incident tersely: '. . . on the same day when the army perished . . . the spirit who was ever wont to attend the King's chaplain returned to Pagan and shook him by the foot and roused him from his sleep saying, "This day hath Ngahsaunggyan fallen. I have been wounded by an arrow. Likewise the spirits Wetthakan of Salin, Kanshi and Ngatinkyeshin, are wounded by arrows." ' Perhaps the fifty-two spirit guardians of Mandalay were similarly handicapped by out-of-date weapons when the British gunboats began their cannonading from the river.

The atmosphere of this town in the days just before the British occupation must have been more macabre than that of Moscow under Ivan the Terrible in his madness. There was a ghastly combination of modernity and crazed medievalism. The telegraph had just been introduced and the town was served by the very latest in steamboats; but wizards went mumbling through the streets, and an English official could be seized and threatened with instant crucifixion if he failed to subscribe to the national lottery.

With a sense of inferiority that was engendered in the knowledge of weakness, every attempt was seized upon to humble the pride of the hated foreigners, unless the king felt that there was any hope of extracting from one of them any of the secrets of their regrettable supremacy in certain matters. Shway Yoe quotes a typical dialogue of the kind that took place between King Mindon and any fresh wanderer to arrive in the city. 'What is your name?' 'John Smith.' 'What can you do?' 'May it please your Majesty, I am a sea-cook.' 'Can you make a cannon?' Whereupon John Smith, if he were a wise man, would agree to make the attempt. A lump of metal would be made over to him, and he would chisel and hammer away at it, and draw his pay as regularly as he could get it.

The contempt for Europeans was rooted originally in Burmese cosmogony, according to which the true human race was concentrated in South-East Asia, which was seen as a symmetrical land-mass, in the centre of which were located, not unnaturally, the Burmese holy places. To the north were the Himalayas, and beyond them a kind of fairyland containing the jewelled mountain of Meru and the magic lake in which all the rivers of the world (i.e. the Irrawaddy, the Salween, the Menam and Mekong) had their source. To the south were dismal seas, and in them the 'five hundred lesser islands' on which dwelt the inferior people from across the sea. Their attitude, with less justice, duplicated that of the Chinese. In the days of Ava they were outraged that embassies should come from the Viceroy of India, and not the Queen of England, and when the envoys came they might be obliged to live, ignored by the court, on an island where bodies were burned and criminals executed. When called to audience they were forced to walk long distances bare-footed and bare-headed in the sun; to pass through a postern-gate in the palace-wall that was so low that the shortest man was compelled to bend. For their benefit the carpets normally covering the floorboards were removed, and their feet were lacerated by the nails which were purposely left protruding.

With the death of Mindon the atmosphere of mania thickened. The ministers of state had manœuvred the supine Thibaw into the kingship in the mistaken belief that he could be more easily controlled than any of the more intelligent of Mindon's numerous descendants. The stage was now set for a traditional and regularly recurrent Burmese drama, but one which, on this occasion, provoked an unwonted flurry owing to the presence of a foreign colony. All the king's half-brothers and sisters who might have been considered dangerous to the succession and had been promptly popped into gaol, were now, according to the current Burmese euphemism, 'cleared'. The English were much impressed by the preparations for this ceremony, which consisted chiefly in the making of a large number of capacious velvet sacks, a piece of exquisite sensibility on the part of whoever was in charge of arrangements. The 'clearing' was completed in a festival lasting three days, in the course of which the victims were placed in the sacks and respectfully beaten to death; princes, by light blows on the back of the neck; princesses, on the throat. The ingenious purpose of the red velvet was to camouflage any unseemly effusion of royal blood, an advance on the method of Thibaw's ancestor, Bodawpaya, who burned to death all his surplus relations, complete with children and servants. Thibaw had shown, too, consideration for the modesty of the female sufferers, an aspect of Inquisitional burnings which was never found altogether satisfactory.

The Burmese have always been ready to excuse such methods of State, as the lesser evil; and even survivors of the Thibaw massacre told English friends frankly that, placed in Thibaw's position, they would have done the same thing. The trouble is always ascribed to the harem system, and the superfluity of potential heirs that it produced. Burmese apologists find excuses for this too. It was expected by the king's feudatories and allies that he would take their daughters into his household, and not to have done so, in the face of immemorial custom, would have given offence. In this way, too, the Empire was held together. Certainly, history does not show the kings as unduly concerned with family matters. The only concubine who is highly praised in the chronicle for her capabilities, is one who knew where to scratch the king's back without being told where it itched. For the rest, the kings are represented as not even being informed of the children born to lesser queens. A principal queen could be returned at her own request to an old lover: the fantastic tests which Brantôme reports as carried out by Renaissance princes to ensure they married virgins, would have filled the Burmese kings with amazement. Even when a queen was seduced, the royal reaction reads more like irritation than wrath. It seems that the kings were content to procreate a polite minimum of a hundred or so descendants, and leave it at that.

Mandalay's foreign colony had hardly recovered from this shock, when another unpleasant affair occurred. A smallpox epidemic carried off two of the king's children; and as epidemic disease was always ascribed to demonic interference, the Indian soothsayers were called in. A formal inspection of the jars of oil buried with Mindon's human sacrifices was made. In the remote past a magic correlation had been established between the condition of the oil thus buried, and the efficacy of the haunting. In this case only one of the four jars of oil was found to be intact; and at the full conclave of court astrologers which followed, it was unanimously voted that the city must be abandoned. When the king's ministers refused to do this, the astrologers presented their alternative: the sacrifice of six hundred more persons. Five hundred were to be Burmese, most carefully assorted to include representatives of all ages and stations. A hundred were to be foreigners.

Mindon had secured his fifty-two victims with tact, giving lavish public spectacles which attracted crowds, from which an odd spectator could be quietly spirited away without attracting attention. Thibaw, lacking Mindon's solid, meditative endowments, went at the thing like a bull at a gate, and ordered wholesale arrests. Accounts of such Burmese customs by the early travellers had been too much for the reason of the eighteenth century; consequently they had been denied in Europe as fictitious: 'an abundance of monstrous and incredible Relations . . . which one would not think could gain credit even with the weakest of their Readers.' But now the Europeans were to see for themselves. A wave of utter terror seized the city, and wholesale evacuation began. The populace crowded aboard the Irrawaddy steamers or stampeded into the fields and hills. The paralysis of the life of the city together with some doubt as to the possible effect on relations with the English of the inclusion of the hundred foreigners necessary to make a success of the sacrifice, produced an official *démenti* of the project. A few of those arrested were never seen again and it was concluded that, in his usual ineffectual way, the king had contented himself with merely tinkering with the problem.

Beyond the walls stretched a desolation of tumbled bricks and weeds I found the spot where, according to a scale-model of the palace which had been erected, the apartments of the white elephant had stood. But of these, too, only the foundations remained. This singular beast dominated the imaginations of all the monarchs of South-East Asia; and although regarded as an avatar of Gautama in numerous previous existences – and therefore primarily of interest only to Buddhists – a kind of collector's fever had developed, seizing such non-Buddhist potentates as the Emperor of Annam. This pressure by the uninstructed — the Hearsts of their day — on a limited supply, only increased the ferocity of the competition between the Buddhist rulers.

The wars between the Burmese and their Siamese neighbours were usually undertaken — in theory, at any rate — for the acquisition, or recovery, of these picturesque symbols of power. 'The king in his title,' said Ralph Fitch, writing in 1586, 'is called the king of the white elephants. If any other king have one, and will not send it to him, he will make warre with him for it; for he had rather lose a great part of his kingdom than not conquer him.' In spite of the alleged rarity of albinism in elephants one could be relied upon to turn up sufficiently often in the days of imperial expansion to keep both kingdoms in a state of devastation.

The whiteness of the elephant was nominal, and its sanctity depended upon so many esoteric factors, beyond the layman's grasp, that a substantial body of literature on the subject grew up. The pinkness of the outer annulus of the eye entered into this, as well as the length of the tail, and the number of toe-nails. Ten toe-nails instead of the normal eight were required in a successful candidate. Black elephants possessing this number were collectors' items, although not entitled to adoration, and were classified as white elephants debased by sin in previous existences. The final test, when all others had been passed, was the water one. If the skin, whether black, grey or otherwise, took on a reddish tinge when water was poured on it, the animal was conclusively white. It was elevated immediately to the position of first personality in the land after the king, accorded white and golden umbrellas, given the revenues of a province, diverted daily by a *corps de ballet*, lulled nightly to sleep by a sweet-voiced choir, and if of tender years suckled daily by a line of palace women — an honour eagerly contested by those in a position to aspire to it.

But of all these spectacles and splendours, not a vestige remained. Nothing had survived the citadel's devastation but a few antique cannon. The largest of them turned out to be imitations, with great immovable wheels made of brick. In the later centuries cannon

[*facing*: THE ARAKAN PAGODA: GUARDIAN FIGURES
TAKEN AT THE SACKING OF AYUTHIA

assumed for the Burmese a purely magic significance, having taken over the protective qualities of the leogryph. As they were never fired, there could be no objection to their being fakes, with enormous intimidating bores and twenty-foot-long barrels. The kings were usually ready to offer its weight in silver for any piece of ordnance however old or cracked, and the palace of Mandalay where all the firearms in the country were stacked up, was a repository of strange museum pieces. They were drawn, when mobile, by teams of auspiciously marked bullocks, which were trained at the word of command to kneel and bow their heads to the ground. The gunners' personal kit was stored in the muzzles. Occasionally a cannon would become, like Alaungpaya's three-pounder, the centre of a cult, and receive offerings of flowers and libations of brandy.

By the end of Mindon's reign it must have been clear that nothing could save Burma. The Burmese, together with all the rest of the Easterners, except the Japanese, were the prisoners of a cosmology composed of interlocking systems, all complete and perfect, and founded in error. Everything had been decided and settled once and for all two thousand years ago. No question had been left unanswered. It was all in the Three Baskets of the Law, its commentaries and sub-commentaries; dissected and classified beyond dispute: the seven qualities, the five virtues, the six blemishes, the eight dangers, the ninety-six diseases, the ten punishments, the thirty-two results of Karma. Although Burma was a young nation it had inherited a civilization with the hardened arteries of senility. By comparison with the certainties and self-sufficiency of Eastern Asiatic thought, the people of medieval Europe lived in intellectual anarchy. When the end came, the Burmese were beaten not so much by nineteenth-century gunners, as by the Galileos of three centuries before.

That day I was invited to Tok Galé's house for lunch. He lived in the sere reflection of an English suburb, in a detached villa with front garden, gate and path. It was about two miles from the town's centre, in the dacoit belt, and two to three miles from the White-Flag Communists' frontier which ran through some low hills to the east.

facing: BY THE WALLS OF MANDALAY]

The Tok Galés were grandchildren of the Burmese ambassador to France under King Thibaw, and there was a faded photograph in the drawing-room of this dignitary in his court uniform, looking rather sullen, as a result, perhaps, of the long period of immobility imposed by the time-exposure. The family had adopted the Baptist creed, in its tolerant and accommodating Burmese form, and had taken English christian names. The youngest sister, mild, sweet, and mysteriously unmarried, was Anne, who, in spite of not being a Buddhist had recently been accorded the great honour of acting for a short distance as pall-bearer at the cremation of the venerable U Khanti. Although she had the good sense to retain the Burmese costume, Anne was much anglicized by the friendships she had formed in the old days with members of the British Colony. She produced two autograph albums full of the familiar unrevealing snippets in which their memory was enshrined. An American officer had called her, unjustly I thought, a yellow Burmese rose, never having noticed, I suppose, that the complexion of the so-called yellow races is rarely yellow. In any case, if obliged to employ a floral analogy, I should have found this charming lady's grace suggestive of the lily rather than the rose. Although the foreign colony of Mandalay was now completely dispersed, Anne maintained her westernization at full strength by correspondence. She was a member of the Robert Taylor fan club, through which she had made many pen-friends, both in England and the United States.

Lunch consisted of various curries, served in the Burmese style with soup, which was supped throughout the meal. The Tok Galé servitors stood behind our chairs, fanning us vigorously, while we maintained a gently platitudinous conversation that was at once both oriental in flavour and curiously Victorian.

After lunch Tok Galé asked me if I would like to be presented to distinguished neighbours of his, the last surviving members in direct descent of the Burmese royal family; children of King Mindon, by different queens, who, in accordance with custom, had married each other.

We found the Prince Pyinmana and the Princess Hta Hta Paya

living in what is usually described, with grim understatement, as reduced circumstances. The Prince was much embarrassed because dacoits had broken into the house a fortnight before, and stolen all his clothes. Before I could be received, Tok Galé went home and came back with a jacket for the Prince to wear for the interview.

The old couple received us in their living room. They looked very fragile, and Tok Galé said that in recent years audiences had very rarely been granted. The villa, which might have been damaged by bombing, was in a state of advanced disrepair. Plaster was flaking from the walls, which had been repaired by sheets of asbestos and iron grilles. The only pieces of furniture were a few worn-out chairs.

Flanked by Tok Galé and myself, the Prince and Princess sat side by side on two of the broken chairs. They were waited upon by a female servant and her husband, who also served as interpreter. Coming into the royal presence from opposite directions, they shuffled along at a surprising speed on their knees and elbows, smoking large cheroots which were rarely out of their mouths. When a respectful proximity had been reached, they dropped into a comfortable kneeling position and awaited the royal commands with the benevolent patience of spaniels. Occasionally the interpreter leaned forward, took the cheroot out of his mouth, grasped the end of the Prince's ear-trumpet, and bawled a translation of my remarks into it. Once, after shuffling backwards a short distance, he turned and made off to fetch some object of interest the Prince had called for, and on returning collected his baby which was shrieking in a back room, and came into sight still crawling, but this time on one elbow, the baby gathered in the other arm.

In vain I sought in these aged, placid faces some vestige of the magic presence of their ancestor Alaungpaya, the village headman, who had conquered the Burmese throne with followers armed only with cudgels, driven the French from Syriam, spurned the English, waded in the blood of his enemies. It was generally acknowledged that fire streamed from Alaungpaya's personal weapons; that, like the heroes of the Ramayana, he fought with fairy javelins and thunderbolts, and that wherever he stopped gorgeous birds and butterflies entered his dwelling. Here his race had come to an end, in these two feeble, affable old per-

sons, subdued by resignation, and possessing no more than the normal
dignity of old age.

Occasionally there was a shrewdness in the Prince's expression,
inherited from his father, as well as evidence of a sense of humour,
inappropriate in a ruling monarch, but which now in lustreless
adversity could be given its wings. He was one of four brothers
who had escaped the famous massacre, having been considered too
young and unimportant for the dignity of the red sack. Later, to avoid
the possibility of any second thoughts, he had become a monk. He
was clearly well prepared for certain standard questions; particularly
when asked for his opinion of Queen Supayalat, commonly considered
to have been Thibaw's evil genius. Why did Queen Elizabeth have
Mary Queen of Scots killed? asked the Prince, apropos of Supayalat's
Borgia-like methods with rivals. The Prince's eyes were twinkling
merrily; he was obviously enjoying himself, and had suddenly taken
over from the interpreter, and relapsed into fluent English. It was
clear that he liked to stagger his visitors over matters of Burmese high
policy in the past. 'Supayalat', said the Prince firmly, 'was as good as
the average Burmese lady. If an ordinary woman comes across her
rival in love, she'll do everything she can. Supayalat had the power,
that's all.'

The Princess was the daughter of a Siamese lesser queen, and was
also considered too insignificant for inclusion in the massacre. She was
only fourteen when her mother took her by the hand and they went
together out on to their balcony to watch the British troops march in.
All she remembered of them was the shining helmets and the plumes.
The Burmese, who had expected a sack and massacre of the traditional
kind, were much amazed at the mildness of the soldiers.

On the whole the Prince and Princess seemed to regret the old
colonial days. Perhaps this was natural because, since Burma had become a free nation, their allowance had been reduced from eight hundred rupees each a month to four hundred rupees. The Prince also
complained of the lack of intellectual nourishment these days, and
asked me to try to send him a volume of Thomas Hood's poems from
England.

CHAPTER X

ANAWRAHTA'S PAGODA

BEFORE coming to Mandalay it had been my intention to visit, if I could, the village of Taungbyon. Taungbyon lies only about twenty miles south of the capital, but I now realized that in the South-East Asia of today it might have become as inaccessible as Lhasa in the last century. This village was associated in about 1070 with Anawrahta's attempt to stamp out the indigenous Burmese religion of nat-worship. Anawrahta was a kind of minor Charlemagne of Buddhism. Conducting a crusade against the kingdom of Thaton he captured the unprecedented total of thirty-two white elephants, each of which was loaded with sacred books for the return to the capital. He also obtained by conquest or negotiation, the Buddha's collar-bone, his frontlet bone and an authentic duplicate of the tooth of Kandy. As a result of these triumphs he was acclaimed the foremost champion of Buddhism of his day.

Anawrahta's method of combating the older faith was to order the destruction of the nat shrines found, at that time, in every house in Burma, and to limit the practice of the religion to one village only — Taungbyon. Here elaborate arrangements were made for the celebration of the rites. The site was inaugurated by a spectacular assassination. On the pretext that they had failed to contribute a brick apiece towards the building of a pagoda, the king's chief generals, the Shwepyi brothers, were executed by castration. Reading between the blurred lines of history, it may be supposed that the king was disappointed at the failure of their expedition to China which immediately preceded this event. Sent to obtain another Buddha tooth from the chief of Nanchao (Yunnan), they were fobbed off with a mere jade replica, which had been allowed by contact to absorb a trifling amount of virtue from the original. The generals happened also to be popular heroes, victors of numerous campaigns undertaken to carry the light of religion into adjacent countries; and the king perhaps felt they had usurped some of the lustre that was rightly his alone. As twins, and the sons of a well-known ogress, it must have been clear that they had the makings of superior nats, and it only required such a piece of monstrous regal caprice as their murder to complete the process.

The Shwepyi brothers became the most popular and the second most powerful of all the members of the Burmese nat-pantheon. They are still worshipped at Taungbyon, with a corps of female mediums in attendance to transmit their oracles. Their annual festival is the most important of Burmese animistic ceremonies, and draws huge crowds from all parts of the country.

Since frequent reference to nats is unavoidable in any work dealing with Burma, I must attempt to define the nature of these powerful supernatural entities. The word is used in a loose, generic sense to cover all members — whether ghosts, ghouls, vampires, or merely lost and starving souls — of the spectral world. There were nats called into existence by an intellectual effort, such as Alaungpaya's gun nat. This modernistic demiurge was reverenced in the form of the king's first three-pounder, which, scented, coated with gold-leaf, and wrapped in silk, was propitiated with bottles of liquor. But besides this *déclassé* and miscellaneous ghostly riff-raff a category of sentient beings exists, having its own fairly elevated place in the Buddhist hierarchy of souls. These are the local tutelary spirits, whose worship preceded (and in the case of the Vietnamese, actually outlasted and replaced) Buddhism. Of these there are many thousands; although only thirty-seven, the indigenous Burmese gods, are adored — or rather, propitiated — on a national scale.

According to the cosmogony which the Burmese borrowed from India, there are eleven principal stages or levels of the 'corporeal and generating' soul; four being unhappy, and seven happy. Unhappy souls are those confined in hell, or existing as miscellaneous ghosts, or incarnated in animals. Until recently souls imprisoned in the bodies of foreigners were included in this last category. At the bottom of the scale of happiness come human beings, and immediately above them in the soul's evolution are located the true nats. The situation of a nat is preferable to that of the most fortunate human being, although it is still far removed from the felicity of the ultimate heavens. Nats, although exempt from the ills of humanity, are still subject to sensual passion, which sometimes leads them even to form unions with human beings. From such attachments — whether temporary or otherwise — arises the recognized class of nat-ka-daws — spirit mediums or wives — so numerous that it has been seriously suggested that in the forthcoming census of the population of Burma they should be described as a separate occupational class.

The land of the nats, then, is a kind of Mahommedan paradise, whose occupants are able to make the best, such as it is, of both worlds. With the soul's progress upwards, however, the intellectual pleasures begin to assert themselves, and the more typically human distractions to lose their appeal. Finally, after passage through numerous heavens, a formless and incorporeal state is attained when the soul, imagined as an immaterial sun, hovers on the threshold of Nirvana, a strange, archaic version of the Shavian Life-Force, the pure intellect functioning in the void.

From an examination of the attributes of the thirty-seven nats the influence of the thirty-three devas of the Hindus may be suspected; but it is also evident that their legends enshrine memories of Mongol heroes of great antiquity, some of them shared with the Thais, the Cambodians and even the Vietnamese, and the peoples of Southern China. The legends are confused and vary from district to district. U Shin Gyi, for example, the guardian spirit of Rangoon and the lower Irrawaddy, is there known as the greatest harpist of all time, who, having fatally charmed the sirens of the river, was drowned by them. In Northern Burma he is no more than the son of a king of Pagan, who was killed by a fall from a swing while at play. To enter this pantheon of the nats, a tragic death seems, above all, to have been essential. Many of the thirty-seven were kings while they lived, but no king who died comfortably in his bed could enter this magic circle. This strange immortality was only to be achieved by touching in some unpredictable way a chord of popular imagination. Of an ancient tyrant's memory nothing remains but the legend of his perfidious handling of a blacksmith, who became the most powerful of all the nats and the guardian spirit of every Burmese house.

Those who became nats died by murder, of grief or fright, from snake-bite, an overdose of opium or the unlucky smell of onions. Among their numbers was a general who took up cockfighting when he should have been leading the armies, and was buried to the waist and left to die. There was also a politician who, when the king's wrath turned against him, tried to get away on a marble elephant, which, however, he failed to vivify by well-tried magical methods. The Burmese people never forgot this picturesquely tragic episode. Nor were they able to forget the grotesque end of King Tabinshweti, the conqueror who united all Burma and left it at the height of its prosperity in the days when the Portuguese first entered the country. Tiring of the panoply of power, Tabinshweti took to drink and was finally assassinated. According to one tradition he was killed while seated upon a close stool, suffering from an attack of dysentery. Of this king nothing has come down to the Burmese man in the street but this one foolish fact. The marchings and the counter-marchings, the sack of towns and devastations of provinces, have all been forgotten. This founder of the Burmese Empire, this scourge of God, is now no more than a man who died ridiculously while on a lavatory-seat, a dysentery nat, who receives offerings of fruit and flowers from sufferers from that disease, and even used to be worshipped in effigy in the ludicrous posture in which he died.

This strange reversing process, that makes clowns of kings, and that in death takes ordinary unlucky mortals and places them in the ranks of the heroes, is no better exemplified than in the case of Nga Pyi, a messenger, a silly man, who while riding, about eight hundred years ago, a bearer of bad news, to the camp of his prince, dared to break his journey to sleep. For this delay he was executed, becoming the Spirit Rider of the White Horse, a national champion, a Burmese Santiago. White horse-puppets are offered at his shrines all over Burma, and he has made frequent historical appearances like the Angels at Mons, brandishing his sword at the head of the armies, when the issue of the day has been in doubt. Lately he was reported in the Rangoon press to have been in action against the Karens.

Thus Burmese history is seen, dreamlike and inconsequent, in the popular imagination, just as the average Englishman remembers little of King Alfred but the story of the burnt cakes, and nothing of Robert the Bruce but his encounter with a spider.

My friend, Tok Galé, thought that a visit to Taungbyon could be arranged through the good offices of the Superintendent of Police; so when in accordance with my instructions I paid a routine call on this gentleman, the matter was mentioned.

The Superintendent was an Anglo-Burman, of a type frequently to be met with, which takes after the English father in an almost exaggerated way. This variation is tall and of military bearing, favours a close-clipped moustache, and possesses a bluff inhibition of manner to be found in England among minor executives of substantial insurance companies, or army officers of field rank. It seemed impossible that a tiny Burmese mother could have produced so stalwart a son as this.

Smiling shyly, the Superintendent held out a huge hand. There would be no trouble in going to Taungbyon. Absolutely no trouble, old boy. Lay on an escort just in case; but actually things were pretty quiet. Touch wood, and all that. The Superintendent was a man of few words, and one felt a habit of understatement might be concealed by these clipped and unemphatic utterances.

A large map of the Mandalay area covered half of the walls. It was patterned with interpenetrating colours, swirling contours and isolated blotches. By reference to the key I learned that Communists, either the 'Red' or 'White' Flag varieties, held the country immediately to the north-east, east and south-east of the city. The centre of Mandalay itself was described as 'under effective Government administration', which, however, did not extend to the suburbs, where administration was admitted to be 'non-effective'. Across the Irrawaddy, to the west, the situation seemed to be vague, or 'liquid' as the military euphemism usually puts it. This area was left uncoloured. To the north and south a hideous yellow stain was spreading, flecked here and there with a red rash of Communism. Here the 'White' People's Volunteer Organization held sway; the once patriotic force which had been raised to fight the Japanese, and then, with the war at an end, had refused to be disarmed, and turned to banditry. There were also, said the Superintendent casually, a few 'Yellow' P.V.O.s who, after surrendering to the government, had revolted again, and gone underground. In some sectors the P.V.O.s were supposed to have accepted temporary Communist leadership, and in other places they were fighting them. There, where the map was striped so garishly, the 'White' and 'Red' Communists had united, dissolved their association and re-united again. The present situation was uncertain. The map-makers hadn't bothered to mark in a few villages held by army deserters, who might quite well by now have thrown in their lot with any of the other organizations.

So there it was, said the Superintendent, with a suspicion of boredom. A bit of a mess, and so on, and so forth, but nothing that couldn't be put right in the end. Taungbyon, I might have noticed, was deeply embedded in P.V.O. territory; but nothing was to be thought of it. With a wave of the hand, the map and all it represented was dismissed. An escort would call for us at eight in the morning.

And at eight precisely the escort was there; but instead of the cheroot-smoking private I had expected, a three-ton lorry had arrived with a squad of tommy-gunners, and a Bren gun mounted on the roof. A spruce young lieutenant came over, saluted and clambered into the back of our jeep, and we were off. This display of force was in flagrant opposition to the advice I had always been given in Rangoon; never to travel with the police or the military. To do so, said my informants, was to run the risk of falling into an ambush, whereas by travelling alone or with unarmed companions, one increased the possibility of robbery, but very much lessened that of sudden death.

Out through the southern suburbs of Mandalay we went, plunging and bucking painfully, through the dust curtain already raised by the thousand bullock carts of the morning. Away to the left lay the abandoned pagodas of Amarapura, glinting dragon's teeth sown thickly in a stony plain. In 1857 this capital city was deserted by order of King Mindon, because its luck was supposed to have become exhausted, and also because the king felt himself drawn towards the sacred Mandalay Hill, of which he had dreamed on two successive nights. In a few years all the lay buildings, constructed of wood, had mouldered away completely, and now only these gleaming cones remained.

Our road floundered on through the exhausted earth. This plain had endured ten kingdoms and a hundred generations, and now it was sapped and vanquished. We were encircled by a ghostly decrepitude, roads that lead to nowhere, canals holding pools of brilliant, stinking water, a few nat-haunted banyan trees, grotesque with old muscled trunks and bearded roots. A row of sickly flamboyants wept their blossoms into a swamp, in which a stork waded away, as if through blood, on our approach. Having taken the wrong road many times, we stopped to ask the way from a girl in a green silk longyi who had come down to a canal for water. As she dipped her petrol cans, first one then the other, into the slime, the whole stagnant expanse suddenly boiled into life as frogs went leaping and splashing away. Before turning back she cupped her hands and drank some water from one of her cans.

Two enormous leogryphs guarded the approach to Taungbyon. They were as large as the monsters that stand before the Shwedagon Pagoda at Rangoon, but painted stark white, and eerie and forbidding in these cheerless surroundings. Beyond, reared up Anawrahta's pagoda.

We roared into the village and pulled up by a structure like a roofed-over market-place in an English country town. The soldiers came tumbling out of the lorry, cocked their Sten guns and formed a widely spaced circle round us and the sacred places. Beyond them we could see the villagers, temporary dependents of the P.V.O., gathered at the doors of their huts and watching us without either hostility or enthusiasm. It was correct first to visit the pagoda. With our shoes respectfully removed, we were led by a guardian to the entrance and shown the two spaces still left vacant for the bricks of the Shwepyi brothers.

Apart from building pagodas, the ancient Burmese seem to have set extraordinary store by the act of completing them. Just as in biblical times battles were sometimes decided by individual combat between champions, there are many examples in Burmese history of conflicts being settled without fighting in favour of the side which could first complete a pagoda. The chroniclers relate with relish the obvious and childish stratagems practised by the victors, who usually had a canvas imitation finished while the incredibly gullible adversary was still busy with the foundations of a traditional building of brick. Perhaps, after all, there was something in the nature of high treason about the Shwepyis' defection.

One of the soldiers now brought up the guardian of the nat shrine, which was in a building under the market-like structure. Padlocks were unfastened and heavy double trellis gates slid back. It was like being let into a bank after hours. In an interior lit by strings of electric fairy-lights and behind a bank of flowers sat two gaudy dolls, with high spiked helmets, and drawn swords carried upon their shoulders. They were quite unmartial in appearance, and yet, in some way, sinister. Unlike the Buddha images with their placid, even smug expressions, these golden faces were shrewd and scheming. What a decline attends the mighty after death! These great captains who had fought their way to China and back, and had plagued Anawrahta after their killing by catching at the rudder of the royal raft so that it could not move (a classical Burmese form of haunting), were now a couple of slightly disreputable Don Juans of the inferior heavens. Legend remembered that they had died by castration, and appeared to attach some tortuous and topsy-turvy significance to this. By a kind of logic in reverse the king who is supposed to have died as a result of an attack of dysentery is worshipped by dysentery sufferers, and the castrated heroes become the patrons of sly amours. At their annual ceremony the chief mediums, who are females, dress themselves in the special costumes attributed to the brothers; in waist-cloths with an ornamental border, wide-sleeved jackets, white scarves thrown over the shoulder, and light red helmets on their heads. They are attended by junior mediums dressed as Burmese princesses. The ceremony begins with the chanting of the traditional song in which the brothers' lives and deaths are briefly described. This ends with the words: 'Now all ye pretty maidens, love ye us, as ye were wont to do while yet we were alive.' In this lies a hint of the mild element of the saturnalia that appears to enter into this feast. As the lieutenant put it, on our way back, 'to accomplish this celebration we proceed not with our wives, as there are many pretty ladies assembled there, also not in company with their spouses'.

CHAPTER XI

BY LORRY TO LASHIO

A T eight next morning I climbed into the gharry called Ford, setting in brisk motion its resident gnats, and ordered the driver to take me to the airport. In accordance with my declared itinerary I was to fly to Myitkyina, leaving Mandalay on approximately the third of March and returning, by river, on the eighth. On the ninth I was to set out for Lashio by road. One day was allowed for this considerable journey; but the War Office had generously allotted five days to get to Taunggyi, which was hardly farther. There was some vague talk of occasional caravans of lorries plying by stages between these two towns, but no suggestion had ever been made that there was any way of getting from Taunggyi to Mandalay, a section for which three days had been prescribed. Having reached Mandalay again, I was to board a boat, which the General Staff Department seemed to imagine would be waiting for me with steam up — since no delay was assumed in the city — reaching Rangoon seven days later, the minimum, taken by the trip, in favourable circumstances. It had seemed to me at the time ambitious, when allowing for Burma's condition, to try to draw up an exact timetable, in the way one might have done in preparation for a Cook's tour in the Dolomites. And now at the airport it soon became evident that an immediate break-down in the original planning was likely.

Nothing had been heard of the plane that was due to arrive at nine o'clock. Nor did the airport staff seem in any way surprised. The plane that had been due four days before, on the Monday, had not arrived either. At that season, thick ground mists often prevented the planes taking off at Rangoon in the early hours, and unless they could make an early start there was no time to go to Myitkyina and back during the day. But there was still hope, and I was invited to make myself at home in the picturesque huts which served as waiting-rooms.

One of these had a notice across it which said it was a restaurant. Here in surroundings to which a Hindu ascetic would not have objected I seated myself and ordered breakfast. I was soon joined by a police official, who began to probe me in the most urbane fashion, between mouthfuls of eggs and chips, as to my intentions. Refusing, perhaps through irritation caused by the delay and the heat, to enter into the conventions of the game, I silently produced and spread across the table the whole of my many documents. The officer was hurt at such bluntness, and said that he was only trying to do his job in the most reasonable way. There was no gainsaying this; I apologized, put the permits away uninspected, allowed myself to be drawn forth in a civilized manner, and our interview terminated cordially.

Several hours dwindled away. With their passing the excited anticipation drained from the passengers who now squatted, resignation drawn over them like a shabby cloak, in corners of the airport huts. A group of pongyis, released in these days, it seemed, from the prohibition on such mundane forms of travel, had ceased to examine their tickets and relapsed into holy meditation. Only a few crows turned in the grey, empty sky, in the rim of which the far hills flickered and stirred as if about to dissolve. Occasionally a member of the airport staff came cringing past under the sun. At about midday an official went round whispering to the various groups, as if a great man had died, that the flight had been cancelled.

Back at the airport office, they refunded money on tickets, re-booked those who insisted on a hypothetical Monday-plane, drove the despondent crowd into the street and barred the door. A huge barrel-chested Sikh came up and clutched at me moaning, 'I can't stand this heat'. He wanted to go to Bhamó, and knew a man who might be persuaded to hire him a jeep, with a driver, for five hundred rupees. What would I say to splitting the cost? I hadn't intended to go to Bhamó, but it was in the right direction; so I agreed, and in a moment the Sikh had leaped into the nearest gharry, which bore him swiftly away, his head thrust out of the window, beard quivering with excitement and despair, shouting alternately instructions to the driver and counsel to me. An hour later he was back, heartbroken. The man was a villain who wanted to profit from the misfortunes of others by charging twice the price offered. Now he was off again to comb the city for an honest jeep-owner, and with a furious wave to the driver he went rattling away.

It now seemed to me that I might as well, to use an army phrase, 'find my own way', going perhaps to Lashio and Taunggyi first, and working in the Northern Shan States part of the trip at a later stage. I therefore made inquiries in the neighbouring tea-houses and found that a lorry was expected to leave for Lashio next morning. With the aid of an English-speaking gharry driver, this was located. The driver was either working or sleeping underneath it, since only his legs protruded, but after the gharry-wallah had jerked them furiously, he crawled out and admitted that he would be leaving for Lashio early next morning. Still not completely weaned from Western conceptions of travel, I tried to fasten him down to something less vague. Through the ever-present language difficulties there was nothing to be done. Around us swirled a flood of bullock-carts and pedicabs. There seemed no way of fixing this definite point in the chaos of the traffic, but that would have to suffice. He would leave from there, early in the morning — when you could see the veins on your hands.

Back to Tok Galé I went to announce the prolongation of my stay. There was another visit to our Chinese friend who with limitless hospitality immediately offered me his room again. Another night was to be endured in the reverberating no-man's-land between the cinema loudspeakers, the pagoda gongs, and the penetrating Chinese sopranos of the tea-house gramophones. Once again I took my wash-bowl to the edge of the parapet, silhouetted there against the neon-pink of the sky, and, trying to convince myself that any previous reaction had been imaginary, poured out the water on the roof below. Once again came back the muffled cry. On my way to the Excelsior a pariah dog turned back and followed me. Remembering the Englishman who was nearly lynched for killing one of these creatures I increased my pace, and the dog did the same. When close at my heels it reached forward and without any particular animosity, in a rather detached and experimental manner, it took my calf between its teeth, and bit. Having done so, it turned back and strolled away, while I was still wondering what the onlookers would do if I kicked it high into the air. In the Excelsior I washed the wound in Fire-Tank Brand Mandalay Whisky, and offer as a testimonial the fact that I suffered no ill effects.

But that night there was a good news. Tok Galé arrived to tell me that a Mr. Dalgouttie of the British Information Service would be arriving next day by plane from Mandalay and then continuing immediately to the British Consulate at Maymyo in the car which would be sent down to meet him. Although Maymyo was only thirty miles along the road to Lashio, it was situated at an altitude of three thousand five hundred feet, and would therefore be a very agreeable place for me to stay for a day or two while making arrangements to go further. I telephoned the Consulate and was told that there would be no difficulty about putting me up.

About ten miles out of Mandalay, the road begins to climb and to wind. There are trees, at first isolated in tangled bush, and then slowly closing in until linked with thinly flowering creepers. According to reliable information, the area through which we were passing was solidly held by White-Flag Communists. Burmese army lorries passed up and down the road and, in doing so, were frequently shot-up; but no attempt was made by the army to penetrate into the jungle where the Communists administered the villages. It was probably not worth while. Even if a major operation could be undertaken to clear every village, the Communists would come back as soon as the troops had gone away. It seemed likely that an unofficial *modus vivendi* had been reached, and for civilians the road was moderately safe, as long as they didn't travel with the police, or with the army. The White-Flag Communists were said not to indulge in acts of terrorism, which sometimes occurred in Red-Flag areas. The trouble was to know who was in control. The traveller's chief security problem was the lack of effective control by one side or the other; because the Communists, no doubt, had the same trouble with dacoits as did the government.

The Consulate station-wagon sped smoothly over the first section of the 'Burma Road' which, still the country's main strategic highway, was in far better condition than the terrible tracks on which I had hitherto travelled. In about an hour we were in Maymyo, the former hill-station of the English, and suddenly it seemed as though we were entering Forest Gate at the end of a dry August. With a hissing of tyres we drove up a well-kept thoroughfare called 'The Mall', across which, before us, passed a long, thin snake with whip-like movements. There was also a Downing Street and several well-spaced villas, with names like Ridge-View. We stopped for a moment at the golf course to chat with members of the Consular staff, and then drove on to the Consulate, which was set upon an eminence, above evidences of landscape-gardening; a sweep of lawns, with coarse, whitened grass; flower-beds in which larkspur and nasturtiums fought against desperate odds.

Here at Maymyo I was offered a splendid chance to compare the English and French methods of adaptation to South-East Asia. In the previous year I had stayed at Dalat, the French equivalent of Maymyo in Indo-China. In Dalat, one knew that one was in the Far East. Although it was neither France nor Indo-China, the French had tinkered with bamboo and carved wood and produced an acceptable pastiche, a compromise that was sometimes gay and well suited to its surroundings. There were hotels and restaurants where you could eat the local food, Frenchified of course, but still of recognizably oriental origin. In Maymyo there seemed to be no compromise. The atmosphere, by contrast, was austere, sporting and contemplative. Maymyo was very clean, hard-working, hard-playing, exaggeratedly national and slightly dull. Here you began to understand the allegation that the English are an insular people.

But if unadventurous and simple by French colonial standards, life in Maymyo was full of solid comfort. It was quite extraordinary to experience the sensations so often associated with the fatigues and discomforts of remote places in these well-ordered surroundings, to lie at dawn between well-laundered sheets, watching the flocks of green parakeets in the tree-tops, and listening to the early jabbering of exotic birds. Fifty yards from my window, beyond the show of sweet peas, the jungle was kept in check behind an iron railing. The jungle was not particularly exuberant, and had been made to look rather like a gentleman's sporting estate in the Home Counties, by the cutting through it of numerous walks and avenues. In the early hours there was a great scratching of fowls down by the fence, and as it seemed unlikely that the Consul, a dashing figure, should keep chickens, I went down to inspect them. I was amazed to find that they actually were jungle fowl, a cock, with mane and rump of copper and glinting blue thighs, with his numerous harem. As no one had ever bothered them you could get within a few yards and watch their bright, busy foraging among the leaves. Duffy, the Consul, said that they were there every day as he had resisted the servants' implorings to shoot them; he knew that as soon as the first shot had been fired, this decorative adjunct to his demesne would vanish for ever.

That evening the Consul gave a party. Besides the shrunken Consular staff, there were a few Indians and Anglo-Burmese, a Burmese princess with her English husband and her daughter, and a British engineer who was at work on the repair of the viaduct which carried the Mandalay-Lashio railway line over the gorge at Gokteik, about forty-five miles further up the road. Officers of the Burmese Army who had been invited did not appear; a reflection, it seemed, of an officially-inspired coolness.

The work on the viaduct sounded like a Herculean labour. It had been in progress for three years and every so often the territory would pass temporarily into the control of some new insurgent movement, and high-ranking officers would come and inspect the work benignly, in the conviction that they would benefit from it in due course. Recently the Communists had made one or two official appearances, once requisitioning the typewriter, for which an official receipt had been left. The local Communists, not having had to fight Europeans as they have done in Indo-China and Malaya, show no particular anti-white animus. When they were about to remove some of his personal gear, the engineer made the private ownership clear by pointing to his chest and saying, 'me, me'. These articles were left.

The guest of the evening was clearly the Princess Ma Lat, who, apart from the possession of a vivid personality in its own right, had acquired some additional celebrity by a reference to her in Mr. Maurice Collis's book *Trials in Burma*. The passage, which is practically known by heart by the literary-minded section of the local population, deals with the occasion when, some thirty years ago, Mr. Collis, who was then a district magistrate, solemnized the Princess's marriage with a local bookmaker. After commenting with great enthusiasm on the Princess's beauty and dignity of demeanour, the author permits himself an expression of surprise that he should have been called upon to perform this particular ceremony.

Ma Lat's party had settled down at the other end of the room, and I found myself engaged with an Anglo-Burman. He was the opposite of the Police Inspector of Mandalay, dark and Burmese-looking where the other had been Anglo-Saxon; unable to throw his lot in with the Burmese from whom he felt separated by blood, he was permanently wretched as a result. This man clung desperately, pitifully, to the English in him, of which so little could be externally recognized. In some way or other, he and his fellow Anglo-Burmese had been 'abandoned', left to some kind of nameless fate under the pure Burmese whom they so clearly despised. Such unfortunate people are, of course, always followers of some nonconformist Christian sect, which further impedes their comfortable and happy absorption into the human mainstream of the country where they live.

As the man was becoming lachrymose I was much relieved by the approach of Mr. Bellamy, Ma Lat's husband, a man of genial and confidential manner, who still occasionally makes a book. Mr. Bellamy said, 'If you want to talk to my mem-sahib, you'd better come over now, because we're going in a moment.'

The Princess Ma Lat was at this time fifty-seven, although in the way of many Asiatics who do no manual labour, she looked much less than her age. She was dressed in conservative Burmese style, and her still handsome features were continually enlivened by an expression which made one feel she was amused by something of which she did not entirely approve. Since it had been brought up several times in the evening, I had an intuition that a tactful allusion to the famous passage would not be badly received. The Princess's characteristic expression deepened. 'I object to the book,' she said, 'only because of its inaccuracy. Mr. Collis said that although a member of the royal family, I could not be admitted to any of the European clubs of Rangoon . . . My father was an honorary member of *every* club.' When she had said this, the amused disapproval brightened into quiet triumph.

The Princess's grandfather was brother of King Mindon and Crown Prince — a perilous situation for any Burman to be in. In due course, in the preliminary manœuvring for the succession, he was murdered by one of his many nephews, and as Burmese liquidations were usually extended to include any members of the family who happened to be about, his son — the Princess's father — escaped, to take refuge with the British. Later he went off to the Shan States where he was recognized as 'King of Burma', and raised an army to attack Thibaw, but was forestalled in this by British action.

In these days Ma Lat had become the moving spirit behind various charities, particularly the local maternity hospital. She is the recognized expert in all matters pertaining to the cinema, and is able quite effortlessly to name the stars playing in any American film shown in the last twenty years. I mentioned my recent visit to her cousins in Mandalay, describing in passing the servants' habit of crawling into their presence. Ma Lat nodded with approval, and said that she could remember the time when hers did the same, but, there — you knew what servants were nowadays. Discovering that we both expected to be in Rangoon in about a month's time, we arranged to meet, and I promised to escort her to see the film of Cinderella.

The daughter of the union, June Rose, who was about twenty years of age, allied to the graceful beauty of the Burmese a quite European vivacity. She had recently been co-winner of some sort of competition, and as a result had been invited with the other successful competitor, a Burmese boy called Richard, for a three months' tour in the U.S.A. There they had learned to jitterbug. When the family were about to leave, in an elderly and ailing British car, June Rose showed much skill in locating a short in the wiring, and much tomboyish energy

in winding the starting-handle until the engine fired. On recon-
sideration of the whole episode I cannot really think that the Princess
was any worse off as she was, enthusiastically immersed in the
interests of any English or American woman of her age, than she
might have been in the old days, living the stifling life of the Burmese
royal seraglio, with the shadow of the red sack looming with each
change of kingship.

It was now time to think of the journey to Lashio, and the Consul
sent his chauffeur with me down to Maymyo bazaar, to make inquiries.
We were told that the trucks leaving Maymyo that day were going no
further than the towns of Naungkhio or Hsipaw. There might be
some kind of transport coming through next day, from Mandalay,
but no one was sure.

Maymyo bazaar itself was wonderfully lively. We were already on
the edge of the Northern Shan States, and there were swaggering,
sword-bearing hill men about the street in turbans and the short
pyjama-trousers worn by the Shans. Some of them were tattooed so
closely wherever their flesh showed, that they might have been wearing
skin-tights of knitted blue wool. In the big, walled market they sold
a fine selection of the bags the Shans carry over their shoulders, wonderfully woven in colours and sometimes decorated with small cowrie
shells. There were piles of enormous coolie hats, some of them
finished in a central cone of silver, any number of patent medicines,
and towels with 'good morning' on them. Maymyo had many
barbers' shops, which had found a use for the waste products of the
local 'tyre surgery'. Lengths of outer covers were mounted complete
in sections of rims on the bottoms of the barbers' chairs, in which the
customers rocked themselves in perilous abstraction while the razors
hovered over their chins. There were ranks of gharries that appeared
to do no serious business, although occasionally a group of Shans
would wake up a driver, bundle into one and go for a quick spin round
the bazaar, much as in the old days one took a five shilling flip round
the aerodrome in a plane. In Maymyo the exuberant fantasy of the
Mandalay gharries was diminished, but I saw a pedicab with three

[*facing:* OLD MAN (RACE UNKNOWN) MET IN
MAYMYO MARKET

pairs of handlebars, twenty-seven lamps and fourteen horns, one in the shape of a serpent.

At the Consulate, Duffy thought it a good thing to wait at least another day, to see if I could pick up a truck going all the way to Lashio, rather than run the risk of being stranded for a time in one of the smaller towns between. I felt ashamed of the eagerness with which I seized on this short respite.

In the afternoon we visited the local gardens. There was a small, trim lake, a few well-spaced trees and shrubberies in the English style, and here, said the gardener, in the early mornings passed a gaudy, transient population of hornbills, orioles and parakeets. But always with the mounting of the sun these exotics vanished and were replaced by the drab, skulking bird-life of the European woodlands. Where peacock and silver pheasant had strutted now only hardy, unabashed thrushes and sparrows hopped. But always the background was dominated by the mysterious calls of birds, aloof and invisible in the jungle; the sad hooting of the Burmese cuckoo, which is the call of the cuckoo we know with the notes reversed; the midnight rendezvous-whistle of the brain-fever bird, which repeated without respite, to the victim raving with malaria, becomes an hallucinatory addition to his torments. In the end these sounds become associated with the Indo-Chinese peninsula, and after being away from them for a time, I found myself longing to hear them again.

Dressing next morning I hid a small reserve of money in a bandage round a damaged ankle. The barometer of Burmese travel had fallen back somewhat, since the news had just come through of the slaughter of two tin-miners near Tavoy — a rare and extraordinary occurrence, as foreigners have not been singled out for attack in Burma. They had been taken off a truck in which they had been riding with Burmese passengers, and riddled with Sten-gun fire. The truck had then been sent on its way, without any of the other passengers being molested. This was supposed to be the work of Red-Flag Communists, or perhaps local Mon insurgents, or perhaps a combination of both. Fortunately it was believed that there were no Red-Flags in the Lashio area.

At seven o'clock the Consul's driver was sent down to the bazaar
to find out if there was any news of transport. Soon after, he was
back again to say that a truck was just about to leave, but that it would
wait ten minutes for me. I said goodbye to Duffy, who gave me the
usual advice about non-resistance and a smile when dealing with Burmese bandits, and we were off.

But at the bazaar there was no sign of the lorry. Backwards and forwards we went, from the tea-shop to the tyre-surgery, from the tyre-
surgery to the petrol filling point. The lorry had vanished, and while
we were combing the back-streets of Maymyo, it might, of course, be
already putting the miles between us on the road to Lashio. Finally
the driver decided that it was no use looking further in Maymyo, and
we went sprinting off, down the Lashio road. After a mile he pulled
up to make inquiries from a man who was sitting outside his workshop, making a coffin. Only a minute ago, said the man, such a lorry
had gone past. But to one engrossed in creative labour time's relativity
is very real; a minute may be an hour. On we went, full speed ahead;
the last bullock-cart dropped behind, the jungle closed in.

It is well known that the natives of all races who have only recently
been introduced to mechanization, drive in emergency with a special
élan, but my driver was handicapped by a mysterious ailment of the
jeep, a disfunction which I have never met before or since. We would
accelerate, sometimes to nearly fifty miles an hour, and then suddenly
the car would be seized by a violent convulsion, whose epicentre
seemed vaguely located in the gearbox. Once in the grip of this palsy,
the driver would be obliged to bring the jeep practically to a standstill,
before the tremors died away, and we could accelerate once again.
This rebellion of the mechanism could be avoided by keeping, say, at
a steady thirty-five miles an hour, but it was clear that if we did this
the lorry might be gaining upon us.

On we went in this way, mile after mile, over hills and through
valleys inundated with a frothing, vernal vegetation and filled with the
odour of newly watered ferns in a glasshouse. We had been travelling
for half an hour when I was alarmed to see that the needle on

the petrol gauge had fallen nearly to zero. This I pointed out, but the driver shook his head reassuringly. He had probably laid some kind of wager with himself, and had become seriously interested in the outcome of our chase. Along we hustled, taking full advantage of the rolling downhill slopes when the speed could be kept up with relatively low engine revolutions, which did not bring on our mechanical ague. To me, it was incredible that the lorry should have covered such a distance in so short a time. Whenever we turned a bend, I expected to see it trailing its billows of dust along the next straight, but all we saw was an armoured-car with tyre trouble, and a couple of the crew covering with their rifles a third man, while he got on with the repair. The petrol gauge now said empty and I gesticulated at it dumbly again; but the driver had become possessed by his purpose and paid no attention, leaning away out of the car to sweep round a right-hand curve. Down a hill-side we dropped through half a dozen hairpin bends, while large, winged insects, seemingly sucked up out of space, struck us in the face. We swerved wildly to avoid a rotten tree trunk that had fallen half across the road. Again we were stricken of our palsy, slowed down, re-accelerated, and there, at last, were the few huts of a hamlet, with the lorry, lying at an angle in the road's camber, outside a tea-shop.

The third of the Three Great Works of Perfection prescribed by the Buddhist faith, is a benevolent disposition towards all sentient beings, and I believe that apart from unfortunate incidents arising out of dacoity and warfare this is much observed by the generality of the Burmese people. But until one comes to know them better, there is sometimes a lack of expansiveness in first contacts, which tends to mask this. A number of faces looked down at me inscrutably from the lorry. Wishing to hear a confirmation of my driver's assurances, I asked if they were going to Lashio. There was a long silence, and then a young man who had been scrutinizing me from between narrowed lids said, 'This car will go to Lashio.' I then asked when it was expected to arrive, and there was another long pause. When I thought that my question had been ignored, the reply came, with slow and clear enunciation: 'We do not know when it will get to Lashio.' There was something about the spokesman that set him apart from the rest of the passengers; a piercing, speculative gaze, a quality of rather sinister deliberation, of the kind which might have been observed in the originals upon which Hollywood film directors modelled their Chinese generals. With slight nods and gestures he controlled the disposition of persons and baggage in the lorry. A lifting of the finger and a few murmured words, and I found a place made for me up in the front, but one place removed from the driver. Before we started off, I hid my two cameras in tool-filled cavities.

The road now became steeper. Painfully we ground our way up the hill-sides, or lurched down them, never travelling fast enough to sweep the engine-heated air from the cabin. In these virgin forests the bird-life was more distinguished than at Maymyo. There were many bee-eaters, hoopoes, and swallows with iridescent blue backs. Jungle fowl scuttled across the road with the foolish panic of barnyard chickens. Vultures wheeled in the sky, and in alighting chose leafless trees — perhaps to leave a clear field of vision — about which they spaced themselves with curious regularity. Once when we stopped on a hill, where a precipice rose from the teak woods above us, I heard a thin, staccato shrieking and saw something which I had heard of but never before seen, a peregrine attacking a vulture, which avoided its furious stoops by negligent dippings of the wing. Besides this one heard continually a shrill, bird-like whistling, which was made by colonies of squirrels.

My immediate neighbour in the driver's cabin was a thin, lively Burmese lady, who at frequent intervals raised her longyi to dab at her left leg, which was thickly coated with mud and stained with blood. When we stopped she had some difficulty in getting down, and sometimes groaned slightly. Encouraged by the general acceptance of my cigarettes, I asked the admittedly chief passenger what the trouble was and received the astonishing information that she had fallen off a motor cycle. At one of our halts she washed her wounds in petrol, but then, although she hunted about and mixed up a few trial samples with water, was unable to find any suitable mud to replace the application.

Frequent repairs to the lorry were called for. Minor engine parts were made fast temporarily by surplus strips of rattan torn off bales of cargo. All tyres were reinforced by patches of cover, held in place by nuts and bolts. Occasionally the engine would falter and choke, and the driver, jumping down and flinging up the bonnet, would utter the word 'short', which is now Burmese. At that, the chief passenger would lower himself from his perch on the highest point of the cargo, and after a brief, judicial scrutiny, point out what had to be done. Sometimes a screwdriver would be wiped and put into his hand, and with this he would operate while the driver and his various mates looked on as if at delicate surgery. This was the general condition into which Burmese road transport had fallen. I wondered what would happen when the day came when all these old ex-army lorries were utterly and finally worn out, when the ruined mechanisms could no longer be kept revolving by ingenious patching and by spare parts taken from other crocks which had completely disintegrated.

We passed through several small towns. They had no particular character and consisted of no more than a street and a square where the markets would be held. As we were deep in the Shan country, there were no more pagodas, but shrines had been erected on the town's outskirts to the tutelary spirits, and some of them were hung with votive offerings of puppet-horses. Among the jumble of Burmese and Chinese lettering on the shop fronts, a single notice in English jumped out, 'Pickle sold here'. At Kyaukme we stopped to unload a cargo of small green tomatoes. Here there was to be an hour's wait, and the chief passenger took charge of my movements and told me that he would show me round the town. He now introduced himself as Tin Maung. As he was then delayed by being called in to consult on more engine trouble, I wandered over to a tea-house. In this tea-growing country, plain tea is considered unbearably dull. It is served with a sediment of some kind of cereal, and many of the Shans, unsatisfied with this consistency, poured it into their saucers and proceeded to make up a kind of minestrone by mixing it with the contents of a small dough pie, for which the tea-house charged four annas.

After a few minutes Tin Maung made a dignified appearance to take tea. There was the usual preliminary silence, then he asked, 'Are you carrying a weapon with you?' I said no, and Tin Maung said 'That is a good thing. Before the war we used to carry guns for tigers. But now it is not a good thing to carry guns any more. If we carry guns we shoot.' I nodded understandingly. The market here was exceptionally lively. Some of the local tribespeople wore patch-work cloaks in bright colours, with Moroccan-looking hoods. I asked Tin Maung if he thought I could photograph them and he went over, and, to my mind, with undue formality, called for the head of the family. There was a long discussion, followed by a refusal. Since all Tin Maung's utterances were preceded by the intervals of silence occupied by the marshalling and translation of his thoughts, I shall cease to mention these pauses. On this occasion he said, 'They do not refuse from shyness, but from superstition.' Later when I thought the incident had been forgotten, he said, 'Our minds have to be adjusted to the medieval conditions, which are variable.'

Here in Kyaukme there was a legless leper, who propelled himself along on his haunches, with pads fitted to his hands. He was assisted most tenderly in his passage round the market by a small boy, whose arm was round his neck. From experience gained in Mandalay, I judged that the boy was in the first stages of leprosy.

Through the brazen hours that followed high noon, we crept onwards through a tunnel of glittering verdure. Then in the early afternoon came the official stop for breakfast. We were in a tiny hamlet, a few branch-and-leaf huts round a well. A single half-blind pariah dog slunk up to inspect us and was immediately chased away by a pair of lean, hairy swine that came rushing out of one of the huts. A cavern had been hollowed out of the wall of rock that formed the background to the village, and wisps of smoke trailed up through a sort of bamboo veranda that had been built over the mouth of it. This infernal place was the restaurant.

The moment had now come when all European prejudices about food had to be abandoned; all fears of typhoid or dysentery had to be banished resolutely from the mind. Even if I held back now and refused to enter this murky grotto, there was a long succession of others awaiting me, and ultimately sheer hunger would settle the matter. Remote journeyings had their advantages, the occasional sense of adventure, the novelties of experience. They also had their drawbacks, and this was one of them. And as there was no turning back from them, it was just as well to be bold.

In the dim interior — a model of most remote oriental eating-houses — we were awaited by a cook who was naked to the waist. Tattooed dragons writhed among the cabalistic figures on his chest and arms. A snippet of intestine was clinging to a finger, which, shaken off, was caught in mid-air by an attendant cat. Tin Maung gave an order and in due course the head-waiter arrived, a rollicking Shan with shining bald head and Manchu moustaches, carrying a dish heaped with scrawny chickens' limbs, jaundiced with curry, a bowl of rice and a couple of aluminium plates. When uncertain how to behave, watch what the others do. A few minutes later I was neatly stripping the tendons from those saffron bones; kneading the rice into a form in which it could be carried in the fingers to the mouth. But the *spécialité de la maison* was undoubtedly pickled cabbage, with garlic and chili-pepper. This Shan delicacy was gravely recommended by Tin Maung as 'full of vitamins'. It had a sharp, sour flavour, for which a taste was easily acquired; I should certainly have missed this and many other similar experiences had I been able to follow the advice given in the *Burma Handbook*: '. . . there are no hotels, and the traveller, when he quits the line of railway or Irawadi steamer, must get leave from the Deputy Commissioner of the district to put up at Government bungalows, and must take bedding, a cook and a few cooking utensils.'

Although Tin Maung had said that it was most unlikely that we should reach Lashio in one day, we found ourselves by the late after-noon within a few miles of the town. We had just crossed the Nam Mi river, where I had admired the spectacle of landslides of the brightest red earth plunging down the hill-side into deep, green water, when we were stopped by a posse of soldiers. They told us that Chinese Nationalist bandits had temporarily cut the road, only four kilometres from Lashio, and had shot-up and looted the truck in front of ours. As this had happened several hours before, it was not exactly a narrow escape. But there was a delay until an officer of the Shan police arrived to tell us we could carry on. As we came into the outskirts of Lashio, the sun set. Flocks of mynas and parakeets had appeared in the tree-tops, where they went through the noisy, twilight manœuvres of starlings in a London square.

In accordance with the recommendations already quoted from the *Burma Handbook*, I asked the driver of the lorry to put me down at the Dak Bungalow, but there appeared to be some difficulty, and Tin Maung told me that it had been taken over by the army. He invited me to come to his house, where I could leave my luggage while making further inquiries. Lashio had been partly destroyed by bombing but, it seemed, rebuilt along the lines of the English hill-station it had once been, with detached bungalows, each with its own garden. We stopped at one of these. It was now nearly dark, and a young man clad only in shorts came running down the path, and opened the gate. Approaching us, he crossed his arms and bowed in a rather Japanese fashion, only partially straightening himself when he turned away. Tin Maung nodded towards the baggage, and uttered a word, and the still stooping figure snatched up both suitcases and hurried away to the house with them. He was not, as I imagined at the time, a servant, but a younger brother.

I was then invited to go and sit on the balcony of the house, where I was met by Tin Maung's father. U Thein Zan looked like a lean Burmese version of one of those rollicking Chinese gods of good fortune. Even when his mouth was relaxed his eyes were creased-up as if in a spasm of mirth. He had learned, in fact, as I soon discovered, to express his emotions in terms of smiles: a gay smile (the most frequent), a tolerant smile (for the shortcomings of others), a roguish smile (when his own weaknesses were under discussion), a rueful smile (for his sharp losses, the state of Burma and humanity in general).

In the background hovered the mother. In her case no formal

presentation was made. The three of us, father, son and myself, sat there on the balcony making occasional disjointed remarks about the political situation. From time to time the younger brother came out of the house, bowed and went in. The mother appeared, curled herself up in a chair well removed from the important conclave of males, and lit up a cheroot. There was no sign of stir or excitement. Later I learned that this was the return of the eldest son after an absence of two years, during which time the brother next in age to him had been killed by insurgents. I could have imagined Chinese etiquette imposing these rigid standards of self-control, but it came as a great surprise that old-fashioned Burmese families should follow such a rule of conduct.

The matter of finding somewhere to sleep now came up, and the younger son was sent off to make inquiries about a bungalow belonging to the Public Works Department. He was soon back to say that it was full of soldiers, although there might be a room free next night. Upon this Tin Maung said that I would have to sleep in his father's house, and signalled for my baggage to be taken inside. I apologized to the old man for the trouble I was putting him to, whereupon he handsomely said, 'Anyone my son brings home becomes my son,' accompanying this speech with such a truly genial smile that it was impossible to feel any longer ill at ease.

But before there could be any question of retiring for the night, U Thein Zan said, there were formalities to be attended to. He thought that owing to the unsettled local conditions I ought to be on the safe side by reporting, without delay, to the Deputy Superintendent of Police, and after dressing himself carefully, he took up a lantern and accompanied me to the functionary's house. The D.S.P. soon mastered his surprise at the visit, seemed relieved that I was under the control of such a pillar of local society as U Thein Zan, and found me several forms to fill in. In the morning, he said, I must report to the office of the Special Commissioner for the region, and to the commanding officer of the garrison. The latter obligation was one of which nothing had been said in Rangoon, and I decided to avoid it if possible. With Chinese bandits in the vicinity I could imagine this officer considering himself justified in putting me under some kind of restrictive military protection, or even sending me under escort back to Mandalay. When I brought up the matter of the attack on the truck, the D.S.P. firmly announced that it had been the work of local Shans.

We went back home and sat for a while chatting desultorily and listening to the radio. Two stations were coming in fairly well: La Voix d'Islam broadcast on a beam from Radio Toulouse, and a station which might have been Peking, because the announcements were in Chinese, and the music Western and evangelical in flavour, with the exception of one playing of a marching song of the Red Army. U Thein Zan was a fervent Buddhist and liked to talk about his religion whenever he could. He was delighted because next day a famous abbot would be preaching several sermons at the local monastery and he was to play a prominent part in the welcoming ceremony.

Soon after this the family retired to bed. The house was a rather flimsy construction raised on piles about three feet from the ground. It consisted of two main rooms and a kitchen, had a palm-thatched roof and a floor of split bamboo. I was left to myself in one of the rooms, while the five members of the family — another brother had just turned up — were to sleep in the other. Clearly the old mother did not approve of this arrangement, which I gathered, from her gestures, probably went against her ideas on true hospitality. Perhaps she felt that I was not being treated as a member of the family. At all events she protested and was with difficulty overruled by Tin Maung, who probably told her that communal sleeping was not a European custom; and with a shrug of bewildered resignation she let the thing go as it was. Bars were put over the door and a shutter fitted to the window. The younger brother appeared carrying a camp bed which he erected in a corner. By the side of this Tin Maung set a stool with a lamp, a glass of water, a saucer of nuts and several giant cheroots. Before going into the other room he told me not to put the lamp out. I wondered why.

Taking off my clothes, I put on a cotton longyi which I had bought in Mandalay. It had been recommended as the coolest thing to sleep in. Turning the lamp low, I lay down on the camp bed, and was just dozing off when I heard a slight creaking, and through half-opened eyes saw Tin Maung, going slowly round the room, flashing an electric torch on the walls and ceiling. I asked him what he was looking for, and he said, 'Sometimes there are moths.' He then tip-toed quickly from the room. My eyelids came together and then opened, reluctantly, at a faint scuffling sound. The bungalow consisted of a framework of timber upon which sheets of some white-washed material had been nailed. It was like a very ramshackle example of a small black-and-white Essex cottage. On one wall, just above my feet was a Buddha shrine, containing a rather unusual reclining Buddha and offerings of dried flowers in vases. From behind this there now appeared several rats, not large, but lively, which began to move in a series of hesitant rushes along the beam running round the room. There were soon seven of them in sight.

I watched this movement with dazed curiosity for a time, and then began to doze again. Then, suddenly, an extraordinary protective faculty came into use. Once during the recent war, I had noticed that whilst my sleep was not disturbed by our own howitzers firing in the same field, I was inevitably awakened when the dawn stillness was troubled by the thin whistle of enemy shells, passing high overhead. Now, on the verge of unconsciousness, I felt in the skull, rather than heard, a faint scratching of tiny scrambling limbs. Something, I half-dreamed and half-thought, was climbing up the leg of the camp bed. Turning my head I caught a brief, out-of-focus glimpse of a small black body on the pillow by my cheek. Then in a scamper it was gone. It was a scorpion, I thought, or a hairy spider of the tarantula kind. I linked its appearance with Tin Maung's mysterious inspection of the room with his torch. What was to be done? I got up, thinking that whatever this animal was, it would come back to achieve its purpose as soon as I fell asleep. I thought of sitting in the chair and staying awake for the rest of the night, but when I picked up the lamp to turn up the wick, it felt light, and shaking it produced only a faint splashing of oil in the bottom of the container. In a short time then, the lamp would go out, and my scorpion or whatever it was, with others of its kind, would come boldly up through the interstices in the bamboo floor. The next impulse was to spend the night walking round Lashio, and I went to unfasten the door bar. Immediately the pariah dog that lived under the house, where it lay all night snuffling and whining, burst into snarling life, furiously echoed by all the dogs in the district. I thought of the trigger-happy police of Lashio, who would have Chinese bandits on their mind.

The best thing, I decided, was to use my mosquito net and hope that I could sleep without any part of my body coming into contact with the sides. Fixing it up as best I could, I crawled in and tucked the net well under me. For a while I watched the movement, blurred through the net, of the rats; then consciousness faded again. I was awakened by a not very sharp pain in the lip and putting up my hand found myself clutching a cockroach which had fastened there. This was the last disturbance; when I next woke it was to the mighty whirring of hornbills flying overhead, and the daylight was spreading through the shutters.

CHAPTER XII

THE NORTHERN SHANS

LASHIO was taking shape in the calm morning light, its roofs and palisades touched with mist-filtered sunshine. Two-thirds of the town lay below U Thein Zan's veranda, clinging to slopes that slid down into a vaporous valley. Sashes of mist wound through the town, isolating hillocks, huts and clumps of trees. From some distant meadow concealed in the hazy depths arose a thin, pastoral piping. Beyond the valley a tuft of cotton-wool balanced on a thinly drawn line joining the summits of a distant mountain range.

This was the country — as Lashio was the capital — of the Northern Shans, a curious people who provided an example of a huge racial group in a constant state — like some radio-active metal — of fission and degeneration into lesser elements. The name Shan is unknown among the people themselves, and probably originates, as do also Chin, and Kachin, in a common Chinese term for hill-savage, or barbarian. The Shans call themselves Thai, meaning 'free', and remnants of their race are spread right across Southern Asia, from Canton to Assam — the greatest single unit being the Siamese. It is their singular passion for freedom which has kept the Thais disunited. In general, those peoples that remain in the mountains reflect in their character the physical division of their environment into hills and valleys. The smaller the tribe the greater the freedom. These arch-republicans of South-Eastern Asia sometimes carried their democracy to a point where there were no chiefs and not even a village council.

Only when such people are driven by some invader from their valleys, and forced down into the plains — as were the Siamese — can they be united, and prepared for civilization, under victorious tyrants. The Burmese, having reached the plains of the Irrawaddy first, turned themselves into a nation of rulers and ruled, organized themselves, increased and multiplied, and bought the latest weapons. In this way they were able to hold the later waves of immigrants — the Shans, and Kachins — back in their mountains.

Surfeited with democracy, the Burmese organized the Shans politically whenever they could, allowing them otherwise to cling to their natural customs. They are notably uxorious, and those who can support them are permitted three official wives. Miscellaneous concubines are styled 'little women'. Divorce is easy, and women retain their property. The democratic principle is followed even in the matter of seduction. An official who seduces the wife of a non-official is heavily fined, and obliged to restore the woman. The non-official in a similar case, escapes a fine, and may even keep the great man's wife, if she agrees to forfeit her property. It is curious that there are racial groups which have lived for centuries among the Shans, which, far from being influenced by this liberality of outlook, have marriage taboos and restrictions only equalled by those of the Australian bushmen. The Bghai Karens strangle in a pit those who marry out of their station. The Banyangs' endogamous system is so exclusive that it has reduced the tribe numerically to a point when it is no longer possible for a marriage to be contracted within the permitted relationship groups. Having therefore resigned themselves to extinction, the people can only be kept in existence by state compulsion. Once a year an official arrives in the village, a suitable couple are selected, detailed for marriage, conveyed by force to the bridal chamber, and kept there under governmental seal, tormented, no doubt, by incest-guilt, for three days. Meanwhile, the Shans fill the surrounding villages with their children.

The youngest brother was already up, moving stealthily about the garden, watering the snapdragons, geraniums and roses with the solemnity of one tending the flowers before the high altar. His face was respectfully averted, and occasionally, when forced to pass within a few yards of me, on his way to refill his watering can, he did so in a hunched-up rush. Soon after he left to go off to some kind of clerical occupation. He was dressed in shorts, a kind of Alpine jacket and a Gaucho hat, with a chin-strap, from the bottom of which hung down a three-inch decorative knot. Under his arm he carried a brief case. Later, U Thein Zan made an appearance, dressed in his best longyi, worn under an American Army greatcoat; he was ready for early-morning prayers at the pagoda. Next Tin Maung, about whom the household clearly revolved, came on the scene. He asked how I had slept, and I assured him that I had rarely passed a more peaceful night. After we had drunk tea, he suggested a stroll along to the market.

Although it was no more than eight o'clock, animation was at its height. Every swaggering Asiatic mode was displayed here. A group of Kachin women wore with demure elegance their black Chinese smocks of some good, coarsely woven material, relieved only by spiralling silver links at the neck-fastening, and a few negligently worn strings of amber beads. There were turbanned Palaungs with infantile faces, and teeth and lips blotted out with betel. They were dressed in dressing-gowns slashed with many colours, and gaily-woven anklets, and had massive silver rings round their necks, which made their wearers look as if they had been won by someone at a game of hoop-la. The Taungthus were in shapeless penitents' chemises of indigo sacking and wore with raffish effect a towel wound several times round the head. Shans, slender and willowy in their long gowns, were the sophisticates, the bourgeoises of the market. Until they looked up, they were extinguished by their huge, mushroom hats; then sometimes one looked into the face of a severe beauty, with the regularity of feature of a fine ivory carving; primly pursed lips and wonderfully shaped eyes – to a Westerner all the more piquant from the invisibility when the eyes were open, of the upper eyelids. Besides these groups there were occasional representatives of more distant peoples; a Lisu, with satchels strapped about him like a medieval palmer, and turban wound with intricate regularity; an unidentified pair in waisted and loose-sleeved Cossack coats. Behind their stalls Shan young ladies viewed their clients with the aloofness of haughty sales-ladies of model garments. Tin Maung said that it was better to deal with the Chinese – perfect shopkeepers who held to the principle that the customer was always right.

On our way back, five beautiful Chinese Shan girls, in blue jackets and trousers and wide cummerbunds, came tripping down the street towards us. They were jolly and free in their manner, and pink-cheeked under their slight tan. I asked Tin Maung if he thought I could photograph them, and after considering the question until it was too late, he gave his verdict, with sensibility, I thought. 'In their own village, they will be pleased for you to photograph them. But here, they are visitors.' He then added an odd corollary, 'They are too slow moving to dance the rumba.'

It had been arranged that a friend of Tin Maung's, who was supposed to have some contact with the Special Commissioner, should accompany me to his house. Afterwards I was to return to breakfast with Tin Maung. The Special Commissioner was also the Sawbwa of Hsenwi, the most powerful of the Shan feudal princes in the Northern Shan States, who had now been turned by the Burmese into a kind of exalted civil servant. The Shan, Kachin and Karen minorities have always been more or less hostile to the Burmese, for much the same reasons that the Irish have not agreed with the English. Lacking the organization, or perhaps even the natural military genius to defeat the Burmese in the field, they have rebelled whenever they could, allying themselves – with usually disastrous results – with any invader, whether Chinese or Siamese, and suffering in due course the frightful retaliation that has always been commonplace in South-East Asia. The Burmese have always accused the British – probably with justice – of trying to separate them from the minorities, in accordance with the principle of 'divide and rule'. There is little doubt also that the Shans did their best to play off the British against their old enemies. Traditionally the Sawbwa were educated outside Burma, often in Siam, and the Burmese are still said to suspect them of plotting with neighbouring states to the detriment of Burmese sovereignty. There were, for instance, in Rangoon all sorts of rumours – and not from Burmese sources – of machinations aimed at turning over part of the Kentung province to Siam. I was therefore warned that any approach to the Sawbwas would certainly be misconstrued by the Burmese, and might even land me in some sort of trouble. However, although the Sawbwa of Hsenwi was said to have been in difficulties with the

Burmese over the Karen insurrection, he was now a Burmese Special Commissioner, and as such it was not only in order but obligatory to call on him.

The Sawbwa lived in a large villa of European type. My sponsor having explained the nature of my visit to a servant, I was shown into a lounge and left to await the great man's pleasure. The walls were decorated with Chinese silk panels of natural history subjects. A large silver cup of the kind awarded for athletic distinction stood on the mantelpiece. Facing me was a partially curtained stairway, and several ladies of the Sawbwa's household took turns to peep at me from behind the curtain. After a reasonable interval the Sawbwa appeared. He was dressed in loose pyjamas of white silk, possessed a handsome, unlined face and a manner of cultivated tranquillity. Shan rulers were clearly modelled on Chinese rather than Burmese patterns. In spite of the conventional British praise for everything to do with the hill peoples of Burma, I must confess to a preference for the easy-going affability of the Burmese notables, well typified by the Premier, Thakin Nu, by comparison with the well-bred Shan aloofness. I have no doubt that every kind of sterling quality is concealed by this habit of reserve.

After reading my credentials the Sawbwa asked me where I wanted to go, and I told him that my intention had been to make my way to Taunggyi. The Sawbwa thought about this for a moment, and said that it would be easier to go north than south. He could give me a letter to his brother, also a Sawbwa, who was now living at Hsenwi, and who would look after me, and pass me on via Mu-Sé to Nam Hkam. After that I could easily get to Bhamó, where there were no troubles of any kind. This was indeed a tempting alternative to my original plan. Such a route would take me for a considerable distance along the Chinese frontier, and Nam Hkam had been described as, ethnologically speaking, the most interesting town in the Northern Shan States, although hopelessly inaccessible in these times. I mentioned the matter of a further army permit to travel in these areas, and the Sawbwa brushed the question aside. 'This territory,' he said, 'comes within my jurisdiction. I will give you whatever is necessary.'

I wondered if, in these words, that utterly efficient facial control cloaked a hint of quiet satisfaction. It then occurred to me to obtain an official ruling on the nationality of the authors of the previous evening's incident, and I quoted the D.S.P.'s opinion that the lorry had been attacked by Shans. Without emphasis, the Sawbwa said, 'The Shans have never done such a thing. They have never committed an act of banditry. The attack carried out last night was by Chinese Nationalist troops, of whom there are several hundreds in the neighbourhood.'

Old U Thein Zan, however, was very worried about the idea of my going off along the Chinese frontier without additional army sanction. I said that surely a letter of authorization from the chief civil authority in the Shan States was enough, but U Thein Zan said, 'You do not realize. You will encounter ignorant, uneducated soldiers, who will not understand the Sawbwa's letter.' Well, then, I said, if they wouldn't understand the Sawbwa's letter, what use would an army permit be? Ah, said U Thein Zan, that would be different. An army permit would be written in Kachin, which these ignorant, stupid soldiers from the hills could read . . . Very well then, I would have the Sawbwa's letter translated into Kachin. But still the old man shook his head, with the gravest misgivings. For my part, I was quite determined, at all costs, to keep out of the army's clutches. I had found that I should have to wait an indefinite time in Lashio before finding any kind of transport going in the Taunggyi direction, so that the choice lay between pushing on northwards, and an ignominious retreat to Mandalay. There was, therefore, no choice.

On the way back we called on the S.D.O., who was in charge of the bungalow of the Public Works Department. In the old Burma it was considered ill-mannered to call a man by his name if he held any office. Imaginary and unpaid positions were often created by the king — the non-existent glass manufactory with its hierarchy of officials was one — to allow worthy men that kind of satisfaction which inhabitants of the Southern States of the U.S.A. are said to derive by calling themselves doctor or colonel without the possession of the usual qualifications. This usage is still reflected in the modern Burmese custom of referring to a man not merely by his function but by a series of initials. I could never remember what those mysterious initials stood for, but everyone in government service had them. They became hopelessly entangled in my mind with similar ones in the British Army. The letter D for instance, in S.D.O. — what did it stand for, District or Deputy? But in this case it was Sub-Divisional Officer.

The S.D.O. was a Southern Indian, cultured and genial, with a thin, home-sick wife, and a pretty doll-like child, with eyes clouded with malaria. He had inherited his comfortable bungalow from an English predecessor, and was obsessed by the fate of the sweet peas that had gone with it. They were still vigorous and profuse of blossom, but since the country had gained its independence had quite lost their colour, all the sharply-divided, original shades having faded to a wishy-washy pinkish-blue.

With the S.D.O.'s permission I went down to the Inspection Bungalow to take over a room left by soldiers who were just moving off. It was like an ample prison-cell, with barred windows and scaling walls. There was no light, and the only piece of furniture was a frame raised on legs, recalling some obscure instrument of torture, across which string had been stretched, criss-cross. On to this I flung my bedding, upon which a few minute red insects immediately appeared. Looking up I saw that the ceiling was entirely screened from view by thick, old cobwebs, which I judged to be no longer tenanted. The door was much splintered and repaired about the lock, and appeared to have been broken in on many occasions.

Having completed these arrangements, I went back and joined Tin Maung for breakfast. An omelette had been prepared, and Tin Maung and I sat opposite at the table and dug into it with ladle-shaped spoons which had been miraculously produced. In the background, her legs drawn up on a chair, sat the old mother smoking one cheroot after another. She never took her eyes off me, and sometimes shook her head sadly. Tin Maung said, 'The old woman says that you remind her of her second son. He was killed by the P.V.O.s last year. No question of politics entered into this occasion. He chanced, according to circumstances, to be passing in his car, and being unsuccessful in their desire to shoot ducks, they shot him.'

That afternoon, the surviving second brother, a gay, philandering fellow, turned up with a jeep he had borrowed for my benefit from some government department. This be-ringed young blood, with his gold bracelet and wrist watch, his American cigarettes, and the chic severity of his longyi of grey chequered silk, was the antithesis of his austere and authoritarian elder brother. With totally oriental insouciance we motored out into the bandit-infested countryside. Climate seems, after all, to have little to do with temperament. Here in the Eastern tropics you felt that while swaggering bravado was probably unknown, an emergency would be met with more than Anglo-Saxon phlegm. Perhaps the whole-hearted belief in the immutability of one's horoscope had something to do with it. I found the Burmese imperturbable.

Although Tin Maung was as near a free-thinker as a Burman could be, our country jaunt resolved itself, inevitably, into a pilgrimage to the local holy places. We did not attempt to enter any of the monasteries. It was sufficient to pull up for a few moments within the aura of beneficence that emanated from them and to gaze meekly at the tiered roofs projecting from their shading trees, before moving on from one to the next. In these rustic areas, the 'no foot-wearing' rules were more strictly applied. In the great pagodas of the towns it was considered enough to remove one's shoes or sandals in making an ascent, when the actually constructed part of the pagoda had been reached. Here, the mounds on which the pagodas were built were holy, too, and however high they were it was incumbent upon one to toil bare-foot up the roughly hewed-out steps. We climbed one such bell-shaped pagoda and, from the high terrace, spied out the lie of the land. Below us, a caravan of bullock-carts jogged by, with a trotting escort of Shan farmers, sturdy and bellicose-looking agriculturists, with swords carried on their backs, thrust through sashes. In a few moments they had disappeared, swallowed in the belly of a dust-dragon they themselves had called forth, and we were left in an empty landscape chequered with withered paddy-fields, each with its low water-containing bunds, so that from above it was like a vast grey Chaldean excavation. The rare trees that had been left standing were ancient banyans, baleful monsters which had constantly increased themselves by the pathological multiplication of their limbs, till now they were arboreal labyrinths, full of root-screened nooks and recesses from which the spirits look out upon their domain. The pagoda upon which we stood had, in the dim past, marked the Chinese frontier with Burma, and here, as at other selected points, after the line of demarcation had been amicably settled, a selected soldier of each nation had been buried alive, back to back, facing north and south.

A visit was now made, in the manner of a minor sentimental journey, to a spot where Tin Maung had had a memorable experience, some years before. Since no connected account was ever given of his past, I was left to deduce from casual references that he had, at some time, fought with the Japanese Army, probably as a member of the Burma Independent Army, which had thrown in its lot with the Japanese in return for the promise of national independence. This fact had emerged as a consequence of a remark that he liked Japanese girls, because, he observed with one of his rare, half-stifled smiles, they were 'very obedient'. At all events, the Chinese had captured him and here, having with some difficulty found a suitable tree (the banyans were too matted with aerial roots to get a rope over a branch) they set about hanging him. It seemed, however, that his four appointed executioners were extremely weak from sickness and semi-starvation and, with all four hauling on the rope, had the greatest difficulty in hoisting him off his feet. Moreover, they had neglected to tie his hands, and once in the air he managed to haul himself up the rope. As soon as a couple of the Chinese let go their hold to remedy this situation, the others found themselves too weak to keep him in the air. The thing developed into a lurid Disney-like farce, with the Chinese soldiers, who seemed to be squeamish about using their weapons, running backwards and forwards in an ill-concerted and amateurish attempt to pinion Tin Maung's hands while keeping his feet off the ground. Finally they dropped him altogether and he managed to pull the rope out of their hands and run off with it still trailing from his neck. Alas, no evidence remained of this macabre scene. Even the place on the branch which had been bruised by the rubbing of the rope had long since recovered its patina.

On our way back to Lashio we made a detour to visit a hot spring that bubbled up from under a bank to become a stream which, after trailing its sulphurous miasma round several paddy fields, again vanished. The neighbourhood of this source too, was of some sanctity, and had, as a result, the ravaged appearance of public gardens in a slum area. A local erosion had been produced by the feet of many pilgrims, and children had torn at the accessible branches of the trees, many of which hung down by strips of bark. Several small caverns had been excavated in the hillock above the spring, all of which contained Buddha images, where presumably less benevolently inclined figures had once squatted. Silently presiding over this scene were many vultures, distributed in a symmetrical composition among the neighbouring trees. Their presence was entirely congruous in this hallowed spot, ranking high as they do, an honourable and superior incarnation within the animal hierarchy, on account of their restriction to a diet of carrion — a limitation believed by many Burmese to be self-imposed.

A Hindu ascetic who, even as a heretic, had gained extraordinary merit in Buddhist eyes by dedicating his body for the use of these semi-domesticated birds, when nature should have accomplished its course, lived at a slightly lower level in one of these trees, brooded over by his future legatees. Mysteriously he had built himself several aerial huts, although, following the nesting habits of the wren, he occupied only one. It was a kind of large kennel of branches and palm-leaves, reinforced with a valuable find of corrugated iron. Above it drooped white prayer-flags, the banners of a spiritual surrender. Standing below, Tin Maung respectfully called on the recluse to appear and give us his blessing. There was, alas, no response.

Before leaving, it occurred to me to test the temperature of the stream, with the idea forming in my mind of a beneficial sulphur-bath. I found it unbearably hot. Tin Maung, who had been watching, supplied the sombre information that immersion for more than a minute meant death, a fact which had been confirmed empirically on several occasions. I wondered how many wretched beings had been parboiled here throughout history for the equivalent of the Kingdom of Heaven's sake.

On reaching the outskirts of Lashio, Tin Maung suddenly decided to look in at the Inspection Bungalow. What he saw there seemed to shock him and, without a word he grabbed up my bags and took them out to the jeep. While I was in Lashio, he said, I should stay with him. Naturally enough, in view of the previous night's experiences, I viewed this prospect with gratitude, coloured slightly with alarm.

In an attempt to repay some of the hospitality I had received, I invited my host's family out to a Chinese restaurant that night. However, U Thein Zan was keeping strict Sabbath, a term which includes in its definition fasting and meditation. Etiquette did not permit the presence of the mother, and the youngest and self-effacing brother probably felt the honour too much for him. In the end there were four of us: Tin Maung, the dandified brother and a friend who was a schoolmaster, a sincere and rather intense young man. The main street of Lashio, which lay at the bottom of the hill, had been rebuilt in the style, if film reconstructions are accurate, of an American shack-town in the pioneering years. But although there was plenty of drama to be had in the vicinity, there were no signs here to be seen of the aggressive rawness of the old-time American frontier towns. Instead, the night-sauntering crowds were, as ever in Burma, demure and well-conducted. If some of the Shans carried swords on their backs, you felt that it was no more than a habit of dress; and no virtue would be less esteemed than quickness on the draw. If there were tough hombres here, as there probably were, the toughness was dissimulated in a display of the courtesies, and an eighteenth-century turn of complimentary phrase. 'We are pleased that you condescend to pay your visit to Lashio, Sir. You find it hard to travel further from this town? That is our great fortune for us. If you will stay here all the longer it is our very good advantage.'

Entering our chosen restaurant, we seated ourselves at first, at a table in the general room, within sight of the kitchen, a smoke-blackened gehenna in which sweating fiends practised their arts over cauldrons and griddles. The meats were on display in a kind of jeweller's showcase, a glass fixture fitted with lock and key. To this customers were beckoned by the proprietor, for the inspection of a discouraging collection of pendant objects, cellular, membranous or veined, swarthy from judicious hanging, or startlingly coloured scarlet and blue. But estimating our purchasing power he soon shepherded us away from this depressing revelation of the raw mater-ials of Chinese cooking, into a separate room. This dimly-lit cell was of close lattice work. The walls were hung with Chinese pictures of the kind sold in Rangoon under the generic title 'bon-ton'. Eschewing the pin-up girl favoured by the West at similar artistic levels, these have concentrated on the young Chinese matron as their pet subject. She is shown as pink-cheeked, blooming, and usually with a complex hair-style. Sometimes her face is haloed in luxuriant fox-furs, and almost always a modest brood of children sport around her. These are frequently dressed as Little Lord Fauntleroys, or, as on this occasion, they wear sailor suits. Our particular young mother was holding a tele-phone as if inhaling from it a rare perfume. Telephones are a popular motif of modern Chinese art.

Hope, however, was revived when the food was served in the most beautiful bowls, upon which inspired brushes had, in a few strokes of red and gold, sketched a squirming shrimp or a facetious and be-whiskered dragon. This delightful ware was of current Chinese production, and its export from China had recently been revived. As a token of special esteem the proprietor produced his finest glasses for our Mandalay Pale Ale. They were products of the British export drive, which by most devious and mysterious channels — almost certainly via smugglers from Siam — had found their way here. The labels, which said Jacobean Glassware, were still in position, and it was clear that they had been accepted as part of the decoration, since much effort was made to keep them intact. It was evident that these glasses could not be washed. Before setting them on the table, the proprietor carefully wiped each rim with his fingers, an operation which was repeated — special care being taken in the case of my glass — by Tin Maung. There had been a lengthy explanation, accompanied by some descriptive gesturing, of what was to be cooked for us. Evidently a special dish had been ordered for my delectation, and I awaited with resignation the appearance of some formidable Chinese delicacy, the legendary new-born mice in honey, a Himalayan bear's paw served with sweet and sour sauce, a few fishes' lips from a bottle imported at immense cost from the remote China seas. But, alas, I had under-estimated my friends' cosmopolitanism. My speciality, when it arrived, was two fried eggs in separate bowls, with more bowls for their inevitable garnishing of chips.

Table gossip was concerned with the higher realities. In Burma the condition of the soul replaces that of the stock markets as a topic for polite conversation. Between mouthfuls of fried rice and prawns, the schoolmaster discoursed on the hereafter, passing in brief exposi-tion over all the thirty-one possibilities that await the discarnate entity beyond the grave. As ever, the unpleasant states were presented with grimly detailed realism, while the pleasant ones were vague and insipid. Behind his glasses the schoolmaster's eyes glittered. His expression was invaded by a peculiarly Nordic eagerness, particularly when discussing the pangs of souls in torment. In Wales, he would have been a nonconformist preacher.

By now it was as if scales had slowly fallen from my eyes, and at last I could distinguish the character in a Burmese face as clearly as in a European one. For the first week or two I had suffered to a mild and diminishing degree from the obtuseness which makes people say of Mongolians 'I can't tell one from the other.' But now the Mongol physical characteristics which once had seemed to impose a deaden-ing conformity, appeared to be vanishing. There was no longer any sense of strangeness, of not being among people of one's own race. People were resolving into types again. Now there were business-men, politicians, students, farmers, policemen; each class seemed marked in some way which couldn't be exactly defined, by an undefinable stamp set upon him by his way of life. These Burmese and Shan girls in the market were now something more than Mongolian dolls with hardly more expression than the conventionalized beauties of Japanese woodcuts. Now, at last, I was in tune to the expressions that flickered round those eyes and lips; the coquetry, the humour, the contempt. And just as I was beginning to see trousered and turbanned sellers of vegetables who by some trick of expression reminded me of girls I had known at some time or other, Italian film actresses, secretaries or army-nurses, so this Burmese pedant was the living double of someone with whom I had been at school.

While occupied with these reflections, I had gradually become aware of an unmistakable reek, usually described as acrid, as definite but indescribable as the smell of burning feathers or any other pungent odour. The lattice separating us from the next private room was pierced with dimly glowing points of light. Now a murmur sifted through the chinks in the wall; there was a tinkle of laughter, a silence, the sound of a bow drawn tentatively across a single string, producing no more than the rising and falling drone of an insect. This was followed by a rustling, then more laughter. The odour became sharper. An alarmed silence had fallen upon our company. I asked Tin Maung if it was not opium I could smell. After a moment he said, 'I am perplexed.' 'There are Chinese-Shan ladies,' said the schoolmaster, averting his head in deprecation from the offending quarter. 'These ladies are not serious.' The word was used in exactly the way a central European would use it, in harsh condemnation of one who is not right-thinking.

Our waiter had been a small Chinese boy of about twelve, with all the urbanity of a trained hotelier. He was quick to sweep the scattered rice from the table to the floor, where rats of extraordinary tameness made frequent sorties to deal with it. He was swift and merciless in his annihilation of cockroaches which ventured on the table, despite the wincing of the schoolmaster. Having presented the bill — a sheetful of cavorting ideographs — he astounded me by refusing a rupee tip. I tried to press it upon him, but the rejection was no mere form, although as he retreated before us, bowing, to the door, he was clearly delighted. 'He does not take money, as a sign of respect,' Tin Maung

144

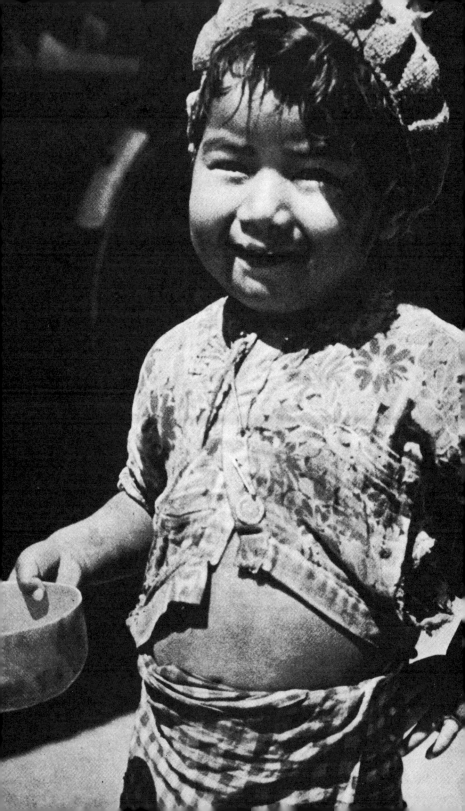

said. 'It is sufficient that you have honoured him by offering it.' A delightful bartering of compliments, I thought, and I practised it on several further occasions. In the end I stopped trying to tip the Chinese, to whom the idea seemed alien — at least, when they are not sufficiently far from their homeland for the old customs to have quite changed. Tin Maung also informed me that in that part of the country, a Burmese, when he is obliged to accept money to which he does not feel entitled, will mark the note or notes in such a way that he will be able to identify them, and give them in alms as soon as he can.

Lashio's main street was in pitch darkness as we strolled back. Chinks of light showed through the tea-house doors, but the only sound to be heard came from a Chinese party in an upstairs room somewhere. An orchestra was playing with spasmodic frenzy, but the undertones were suppressed by distance. The only sound which reached us with rhythmic regularity was that, as it seemed, of an iron saucepan being thrown from a height into the street; a hollow and staccato thud, doubtless to be achieved only after infinite practice at whatever the instrument was.

U Thein Zan had just returned from the monastery and was awaiting us, dressed, as usual, for the evening, in a sailor's blue sweater, which he had put on over his shirt. He had been both chastened and inspired by his visit to the monastery, and it was soon evident that we were to receive a substantial paraphrase of the sermon. First, however, a bottle of rum and two glasses were put on the table, a truly remarkable sight in such a devout household. I felt, indeed, most dubious about committing in the old man's presence what amounted to a deadly sin. But filling up the glasses and raising his in my direction Tin Maung said that if his father wanted an audience, he would have to put up with its wickedness. Shaking his head in fond reproof, U Thein Zan said, 'I do not renounce my son's salvation. Foolishness and laughing is the age and lack of experience. Soon he will come to tell me, "old man, you were right".' With sandals removed, our legs drawn up on the seats of our chairs, and our pernicious glasses before us, we resigned ourselves to U Thein Zan's exhortations. Since in the Orient no one is distracted by mere noise, the Radio Toulouse programme was left at full

K   G.E.   145

strength, although on this night the reception – a concert by the Chasseurs d'Afrique – was fitful and gusty.

Buddhism, as I had gathered from various sermons printed in the Rangoon press, had suddenly become injected with evangelical fervour, a rare phenomenon in the history of the religion. And perhaps with the notion of making the message more palatable to the West, great emphasis was now being laid on its 'scientific' character. Having held back, in the way of religions in which the final and perfect revelation is given once and for all, until it has seen itself in danger of being left high and dry by the times – a survival of medievalism – it has now come forward, almost as if an intolerably compressed spring had been released, with something of a jerk. Buddhist sermons now feature such topics as atomic fission, and the Buddha is sometimes referred to as the first atomic scientist. Even before having been subjected to such propaganda, one cannot have helped noticing that primitive Buddhism, in its rarely found, untainted form, could loosely be described as scientific in its attitude, and in its conception – a feat of great intuitive power on the part of its founder – of the soul's slow evolution through countless ages from lower to higher forms. This foreshadowing of Darwinism is now belatedly exploited by his followers. It is much stressed by the organizers of the Third Missionary Movement – the only previous movements recognized being those of Buddha, and the Indian king, Asoka. U Thein Zan's reconstruction of the sermon was a thick soup; a conventional stock of Buddhist mysticism into which much Freud and Einstein had been stirred. Afterwards he produced a pamphlet by the Venerable Lokanatha of Hongkong, the leading spirit of this movement, of whose previous announcements I had acquired copies in Rangoon. This worthy monk, described as being in the truth-exporting business, was on his way to the United States, where the construction of an 'incomparable Skyscraper Pagoda in New York, dedicated to World Peace' would be the crowning achievement of his work.

As in many Buddhist sermons, there was an earthiness, a downright manner in the attack. This was strong stuff for the squeamish. There were no airy abstractions here. Briskly the venerable monk settled down to a classification of the body's 'thirty-two filthy parts'. He seeks to shatter the image of fleshly beauty and does so in a few, shrewd blows. The body is 'a foul latrine on two legs' he begins, then, warming to his subject with the relish of an Aldous Huxley, he invites our attention to a dead body, '. . . an excellent subject for meditation. The swollen, stinking corpse, bluish-black, with swarms of worms issuing from the nine holes is enough to make any one disgusted with the foul nature of the body. We should sit down and identify ourselves with the horrible corpse, with the following reflection: "As I am now, so once was he; as he is now, so shall I be." By thinking in this way the idea will finally dawn on us that our body is a corpse bound to our neck. And we shall loathe and hate our body and the bodies of others. This is the way to destroy lust for ever.' But in case this exercise in meditation should fail to work we are presented with a monkish technique of taming this disturbing and disgusting machine. It reads a little like one of those slightly repellent chats about fitness and the body beautiful in a sun-bathing journal — the note of obsession is common to both — except of course, in reverse. All you do is take as little sleep as you can — four hours at the most, avoid nourishing food, and above all, never relax. In this way you can be sure of building-up the body unbeautiful in a reasonably short time.

But as the Reverend Lokanatha's appeal is directed above all to the citizens of the New World, he feels it necessary to put in a word about how to get rich. 'Men are born poor because they were stingy in the past. Men are born rich because they were generous in the past. Therefore don't be jealous of the rich man driving in a fancy limousine car. Give as he did, and you too will become rich . . .' A yard-stick for calculation is thoughtfully provided in a quotation from the Master's words: 'Herein Ananda, the yield to be looked for from a donation to an animal is a hundred-fold, to an ordinary non-virtuous man a thousand-fold, to the Saint, incalculable and beyond all measure.'

It is extraordinary how the fascination of America is felt equally by Burmese bobby-soxers and venerable monks. There is no doubt that the U.S.A. has become the Cathay of our times. 'The scientific

American will readily embrace Scientific Buddhism. They are eagerly awaiting for our Atomic Bomb of Love. Our incomparable Sky-scraper Pagoda in New York dedicated to World Peace will surely crown the world. The year 2500 (A.D. 1956) will see the rise of Buddhism, and we must start now by preaching in America . . .' The wheel has turned a full circle and now the Marco Polos and the Francis Xaviers of the Orient set out for the Hang-chow of the West, on Manhattan Island.

That night, I dealt with the sleeping problem more efficiently, tucking the mosquito net under the bedding so that it was under a continuous even strain all round. Shoulders, ankles and outsides of arms, where they might touch the net, were smeared with insect-repellent cream, which I now used for the first time. A few baffled cockroaches soon appeared, silhouetted like coracles on the outside of the net, but after mooching about for a while they went away. Rats rustled behind the shrine and ran squeaking along the timbers. From all quarters of the night horizon came the muffled hallooing of owls. In pleasant anticipation of the next day's journey, I fell asleep.

But the next day brought no hope of leaving Lashio. At the market we learned that the only movement signalled was the return of a lorry to Mandalay. The trouble was that there was nobody who could be approached for definite information, no set point of departure. If a driver got a load, he was likely to move off at short notice, and only those who hung about the market continually could be sure of a seat. Then again an owner might announce his intention of going to a town on my route, and then for any one of a number of reasons, suddenly change his mind, and go off in the other direction. This happened in the case of an Indian who had to make the run to Nam Hkam at some time, to pick up some goods there. But there was a rumour that the Chinese bandits had cut the road; so he said, with a kind of jellied smile, that the Nam Hkam trip could wait for another day. The only offer I got that day was of a ride on a bullock-cart going to Mong Pang, about twenty miles along the road. I was warned that although Burmese bullock-carts are a rather more rapid form of transport than one would imagine, this journey might take two days.

At this moment the market was full of rumours. Without particular excitement the knowledgeable hangers-on who foregathered there spoke of heavy fighting to the south, where a Chinese Nationalist division had been split up by Burmese forces, supported by planes. To lend colour to this account, we had at one time, with the stirring of the breeze, heard a distant thudding which might have been the sound of falling bombs. The incident on the Mandalay road came back to us in thunderous and distorted echoes of slaughter, rapine and destroyed convoys. More ominous was the fact that the post-lorry from Nam Hkam was long overdue, and it was generally assumed that the driver and guard were lying somewhere in a ditch, with their throats cut. Merchants are most phlegmatic and enterprising people, but it was clear that their present attitude to journeyings was tinged with unwonted caution. Into such a state had Burma, and indeed most of South-East Asia fallen! Travel had become almost as slow as in the days of Marco Polo, and probably more hazardous. Certainly the security of the roads under the Mongols' dominion, when the Venetians made their great Eastern journey, was much superior to that of twentieth-century Burma.

And now as the days passed a pattern of life in Lashio began to evolve. There were the hours immediately following the dawn, when the town emerged from mist like the image on a photographic plate, and when I was now permitted to assist the youngest brother in the serious passage with the watering-can from plant to plant. Then would follow the morning walk down to the market to interrogate drivers on their intentions, followed by a ritual drinking of tea, with its accompanying saffron-cake, undesired but bought out of decency because plain tea was always free of charge. Before midday a shower bath was taken in a shed in the garden. I was attended by the youngest brother, who brought the pitchers of water. At this point I learned the prim Burmese method of bathing with longyi in position and then releasing the knot in the wet longyi and stepping out of it when the dry one was in position over it. Such douchings were frequent and obligatory. The Burmese bathe as often as possible, and also use water for their most intimate sanitary toilet, relating as a cautionary tale the fate of one of their kings who, because in his immediately previous incarnation he had been an ogre, scorned these matters of hygienic routine and was in consequence deserted by his principal queen.

At high noon we would relax on the balcony before glasses of lemonade, while a sporadic snow of white butterflies drifted across the now sharply defined landscape. This was the time for the collections of snapshots to be produced, and on looking through them I felt that the camera had confirmed, perhaps more convincingly than anything before, the brotherhood of mankind. There were Burmese parties on a social outing to the pagoda, just as Europeans might visit a road-house. The halt on the way to be photographed against the blurred background of a waterfall, the girls in the group holding their heads at studied angles, their mouths set in the rictus of the film-star smile. And then there were records of more intimate occasions, such as the canoeing trip with the pretty Shan lady, a shorthand typist, by whom 'pleasant expectations were aroused, but with vain outcome'. A Sawbwa's daughter, whose face contained a suggestion of the forceful characteristics of Edda Mussolini, seemed to have been kinder, since Tin Maung's lips were pursed at the memory — so much so that I almost expected a whistle to issue from them.

In the afternoon I would take up a book, while Tin Maung dismantled the wireless set and prepared it with dexterous tuning for the evening tussle with Radio Toulouse. The evening meal was taken in one of the Chinese restaurants, the opium-smoking and non-serious one being virtuously avoided; on our return, U Thein Zan would be ready with a homily. In a moment of mild exasperation Tin Maung gave away the reason for the present phase of religious fervour. 'It is time now that the old man should die. If he should continue too much longer in this existence all the monetary resources will be vanished away.' U Thein Zan's face cracked into a crestfallen smile. It seemed that he had recently fallen into his old vice of gambling, and having staked heavy sums as an outcome of a fatal blunder in the calculation of his horoscope, his losses had been tremendous. 'You should die, old man. You should die,' said Tin Maung relentlessly; a verdict with which U Thein Zan seemed, humbly enough, to agree.

A day or two later, there was another report of a lorry going to Nam Hkam. It was said to be loading in the market — news which sent me hurriedly packing my things. When I was ready I wanted to go straight down and take my seat, and not leave it for a moment until we were on our way. But Tin Maung would not hear of this undignified procedure. A message would be sent for the lorry to call for me, and I could wait in comfort and propriety where I was. It might be hours before it was ready to depart. I wanted to photograph the family before I left, so they all retired for a few minutes to prepare themselves. U Thein Zan appeared dressed with flamboyant conservatism in a taung-mathein, a long, white coat, a sartorial survival of the last century equivalent to a frock-coat. His paso had been wound tightly round the waist and tied in front with a fine, impractical ebullience of material. The made-up turban was replaced by a scarf, tied with the swagger of a buccaneer. It was a fine turn-out, combining the maximum of difficulty of manipulation with good taste. By him stood his wife, wearing all the jewellery she had left to her after U Thein Zan's gambling losses, flowers in her hair, her face powdered ghastly white. The youngest son was dressed as usual for the pampas; the second son with his everyday buckish elegance, which in any case could not have been improved upon; while Tin Maung, undaunted by the heat, had put on an army pullover. I photographed the little group in colour, amongst their flowers, having promised U Thein Zan to give him some lasting record of the rather pallid glory of his snapdragons and sweet peas. This was all done rather hurriedly, with an eye on the road, and my bags standing by the garden gate. But as the shadows lengthened and the hills across the valley began to gather about them their drapings of mist, there was no heartening cough, rattle and thump of well-worn mechanism coming up the hill. In the end, I went down to the market again where I heard that at the very last moment the lorry had been requisitioned by the Army.

Early next morning, without heralding, salvation came. A post-wagon was taking mail to Nam Hkam, or as far as it could go along the road, and someone had told the driver about me. There was a scramble to get my things out. When I said goodbye to the others, the old mother was missing, and just as the lorry was moving off she came rushing out with food for the journey tied up in a palm-leaf bundle. She tried, without success, to persuade me to accept also the contents of a handkerchief, which appeared to be several precious or semi-precious stones — another reminder of the fact that, to the Burmese, liberality is the chief of the ten great virtues, and the second of the three works of perfection.

The post-wagon was undoubtedly the most decrepit, the most ex-hausted vehicle in which I had ever travelled. It was a phantom from a breaker's yard, something which had been unearthed from a bombed building. The treads of all four tyres displayed a rippling pattern of canvas. There was no spare. Before the steering wheel could influence the car's direction, it had to be spun through half a turn. Gaping sockets showed where all the instruments had been wrenched out of the dashboard. The floor-boards above the engine had been removed, releasing a furnace heat and the rattling vibration of a million nails being shaken in a metal box. Above this pit sat the driver, stabbing like a frantic organist at the control pedals, which in some way had lost their normal independence of each other, since the application of the brake slightly opened the throttle, and the engine had to be switched off, or the accelerator held back, whenever this was necessary. When-ever he wanted to blow the horn, the driver, reaching out as if to catch a butterfly, seized two dangling wires and held them together. The body was insecurely fixed to the chassis, but settled down on a straight road to a steady see-sawing motion to which one soon became accus-tomed, although the sudden opening of the doors as we took corners continued to surprise.

Our first stop was at the market-place again where two Shan police-men, armed with swords, arrived in company with a Burmese women. The woman was singing in a penetrating voice, and the policemen

looked embarrassed. All three climbed into the back. The policemen
unbelted their swords, laid them down beside them and settled themselves. Two or three onlookers gathered; the woman waved gaily to
them and started another song. One of the policemen picked up his
sword, leaned over and tapped the driver on the shoulder with it,
nodding to the road ahead. The driver screwed up his face, but said
nothing. More onlookers strolled up and stood about, their faces
amazed under their turbans while the Burmese woman serenaded
them. Another policeman appeared, and checked the travellers' passes,
and then, as with a resounding crash the driver engaged bottom gear,
our musical passenger broke into 'I put my money on a coal-black
mare, doodah, doodah', and away we went.

Within minutes the last of Lashio's cottage gardens was behind us.
We were going down a gradient with a steep, flowering slope on our
right, and then my heart sank. There was another lorry in the middle
of the road, clearly in trouble. From it swarmed like troubled bees a
colourful collection of passengers, Kachin women with a chain-mail
of silver coins over their breasts, Palaungs with hips swathed in metal
bands, and betel-stained holes where their mouths should have been.
In the Far East, the courtesies of the road are observed with punctilio.
We drew up alongside and immediately a team of experts from the
post-wagon was formed to investigate and pronounce upon the breakdown. Petrol lines, pumps and carburettor were dismantled in a
leisurely manner, fiddled with and re-assembled. The engine started,
wuffled for perhaps ten seconds, and stopped. Meanwhile our singer
had reached a number in her repertoire which seemed to give her
special pleasure, and was singing that simple tune, 'Happy birthday to
you', for the fifth or sixth time.

A moment later it became clear that the driver of the post-wagon
had made a generous decision, for there was a sudden rush of whirling
skirted forms in our direction, and in a few seconds we had taken on a
jingling cargo. There was something miraculous about the compression involved. A young Indian girl of distracted Pre-Raphaelite
beauty joined us. Jewels dripped from a nostril, and round her neck
she wore a large iron key. Passing by an act of levitation over the

crowded forms, she subsided in a ballet posture among some vegetable marrows. The Palaungs, a compact racial heap, stared around them with the frightened eyes of children in the presence of violence. The singing Burmese woman had been driven by the invasion into a position immediately behind me, although slightly higher. Every time she moved she struck me with her knee in the back of the neck. Forced thus into close contact, I took in the details of her dress, the grubby, flowered longyi, the unbuttoned blouse and, rather alarmingly, the necklace of beer-bottle tops.

We moved off down the hill, the overloaded post-wagon wallowing with a nautical motion. Whenever we went over a bump there was a sound from the interior like the clashing of circus accoutrements. Having covered a mile or two, we reached a gradient that was too much for us. Everyone got out, and while the passengers trotted by its side the lorry made a groaning, faltering climb. At the top of the hill there was a pause to let the engine cool. The Burmese woman, still singing, leaped suddenly from her perch, easily cleared a low hedge into a field, where, producing a clasp-knife, she hacked down a sugar-cane and began to tear at it with her teeth. I thought this extraordinary because I could never remember having seen a woman run in the Far East before. I got out my notebook and started to write and a young man dressed with striking formality came worming his way through the baggage, pulled my sleeve, and asked courteously, 'What are you writing, sir?' I told him I was writing poetry and received a brilliant smile from under the brown trilby hat.

It occurred to me to comment on the behaviour of the Burmese woman, who was now coming towards us, her sugar-cane held in her hand, in a series of leaps. He said, 'This lady has bad nerves, sir.' I had begun to suspect as much, and now something else struck me. In the Burmese theatre the insane are always shown as Ophelias, distraught and wildly eccentric. Although their condition is pitiable, and sorcerers are called in to heal them by the medieval equivalent of shock treatment, they dance and sing in an absurd fashion, and adorn themselves ridiculously with such things as condensed-milk tins. This then was the recognized pattern of Burmese insanity, and it looked as if the Burmese went mad along accepted lines. It was curious to consider that an element of pose probably lurked beneath the authentic state of derangement. I asked what had been responsible for the woman's misfortune, and my friend, who introduced himself as Seng, said, 'This lady has lost all her children. For this reason her nerves have become bad.' But there was no way of discovering the circumstances of her children's death; my further inquiries only producing flashing smiles of incomprehension. Later he told me that the woman, who had caused a disturbance in Lashio, was being removed under escort to her home village. And where did she learn all these extraordinary hymns, carols, negro spirituals, bawdy army choruses? The answer, when the question had been repeated several times, in different ways, was unconvincing. 'They teach these songs in the schools, sir.' Seng was a Kachin who had been down to Rangoon for his education and was now on his way home. Gradually and rather painfully our conversation expanded. At first there were long pauses while the thoughts in Kachin were translated into English via Burmese; but after a while the sentences began to come more readily, and with their proper Anglo-Asiatic injection of rotundities, euphemisms and prudery.

Our road wound through low hills clothed in formless scrub, and the slow re-animation of secondary jungle, where cultivation has long been abandoned. Occasionally there were patches, ragged in shape as Hebridean islands, which had only recently been given up and where the self-sown maize and the tea-bushes spread in increasing dilution through the ferns, the creepers and the thorns. In this desolation we passed a single, human form, a Shan who wore gauntlets of tattooing and a ring of tattooed dragons leaping up from his waist as if to devour his torso. He stood motionless by the roadside, his arms curled inexplicably round a slender tree trunk, looking, somehow, against this seething background of curving fronds and tendrils, like a capital in a richly illuminated manuscript.

Near here, the Indian girl left us. She was accompanied by an ageing man, who now struggled up from the depths of the baggage, and the pair of them set off down a thorn-lined track, bound, under the relentless sun, for who knows what strange haven of domestic bliss. At Mongli, which although marked on fairly small-scale maps, seemed to possess only one hut, there was a halt for refreshment, and the post-wagon discharged its passengers like seeds exploded from an over-ripe pod. I found that the package Tin Maung's mother had given me contained raw onions and fried meat balls, beautifully done up in banana-leaves and then the locally made, tough, translucent paper. I shared this with Seng, who gave me some tea out of a section of bamboo fitted with a neat, wooden cap. It was here for the first time that I noticed the beautiful baskets carried by the Palaungs, who had gathered in a ball-players' huddle.

Being without anthropological training I do not know whether one is entitled to form theories on so slender a basis of evidence, so I only place on record the fact that although regarded as a Mongolian people, the Palaungs possess beautiful woven and lacquered baskets, of a quite extraordinary shape, which are identical with those made by the Indonesian Mois of Central Annam, which, as the crow flies, is about fourteen hundred miles away. These baskets, which I have photographed in both countries, are not owned by any of the peoples by whom the Palaungs are surrounded. Their construction is very complicated, and they are beautiful on the score of shape and texture, as they are not decorated in any way. I think that the possibility of coincidence is ruled out. It is, by the way, curious that the handicrafts of a people so remote, so neglected, and apparently so low in the cultural scale, should be so much superior to those of the relatively sophisticated Shans and Kachins who are their neighbours. The Palaungs speak a Mongolian language, and I believe that on this linguistic evidence, they as well as so many of the Burmese minorities, have been classed as Mongolian people. From a cursory and superficial study of their features, as well as those of many other obscure racial types I encountered in my travels, I should guess that although these people may have adopted the language of powerful neighbours, and have intermarried with them, they probably also possess pre-Mongoloid Indonesian blood. Many of them have the Caucasian type of eye and thick, wavy hair. The French, who have carried out intense ethnological studies in Indo-China, produce a map showing enclaves of Indonesians clustered along the western frontier of that country, where it is contiguous with the Southern Shan States of Burma. It would be unreasonable to suppose that these cease to be found as soon as one crosses into Burma, when the frontier is, of course, a purely political one. Perhaps if instead of the linguistic classification which has hitherto sufficed, a study were made of the laws, ceremonies, legends, religious customs and the traditional designs of weaving of these peoples, an entirely new light might be thrown on their origins and racial affinities.

Certainly the Palaungs' legend of their origin sounds a Mongolian one, although it may have been adopted in recent times along with the language. The founder of the tribe was hatched from a serpent's egg — a hint of totemism which is echoed by the women's habit of encircling their hips by forty or fifty narrow cane hoops, which rest one on another, to a depth of about a foot or eighteen inches, and provide a suggestively undulant motion as they walk. Such an ancestry is considered utterly reasonable in the Far East, and the existence of a naga in one's pedigree would have caused no comment, at least until recently, in the gravest of academic circles. The Glass Palace Chronicle — a collation of records combined with historical criticism — written in 1829, goes into the question of 'egg-born kings' at length, but the learned commentators are concerned only to establish their reasonable opinion that a certain Burmese monarch — Pyu Sawhti — could not have been born of an egg laid by a naga (a female serpent-god) *as the result of her union with a spirit*, and that since the king was human, one of the parents, at least, must have been human too. However, instances are given, and approved, of the oviparous birth of human beings where only one of the parents was supernatural — a naga, or a fabulous lion.

Hsenwi was an incrustation of huts where, in a bare plateau, the road was joined by another from the east. We crossed a rush-choked river, over which shaven-headed children in blue smocks held their fishing rods. There was a small lake with white ducks on it diving through the reflection of a bare mountain, and storks going round in circles overhead. Horsemen, their feet almost trailing on the ground, came charging through the grass to the verge of the road, and as we passed cavorted like movie-Indians and waved their yellow scarves at us. We passed a line of shops with the shop-keepers outside flying fish-shaped kites. A caravan of ponies, piled high with what looked like bean-sticks, panicked at our approach and, turning, stampeded through the village in a charge like that of the bulls driven before Morgan's pirates at the sack of Panama.

This was Kachin country, although there were still plenty of Shan enclaves. The Kachins, comparatively recent arrivals in these high-lands, have always been regarded by the Shans, whose country they invaded, with a kind of superstitious aversion. Their exceptional ability as hunters was apt to be ascribed to the works of the devil. This charge had some slight basis, because the Kachins had the un-usual advantage of the protection of a powerful spirit called Kyam, in a country where the most that could be hoped for from the average nat was neutrality, bought at a cost of frequent sacrifices. Kyam led the Kachins to their game, which he fascinated, while the hunters shot them with their crossbows, using aconite-tipped arrows. The service was performed without any question of return, and not even a priest had to be paid.

As far as the Shans could, they kept the Kachins back in their moun-tains, often burning the villages of those who tried to establish them-selves in the more fertile Shan country. But the Kachins were under constant internal pressure to emigrate, the result of the destructive type of cultivation they practised, and of their custom by which the youngest son inherited all his father's property, thus compelling the elder sons to set out to found new settlements. When the Kachins reached the stage when they had to expand or burst, they did so explosively, practising a form of warfare rarely known in the West since biblical times. All living beings were exterminated in the terri-tory taken over. The operation was carried out without animosity, and the ghosts of the victims — who received a decent burial — were placated with inexpensive sacrifices.

In their mountains, the Kachins live in long-houses, which are often occupied by several families. The dead are buried under the floor, where it is felt that they will be less lonely. Up to the time of marriage the women enjoy unusual freedom, and often try a succession of lovers before settling down. They then become chattels, descending to a man's heir with the rest of his property.

Beyond Hsenwi we mounted a hill, entered a stockade, and drew up outside the local military headquarters. The driver expected to find the Sawbwa here, but we were redirected to his haw, a mile away on a hillside among a belt of trees. The haw, or palace, as the Sawbwa's residence in usually known, was a substantial, single-storied building of plaited bamboo, with a formal, roofed-over approach, and a kind of exterior waiting-room where Seng and the driver were left, while a servitor conducted me up the steps to the entrance to the haw itself. Here the Sawbwa appeared. We had arrived rather unfortunately in the siesta time, and he showed signs of having dressed hastily. Like his brother, he was polite but without affability. Reading my letter he invited me to be seated at a table in his barely furnished reception room. He then gave an order to one of his sons, a boy of about twelve, who went away and shortly reappeared with cigarettes and air-mail paper and envelopes, which, kneeling respectfully, he handed to his father. The Sawbwa then wrote out an open recommendation to any official I might encounter on the road to Nam Hkam to be of all possible assistance. He advised me to continue with the post-wagon as far as I could go, as it might be some time before another opportunity of transport offered itself. I should have liked to stay a day or two in Hsenwi, but although I made it clear that I did not wish to inconvenience the Sawbwa in any way, this delay was not thought advisable. The village had been thoroughly destroyed by bombing during the war and accommodation was very limited. My interview lasted five minutes. Perhaps the Sawbwa had given up all hopes of the English.

Kutkai was another Hsenwi, except that it was twenty miles nearer the Chinese frontier, and in that distance a marked increase in Chinese influence had taken place. I was surprised to see Chinese women with bound feet pegging along the single street, as if picking their way across a surface strewn with invisible eggs. In one's schooldays one was told that this practice had long been abandoned, and that examples of it were only to be seen in the case of old women, survivors from the Imperial days. At about the time this information was imparted, these women must have been undergoing the minor tortures which had finally moulded their feet into the lotus form. It was an extraordinary quirk of taste that could see the image of a symmetrical bloom in this deformation of the foot-bones.

The village was in a low hollow of the hills. They were covered with whitened grass, a tough, austere growth heralding the vegetable dark-age, when the soil has been utterly exhausted by primitive cultivation. We could see Palaungs converging on the town, moving down from the hills in Indian file, loaded with green grass for use in feeding the animals; grass that every year, one supposed, would have to be brought from a greater distance. Here, at Kutkai, the post-wagon gave in. After its long, arduous and useful life, it had chosen just this day of all days to attain the Nirvana of final disintegration, or so the driver thought. The radiator had boiled steadily all the way from Hsenwi, emitting thin jets of steam and water through various perforations, and lately the even, almost rhythmic clatter of loose tappets, bearings and pistons, and the whine of worn gears, had been invaded by new, irregular and compelling sounds. Suddenly the power had faded away, absorbed in mechanical convulsions preceding the ultimate coma. We had limped into Kutkai at a slow walking pace. Now a line of turbanned heads was bowed, under the bonnet, over the smoking, reeking mechanism, and a murmur of advice in several of the Thibeto-Burman and Thai-Chinese languages arose. And then, the driver produced his diagnosis. A connecting rod had snapped and it was supposed that a macerated piston had dropped into the sump, where it had been ground into fragments by the crankshaft. If parts could be found a repair would take about four days. Otherwise the post-wagon would never travel further. Sadly the passengers dispersed towards the various caravanserais of Kutkai. With them went the crazy Burmese woman and her guards. She was still singing and gambolling with the inexhaustible vitality of her despair.

160

[*facing:* THE KACHIN HEADMAN'S WOMENFOLK

I was just about to look for a tea-house myself, speculating on whether Kutkai could provide even one-star accommodation by local standards, when Seng, who had gone off as soon as we stopped, reappeared in a bullock-cart. It was a vehicle of a kind I had not seen before, high-wheeled and rakish, and having about it something of the chariot. It was drawn by two fine and almost spirited-looking animals, constrained only by a light yoke. They approached in a quick, shambling gait. Directing the driver, a tattooed and muscled Asiatic Ben-Hur, to put my baggage in this contraption, Seng invited me to accompany him to the house of his brother-in-law, a Kachin headman, who lived only a few miles away. Here I could put up in comfort while inquiries were being made about transport for the next stage of the journey. Accepting this very welcome suggestion, I climbed in and sat down with Seng in the bottom of the cart, the driver cracked his whip, and the bullocks moved off at a sharp pace.

A few miles out of Kutkai we turned off the Burma Road into a rough, rutted track leading up into the hills. Within minutes there was a change in scenery. It was like the escape from a concreted highway with the flat boredom of its surroundings into the sanctuary of the undisturbed woods. The dazzling white deadness of the grass was broken by sere but florescent bushes and thickets of bamboo, and among these the trees, pipuls, banyans and flamboyants, massive eruptions of verdure, became increasingly frequent. Huge rollers flew strongly among their branches, their wings flashing with Aegean blues. 'The foolish bird,' said Seng, following my gaze of admiration. 'This is its designation in the Kachin tongue, because it eats its own faeces.' As we penetrated into these high forests, the butterflies threading among the trees had already lost the pallor of those of the tropical steppe-lands and taken on a wash of colour, a token of the magnificence that awaited us in the deep undergrowth ahead. Palaungs, gowned like pantomime witches and bent under their bundles, flitted away into the trees until we had passed.

The headman's house was on a bare hilltop. It was as big as the Sawbwa's haw, an important construction of stone and corrugated iron, which had been smashed in the passage of the war, and half

facing: A CORNER OF THE NAM HKAM MARKET]

rebuilt in woven bamboo. Two or three rifle-armed soldiers of the headman's bodyguard were hanging about outside, and a jeep painted with a vigorous, primitive design of tigers and deer was drawn up outside the door. Seng directed our driver to continue round to the back of the house, where we found a kind of tradesman's entrance, surrounded by much domestic activity, cooking on outside stoves, and babies sitting in the dust eating rice out of bowls. Here also was the headman's private lock-up, a species of chicken-house strengthened with thick, timber bars, in which three inmates were sitting, whom from their blue-cotton clothing I took to be Chinese. The door was unceremoniously opened by the headman himself, a short man of almost theatrical inscrutability, dressed like a Soviet official in a plain loose tunic and trousers. He greeted his brother-in-law without surprise or effusion, and invited me to enter. We went in and sat down in chairs placed against the wall, in a room furnished like the waiting-room of an old-fashioned, poor persons, dispensary. The headman took my collection of permits and letters in English, Burmese, Shan and Kachin, and began to read them with extreme deliberation, his lips silently forming the words.

While this process went on, my eyes wandered round the room, passing over the repetitious bamboo pattern of the walls, then arrested by a crudely coloured picture of a number of figures in vaguely Palestinian dress, who were peering into a cave, which they were prevented from entering by a stern-faced, white-robed form. Under this was printed the legend: 'He is not here, but is risen.' The aristocracy of these parts, it seemed, were Baptist converts. Beneath this picture hung a gong, and when the headman had finished perusing my documents he reached up and tapped it lightly with his knuckles. Immediately a soldier came in. He was dressed in a British battledress, was barefooted, and carried a rifle slung on his shoulder. The headman muttered something and the soldier went out and came back almost immediately carrying a tray loaded with three cups of tea and basins of sugar and salt. In the Burmese hill-country, tea-leaves are grilled, and the addition to the brew of salt as well as sugar produces a result which differs greatly in flavour from tea as drunk in the West. The headman passed the tea, having added the sugar and salt with his own hands. This courtesy accomplished, he was called away to other duties. I could not make up my mind whether I was welcome or not, but resigned myself to Seng, who showed me to a bare chamber leading off a central room, and told me to make myself at home. It was part of the original stone construction, and there was an attached cubicle with a stand, a pitcher and a hole in the floor, where a shower could be taken.

No sooner had I put my bedding down in a corner than a Kachin girl came in. She had a wide Thibetan face with bright pink cheeks which seemed to continue right up to her eyes, which were narrow, black and glinting. She was smiling with abounding good humour, and bounced round the room in a kind of brisk tour of inspection, skirts swirling and hawser-like pigtails flapping on her back. It seemed as though she wished to assure herself that all the non-existent furniture had been properly dusted, and that the towels had been put out. Finally satisfied with the good order of the void, she withdrew with a slight bow, indicating, as she did, the cubicle, where I found a bowl of hot water had been placed. Five minutes, perhaps, passed while I was unpacking a few things; then I heard footsteps in the cubicle, to which there was also an outside door, and looking up I saw that another handmaiden had arrived with a second steaming bowl. The first was removed. Next the beaming Seng arrived with a chair to put my clothes on. Having arranged my wardrobe on this, and laid out my mosquito net ready for use, I made for the wash-place, just in time to see the water being changed for a third time.

I washed and hung up my mosquito net, and was wondering what to do with myself when there was a tap on the door and Seng was back again. 'Do you like rum?' he asked. I said that I did, and followed him into the central room, where the headman was staring severely at several bottles. We sat down and the headman took three half-pint tumblers, half filled them with rum, and topped them up with the now familiar Mandalay Pale Ale. One of these he handed to me. The headman and his brother-in-law raised their glasses in my direction. Seng smiled brilliantly; he said 'Chin-chin'. The headman managed a faint grimace. Two heads were flung back and two glasses drained. The headman looked up with faint reproach while I gulped painfully, fulfilling at enormous effort what was expected of me. Immediately the two bottles were raised, threateningly, and I realized that the abstemious and puritanical Burma of the plains was now behind me and that I had fallen among a race of hard-drinking hill-folk.

The headman spoke a little now, groping for words, about local conditions. In recent years they had seen plenty of fighting. When the Japanese had finally gone there had been a plague of Chinese bandits, and then a Kachin insurrection against the Burmese led by a self-promoted Brigadier Naw Seng, who when defeated had escaped with his adherents into China. The headman supposed that he would re-appear one of these days in the guise of a Chinese-backed liberator of the Kachin people. He was not disturbed at the prospect. 'We Kachins lack education,' he said. 'We like to fight and to drink country spirit.' If the Chinese Communists ever came over the frontier it would be a good scrap while it lasted, although he was the first to admit that it wouldn't last long. Up to the moment there had not been a single instance reported to him of the violation of the frontier by a Communist soldier, although waves of fleeing Nationalists kept coming over. The road ahead, between this and Nam Hkam, had been closed for a week now because of the attacks they had made on traffic, and in the near future he would have to go and drive them out of the area. He had a two-pounder gun that hadn't been used since the war, and now he was hoping for the chance to fire a few rounds. The headman's voice when he said this lacked the ring of conviction. It was more of the sportsman's gesture to a convention of optimism, than a matter of serious hope.

I asked for news of conditions over the frontier. Were, for instance, land reforms being put into practice? Land reforms! the headman echoed scornfully, it wasn't land reforms the hill-peoples wanted. The people over the frontier were Shans, Kachins and Palaungs, just as they were on this side. If they wanted land, there was nothing to stop them clearing the bush and cultivating it. What the Kachin people wanted was not land, but education. That, he understood, their new masters in China were going to give them, although he had heard that the first samples to return from the school in Kunming had soon shown, to the scandal of the villagers, that they had lost respect for their parents. One of the worst things about the present situation was the closing of the frontier to ordinary respectable people. If you were dressed up like a hill savage in a turban and strings of beads, nobody said anything to you — you could cross backwards ·and forwards as much as you liked. But if you wore decent clothes — a pair of trousers and a hat bought in Rangoon — they arrested you as a spy. Draining his glass sorrowfully to the memory of departed liberties, the headman reached over and struck the gong. There was an almost immediate irruption into the room of domestics carrying dishes of food. Along with them came the headman's wife — Seng's sister — a strapping Ludmila of the remote Asiatic mountains, who, relieved of the headman's necessity for high-minded seriousness, giggled frequently, especially when in difficulties with the serving of the food. There was a continual coming and going of flouncing, pig-tailed forms, until the table was closely covered with dishes, scarlet curries with surface currents of ochreous oil, three varieties of what looked like seaweed (inevitably recommended as abundant in vitamins), a paste made of ground beans and chillis, pickled tea-leaves, great bowls of red rice, cups of tea with a container of salt by each. Having brought ·in the food, the female staff bowed, and one by one withdrew. Their place was taken by soldiers, who took up position behind the chairs and helped with the dishes, into which they sometimes let ash fall from the cheroots they were smoking. In between their duties, they knelt down to play with several of the headman's young children who had escaped from the nursery to take refuge here, and were crawling about on the floor.

Later that day, I found out from Seng that his brother-in-law had just received definite information of the location of the Chinese band. They were in a jungle village, about five hours' ride to the north, and next morning the headman would lead a party of his men to attack them. By this time Seng and I were on such good terms that I felt able to ask him to persuade the headman to take me with them. The headman, too, had suddenly thawed out with a revelation of charm that was like the unexpected appearance of the sun on a dull day. We talked about such things as education, particularly the flashier subjects like psychology, to which provincial Asiatics are often specially attracted, finding that the transition to such studies is not difficult after a grounding in, say, horoscopy or in the art of making oneself bullet-proof. In the cool of the evening all the able-bodied household, including the womenfolk, were chased out to do physical jerks in the courtyard while the headman, himself, rapped out the orders in Kachin — knees-bend, knees-stretch. This ritual was thoroughly enjoyed, especially by the women who usually over-balanced while in the knees-bend position. Nothing was said, one way or other, about the next day's expedition.

However, soon after dawn, Seng followed the pig-tailed serving-girl into my room, and said, 'The horses are ready.' He was trying to buckle on a Kachin dah, a weapon of monstrous unsuitability, over his Rangoon clothes. Seng was manipulating the dah — a heavy bladed affair, half-sword and half-axe — with a civilized lack of enthusiasm. 'If I do not carry this,' he said, with an apologetic smile, 'the headman will think I have become soft. But I have lost the habit of the strokes.' The soldiers were armed with Sten guns or rifles, but the headman and his brother-in-law were by tradition invulnerable, and carried dahs for reasons of prestige alone.

I am a plain horseman, content to keep my seat, and unfamiliar with equestrian refinements. The pony provided for me looked well-shaped enough and there was nothing unusual about it, except a certain sheepish quality about the head, and a drooping of the muzzle that reminded me of some other animal, perhaps a tapir. The stirrups were too short, and could not be lengthened enough for comfort. I mounted, and found myself, in this position, nearer the ground than I had ever been since on a donkey on the sands as a child. The short, fat back sagged springily as it took my weight, and I half expected the animal to col-lapse. Once firmly in the saddle I kicked experimentally at the pony's sides, and it instantly threw me backwards, over the tail, with an irresistible oscillation, like that of a dog shaking the water out of its coat. One of the Kachin soldiers caught it by the rein, passed a caressing hand over its face, then smacked it fiercely with the flat of his dah. I mounted again, and sat there quietly. The soldiers went off, stringing out into a thin column, with the headman leading them. Behind him rode a soldier, steering a pony which had nothing but a large ceremonial drum strapped to its back. Then came the straggling column, with the soldiers in their British battledresses, with waistbands tied over them, and dahs stuck through the waistbands; so that they looked like Japanese swordsmen. Seng and I brought up the rear. My pony started when the others did, and stopped when they stopped. Without any urging on my part, it broke, when it was required to keep up with the rest, into a kind of scrambling gallop, but would tolerate no interference on my part; it danced about and tossed its head angrily if I tried to give it any encouragement other than a shake of the reins, or to influence its course in any way. But it was the smoothest animal to ride I had ever sat on, and Seng later told me that a Kachin pony was unsaleable until it could be put through all its paces, with its rider holding a full tumbler in one hand, without spilling the contents.

That morning I had awakened with a vague sense of indisposition, and now as a growling malaise concentrated and defined itself, I realized that I was in for a mild bout of malaria. The fever soon cushioned the edges of sensation, and simplified things wonderfully. To me the jungle itself has never offered the brilliant variegation of the jungle as it appears in an air-terminal mural. It has never been a matter of orchids and black panthers; and now even the few modest highlights that this forest could have offered were suppressed by two or three degrees of fever. The impression remains that from the outside, as we rode through the wide clearings, it was like the trimly arranged asparagus of a bouquet from which, unaccountably, the flowers had been omitted. But as soon as we rode beneath those delicate awnings of fernery we passed into a seedy vegetable disorder, with many sallow, broken grasses, and moulting bamboos; and the sun showered its spears on us through a ragged armour of leaves. There were no serpents, nor startled fawns; not even, in fact, birds of sufficient presence for my fevered eyes to record them. This was a well-worn track, which wild animals had probably learned to avoid. Tribesmen, like any other travellers, are careful to keep out of the virgin jungle, and this narrow path probably carried as much or more human traffic than the metalled high-road.

We rode by the verge of swamps, over bare hill-tops, and down into the untidy jungle again; and thus on and on. Some time in the early afternoon the soldiers ahead broke into a gallop, and a few minutes later we rode into a miserable Palaung village. The soldiers sprang from their horses, crawled into the huts and came out with a few women. They were half-naked, and all had goitre. The Chinese had gone off the day before, they said, but they had left two sick men behind. They took us to a shelter of leaves and branches, under which the two deserted men lay on the ground, half-conscious, and with their bare feet grossly swollen. The Kachins sat them up, tied their hands lightly, and tried to stick lighted cheroots between their teeth; but the Chinese were past smoking. It appeared that the band had gone off down the trail in the direction of the border, so the headman, leaving a man behind with the prisoners, gave the order to ride on.

We rode out of the village, with the half-clothed, goitrous women standing by their huts looking after us, and down into the jungle, which was exactly as before. The thumping behind my eyes deepened, and with it, the monotony of the ride. Hours later we came down to a river. From our position we could not see the water, which at this time of the year was very shallow and split up by islands and sand-banks. There was a fording-place here, and China was on the other side. We could just make out a village, with an insect-movement of humans and buffaloes among the huts. The headman sent soldiers in various directions to make inquiries and, after a long wait, one of them came back with the news that the bandits had been seen crossing the ford. It was evident that the Kachins did not relish being checked by the purely political barrier. Seng explained that the people across the river were not Chinese, but Shans and Kachins; moreover, he said, 'The actual border is in dispute. Every year the river changes its course.'

But the headman was against further action. There might be Communist soldiers on the other side. Not that he was prepared to cross, in any case. To satisfy the men, the big drum was beaten vigorously; and a few seconds later the reply came, a bugle-call, practised, unwavering and definite. That settled it. A new, unsympathetic authority had announced its presence.

Although I had no idea of it at the time, we were at this point actually within a few miles of Nam Hkam, having in the course of our expedition cut across the base of a triangle of country enclosed by the motor-road. In a few days I should be passing once again down the roughly-metalled track running parallel with the river.

That night we slept in a jungle-clearing on the way back. There was a remnant of a hut perched on stilts ten feet high, and into it the headman, Seng and I climbed. Every time one of us turned over, this construction swayed a little. Beneath us, the soldiers thudded with unflagging energy at their drum, and sang a soldiering song with endless verses and an extremely monotonous air. The end of each verse would be signalled by howls of laughter. In the end, as the first wave of fever slowly spent itself, I relapsed into rambling, oppressive dreams. I was soon aroused by a discharge of shots. But it was only a soldier who had been tinkering with his Sten, which was loaded, and had shot off one of his toes.

CHAPTER XIII

PROTECTIVE CUSTODY

THE local section of the Burma Road having been declared open
to traffic, the headman took me down in his jeep to the point
where the hill-track joined it, and where he had established a road-
block, guarded by his men. Seng had come down to see me off, and
here we parted most cordially. The soldiers had already stopped a jeep.
In it were two Chinese merchants on their way from Kutkai to Mu-Sé.
This town was not marked on my map, the production of a very well
known map-making firm, which was vague — and, as I later discovered, inaccurate — about this frontier area. The Chinese spoke of
Mu-Sé as if it were a considerable metropolis, a local nerve-centre
from which well organized transport services left regularly in all
directions. This pernicious optimism in informants is one of the
traveller's worst enemies. They said there were lorries to Nam Hkam
'plenty often'. More than once a day? Oh, sure, more than once a day.
Would we get to Mu-Sé early enough to catch one? Oh, sure we
would, sure thing.

The Chinese spoke English better than the Burmese perhaps because
they had escaped the schools run by religious institutions, with their
hallmark of tedious and involved archaism. By comparison the Chinese made it snappy, and cinema-argot ran like a rich vein of fool's
gold through their speech. Their Americanisms are, of course, dated,
and as the cinematographic diet of the Far East is largely composed of
gun-toting epics, they are drawn largely from the dialects of the cattle-
raising states. 'Well, I'll be a son of a gun,' said the driver in amazement, when he learned of my hitch-hike from Mandalay.

The Chinese jeep reflected in its purposeful, surging acceleration, its
efficient steering and brakes, and also in certain additional equipment,
such as fog-lamps, the tastes and calibre of its owner. Wherever a
plain black handle or knob had existed, it had been replaced by one of

sky-blue plastic. Badges in the dashboard announced membership of motoring associations in places like Hongkong and Cuba, and would have appeared to be of little service to the Chinese member. Sometimes when approaching a corner, round which the odds of an approaching vehicle being hidden were several thousand to one, the driver would touch a button, and a tremendous fanfare of trumpets would flush from the undergrowth an unsuspected population of pigeons and quails.

This landscape was the wild, natural reserve common to most frontiers. Exposed to endless incursions of bandits, it had not been thought worth while to build villages, or to undertake any settled cultivation. From the absence of trees on the low hillsides you could see that the Palaungs or Kachins had moved through at some time, set fire to the forest and snatched a crop of 'dry' rice or maize. The road had been cut, a red whip-lash round hillsides and through valleys filled with a dense low tundra of tropical vegetation. We saw few signs of animal life here, except some lizards in the red dust, one of which was carried off from beneath our tyres in the talons of a hawk, which missed annihilation by inches. After perhaps two hours of shattering the savage peace of this wilderness with our heraldic approach, we dropped down into a long valley running north-south, and beyond the end of this, their bases laced with an immediate foreground of tree-fern, loomed portentous and pallid the bare mountains of Yunnan. At the valley's end we passed out into the unchallenged sunlight of a plateau, soon reaching a cross-roads with a police post and a knot of harassed, sword-bearing travellers. From this point the Burma Road went on to cross the Chinese frontier, at Wanting, about three miles away. The road to the left went to Mu-Sé, and down this broken, calamitous track we plunged, after a cursory inspection by the Kachin frontier police.

Mu-Sé was a place of importance and animation. We pulled up in a considerable square with a market to which a row of Chinese tea-shops with outside tables had given a faintly Parisian atmosphere of graceful leisure. Banners, which might have flown at the fiat of a dictator, were found to advertise the practices of dentists, and were usually adorned

with enormous sectional diagrams of the jaw, the danger-spots filled in
in savage colour. There was a Shwebo Motor Store with an Indian-
Gothic façade in red brick, complete with castellations. Combined
grocers and tea-shops had their shelves well stocked with such com-
modities as nougat and Wincarnis. At one of these the two Chinese
and I took tea together, while glossy, blue-black crows hopped about
our feet or dived under the chairs to pick up crumbs of cake. Women
with bound feet, and conservatively dressed Chinese in long gowns
and Phrygian caps, passed by. As in Hsenwi a few of the shop-keepers
were combating the tedium between customers by flying kites from
the doors of their establishments. This was done with much expertness
and the use of the best equipment, the string being wound on expen-
sive-looking contraptions like fishing-reels. In one case some kind of
competition seemed to be in progress between an Indian executive of
the Shwebo Motor Store and a dentist, some hundred yards away, at
the other end of the square. Their kites, flown at such a height that
they were no more than white slivers in the sky, were going through
the most complicated evolutions, feinting and thrusting, swooping
and ducking. It seemed a most convenient kind of game that one
could play with opponents in different parts of the town without
neglecting one's business.

Inquiring in the market place, I found that there were no lorries
going to Nam Hkam that day. This did not surprise me. I had
learned no longer to expect a dovetailing in such travelling connec-
tions. Mu-Sé was said to possess a circuit house, but supposing it to be
in some exposed position, outside the town, I decided that I might
as well stay in one of the Chinese places in the square. Returning to the
shop where we had had tea, I managed with some difficulty — since the
Chinese are not a gesticulatory people — to make the waiter understand what I wanted, and was led into a dim, lattice-screened interior,
where, upon a board raised a few inches from the earth, I put down my
bedding. Mu-Sé was a hot town, and outside an ardent breeze had
sprung up, carrying processions of whirling dust-genii through the
streets.

I decided to take a siesta, and had just settled down when a form darkened the doorway, which in this room was the only source of light and air. In obedience to a silent beckoning, I got up and went out. My visitor — who had shrunk somewhat in the light — proved to be an elderly Kachin police officer, with a flat, sensitive face. He was dressed in khaki-drill shorts, a grey woollen pullover, and a forage cap, worn, after the fashion of all Asiatics, on the top of his head. His manner was apologetic and discouraged, as with a slightly sad smile he led me to a jeep and motioned me to get in. The Indian who had so recently been flying a kite outside the Shwebo Motor Store, and who was a mildly interested onlooker, now moved towards me and said, 'He is taking you to the police station, sir.' Owing to the complete absence of everything that might have been described as autocratic in the police officer's attitude, I could not decide whether I was under arrest or not. I got into the jeep and we drove away, turning off the main square into a side street, which emptied its dust and ruts after a hundred yards into what looked like a neglected playing field. At the end of this was a long low bamboo construction, raised on piles. This I judged to be the police barracks, as uniformed Kachins were lounging about, or sitting on the steps leading up to the several entrances of the long house. The distant prospect was splendid. Behind the barracks the ground rose gently, scored with paths like intersecting lines drawn idly with a compass. Gradually the groves of trees, the bamboo thickets closed in, till summits of the low hills were covered with frothing vegetation. Somewhere beyond came the dividing line, the true frontier, where the forests of Burma shrivelled and expired on the slopes of the mountains of Yunnan. With this rampart of pyramids the horizon was closed; golden and glowing slag-heaps, other-worldly in the purity of their utter desolation.

Policemen took my luggage out of the jeep, and carried it up to the lieutenant's room. My bedding roll was laid out on the bamboo floor next to the lieutenant's. Between them was a soap-box, on which the lieutenant's washing-kit was exposed in military style. A tommy-gun leaned against the box. A tinted photograph on the wall showed my host, or gaoler, dressed as a Buddhist novice. While I was examining it I felt a light tap on the arm and turned to find myself now also provided with a soap-box, on which stood a bowl of hot water, a neatly folded towel and a tablet of some much-advertised brand of soap. The lieutenant smiled as if at the memory of secret pain, and went out. I washed, got out a camera, and followed him, noticing as soon as I had reached the bottom of the steps, that a policeman had appeared behind me, carrying a chair. When I stopped, he stopped, and put the chair down. As soon as I moved on, he picked the chair up and followed me. It seemed to me that I had better fall in with the inference and sit down. I did so, and in a few minutes the lieutenant came up and squatted beside me. He put a tumbler in my hand. It was a brand new one, just unpacked, and was lightly coated with straw-dust. The manufacturer's label was in position, bright and unsoiled. Raising his pullover, the lieutenant groped underneath, found the breast-pocket of his shirt and brought out a pinch of dried herbs, which he dropped into the tumbler. A waiting policeman now approached with a kettle, and filled up the tumbler with hot water. At the bottom, the herbs stirred with sudden impulse, and blossoms uncurled like moths newly released from their chrysalises. Petals un-folded and straightened, stamens thrust forth, until the bottom of the glass was gay with daisies. While the lieutenant looked on eagerly I sipped, for the first time in my life, an infusion of camomile.

I was still unable to make up my mind whether this was protective custody, or no more than strangely spontaneous hospitality on the police's part. After a few moments, therefore, I decided to define the position if possible. Gesturing vaguely in the direction of a neigh-bouring belt of trees, and incidentally, of China, and at the same time smiling inoffensively, I tried to convey the idea that I proposed to go for a walk. This produced no obvious symptoms of disapproval, so I got up, smiled again and strolled away in a casual manner. Having taken an aimless and wavering course for a couple of hundred yards, I bent down to pick something up, at the same time glancing behind. The lieutenant was no longer to be seen, and as no one was following me, I quickened my pace. On the edge of the level, open space was a cemetery with perhaps a couple of hundred mounds. The recent ones were covered with elaborate miniature palaces made of white paper, stretched over a framework of cane. A few of these were intact, minor works of art; and there were others in all stages of disintegration until, on the old mounds, only a few sticks lay strewn about. Beyond the graveyard, the houses were reached again. A street of bamboo-shacks led almost to the edge of a chasm. Standing on the edge of this I found myself looking across a valley. From where I stood, steep banks dropped away to the bed of a wide river, riven by numerous islands and sand-banks. This was the Shweli River, and the opposite bank was China. Peasants with their buffaloes were cultivating strips of land left by the recession of the waters, both in Burma and in China and on the islands that lay between and came under who knows what jurisdiction. From across the river came the sound of cocks crowing, and most strangely, what sounded like the ringing of church bells.

That evening a lorry went to Nam Hkam, but, for the first time, I learned that even in the Orient a vehicle can be crammed to a degree when not a single passenger more can be taken. Bales had been piled high into the air, so that, in order to reach their perches, the passengers had to scale sheer precipices of merchandise. And either the weight had been unevenly distributed or a spring had given way, because the load tilted most dangerously. Here it was that I began to long once more for a smattering of Chinese, that valuable lingua-franca of all who travel or have affairs in the backwoods of the Far East. It was laborious and a little ridiculous having to keep up this patrol round Mu-Sé bleating hopefully, 'Car (now a Burmese word) Nam Hkam?' Finally an Indian appeared with a polite 'What is your destination, sir?' And from him I learned that there was no hope of getting to Nam Hkam until the next day.

There was a permanent market place in Mu-Sé where a nucleus of traders sold such essentials as liver-salts and vaseline, and a tooth-drawer publicly removed teeth with astonishing speed and address. The market was served by a Chinese restaurant, a grim, open-sided booth with a kitchen in its centre, where the sinister routine of a low-class Chinese eating house was practised without attempt at conceal-ment from the patrons. Here I resolved to tackle the language problem — at least so far as eating went — and persuaded the proprietor, who was grubby as usual in vest and slacks but anxious to help, to accompany me on a tour of his pots. From him I acquired the basic smattering to deal with gastronomic emergencies, and this carried me through Burma. The only adjective that really mattered was *chow* — fried; from which, of course, the American army slang for food was derived. By keeping to fried dishes, I could reasonably hope most of the bacilli had been destroyed. *Mien*, which is usually associated with *chow* in the Chinese restaurants of the West, meant noodles, although here it was pronounced 'myen'. Chicken was *chi*; eggs, *dan*; rice, *fan*; pork, *youk*. If you wanted the pork chopped up and mixed with vegetables as well as fried, all you had to do was to precede *chow* with the onomatopoeic and memorable adjective *tok-tok*. Strangely enough, this system worked, in spite of my repudiation of the notorious tones which are supposed to be so baffling to the Westerner, in Chinese. No restaurant owner ever failed to understand my order or even had to have it repeated, and one even went through the complimentary farce of asking me in what part of China I had picked up my knowledge of the language. The word for salt, *yem ba* was very important. This always seemed to be a rare commodity, only produced grudgingly, on special request. Warm Mandalay Pale Ale was sometimes forthcoming at the average price of a bottle of medium quality wine, by uttering the magic words *ku dziu*. Tea, *sha*, was always silently placed on the table as soon as you sat down.

At this restaurant I was hardly surprised to find the police lieutenant sitting, with eyes modestly lowered, at one of the tables. I went over and joined him and tried to buy him a meal. After a great deal of explanation in which the restaurant owner and several customers joined, I was finally made to understand that my host, or keeper — whichever the case might have been — was a strict Buddhist and was observing some kind of penance, or sabbath as it is known locally, involving a semi-fast and some meditation. He could therefore only be prevailed upon to accept a little plain rice.

While we lingered over tea the day was declining. Children came down from the crest of a bare hill, from which a diminishing cone of light had finally disappeared, dragging at their kites which shone like minute fish against the blue depths of the Yunnanese mountains. The tooth-extractor packed up, unhitching the strings of his trophies from the frame on which they were exposed, and lowering them string by string, as tenderly as if they had been matched pearls, into a bag. The last bullock-cart was driven away, producing with its greaseless axle a plain tune consisting of four notes of the pentatonic scale repeated *ad infinitum*. Suddenly the square of Mu-Sé had lost a dimension, the wooden shop façades, splashed with their vigorous Chinese characters had become a backcloth, dramatic and even menacing, before which a band of posturing actors with pikes and lances might soon present themselves in the nocturnal scene of such a play as 'Stealing the Emperor's Horse'. As the twilight deepened, the restaurant owner went softly from table to table, placing on each a tiny oil-lamp. Over the kitchen he hung a lantern providing a sympathetic illumination for the tapestry of viscera. From various directions came a soft, tentative strumming as if plucked from single-stringed instruments hung in space. Three or four distant voices were raised quaveringly, as if to exorcise this Asiatic mood, in the chanting of a revivalist hymn, a tune to which the words usually sung are, 'Jesus wants me for an angel'. Occasionally, when these sounds subsided, a bugle could be heard, very faintly, being blown in China.

We went back to the police barracks and turned in. The lieutenant dimmed the lamp till there was just enough light for him to be able to pick up his tommy-gun without groping for it, and lay muttering his prayers. Beyond the window ebbed and flowed all the sweet, sleep-inducing, night sounds. The monotonous grumbling gossip of the Kachin policemen was woven through with a silver thread of mono-chordic music. This was blown away by the rush of wind through the bamboo thickets, and into the following silence fell a dribble of nightin-gale notes. The Kachins took up their topic again, and now the sub-dued rattle of monosyllables was coagulating and shaping itself in the rising tide of drowsiness into odd English phrases. As I fell asleep, someone said quite clearly, 'a shortage of timber'.

The chief was up when I awoke soon after dawn, but shortly

appeared with a pot of tea. Both of us were wearing, like the insignia of some exclusive club, those popular oriental towels which bear the words, 'Good morning', and in the language of smiles and signs we passed with each other the time of day.

Afterwards I took a brisk stroll over to the border, noticing, as I had done on the previous day, that within a few minutes a Chinese appeared, wearing semi-transparent white pyjamas, and pedalling very rapidly on a gaily decorated but much under-geared cycle. Separated by some twenty-five yards, the Chinese and I stood, two solitary and insignificant figures poised over the grandiose setting of this natural frontier, while beneath us the peasants of Burma and of China were to be seen leading out the buffaloes to their morning tasks in the fields. When I turned away and made for the village through the lanes of cactus, whose leaves were covered in elegant Burmese script with what I supposed to be amorous inscriptions, the Chinese was still there, but soon he overtook me, legs whirling and garments streaming. By the market place I was met by the Indian of the previous day. 'What are you interested in, sir?' he asked. 'Rubies and jade', I told him. 'But there are no rubies or jade at Nam Hkam.' The tone contained a mild reproof. He was clearly hurt at an unflatteringly clumsy attempt at deception. He had a fine sensitive face, with that brooding nobility of expression one often finds in Indians, even when in mediocre occupations. As he always appeared, to put some new, straightforward question whenever I visited the market, I supposed that he was the informer assigned to this area, just as the flying Chinaman was probably in charge of the frontier proper.

He must have found my explanation unsatisfactory because after our third encounter a new kind of policeman arrived and signalled me to follow him. I soon found myself in some kind of military headquarters where a Burmese officer, handsome and dapper in his well-pressed British uniform, grilled me with extraordinary suavity, while butterflies fluttered in and out of the open door and a blind beggar collected alms from the guard. It seemed that I had fallen into the hands of some kind of frontier force. The Burmese officer's smile became glazed when, in answer to his probings, I told him that I had spent the previous night in the barracks of the Kachin police. My lieutenant was fetched to testify, a rustic and self-effacing figure in these polished military surroundings. A little reluctantly, but with charming resignation, the Burmese officer declared himself satisfied. I could go on to Nam Hkam. A pass and an accompanying letter to the Amat were typed out, to be added to my now bulky collection of official documents. Meanwhile, said the officer, there was no point at all in wandering about the streets of an unattractive place like Mu-Sé. I could wait comfortably in his office until transport was found. Glasses of lemonade were brought in, and then the officer excused himself and went off in a jeep. When I sauntered to the door I found a soldier with a fixed bayonet there. He gulped nervously when I eyed him.

An hour or two later, the transport for Nam Hkam drew up outside. It was a Fordson, externally battered but intact, and scientifically packed with ageing Kachin ladies, who, I later learned, had organized a kind of Mothers' Association outing to the bazaar of Nam Hkam, which was to be held on the next day. They were all dressed, with the sobriety of their years and station, in navy blue, and wore tall, cylindrical turbans in which their hair had been severely constrained. As usual, I was allocated a dignified position in the front. I found myself pinned firmly against the door-handle by the two dowagers wedged in between me and the driver. Unhappily the engine in this particular vehicle is set back and occupies much of the space in the driver's cabin, from which it is only isolated by a housing of metal plates. Owing to the external temperature, plus the terrible roads and the decayed state of the engine, this housing soon became blisteringly hot, so that both my neighbour and myself squirmed and struggled endlessly in our efforts to avoid contact with it. The nudging and kneeing provoked by these conditions probably struck my companion, who was about fifty years of age, as improper, because at the first opportunity she changed places, providing a substitute of not less than eighty.

The journey to Nam Hkam, then, although a matter of only nineteen miles, took several hours, and was endured in the most excruciating discomfort. After the first hour numbness spread from the feet to the waist. Only then could I begin to enjoy the scenery through which we were travelling. A mile or two away to our left across a cultivated plain were low ranges of densely forested mountains, while to the right the land slipped away, down to the Shweli river, an unimportant tributary of the Irrawaddy, which here, mysteriously, for no more than thirty miles, swelled into a shallow, much-divided flood, as wide as the Salween. Terraced paddy-fields came down the mountain sides like the ceremonial stairways of a race of giants, lapping the plains in mighty, rippling waves. Hundreds of buffaloes slogged through the mud and stagnant water, and egrets crawled about them. The villages were screened behind the matting of roots hanging down, almost to the ground, from huge, old banyans. Wells had stone covers like miniature pagodas — sometimes with horses carved on them. The pagodas themselves were on the Chinese joss-house model, with up-swept eaves, often involving much ingenious joining of corrugated-iron, which had been artfully hammered and bent into the traditional shape of wooden logs. Tombs continued to carry their ephemeral palaces of paper. Sometimes we passed a tumulus. Under such mounds the Kachins buried the victims, man, woman and child, of the unlimited warfare they practised whenever compelled by dearth to migrate in force. There were a few isolated houses which advertised the wealth of their owners by the addition to a plain bamboo construc-tion of a carved balcony or some fretwork embellishment of the eaves. Over the Shweli hung a golden mist, composed of particles of sand swept up from the uncovered bed of the river and held in suspension by the wind sweeping down the valley. Just outside Nam Hkam three Chinese Nationalist soldiers in blue cotton uniforms appeared at the roadside. I recognized them from the others I had seen in custody. They seemed to be unarmed, and were probably on their way to Nam Hkam to give themselves up.

CHAPTER XIV

NAM HKAM BAZAAR

NAM HKAM in the white, dusty haze of the afternoon, was a less concentrated Mu-Sé, a sprawling collection of bamboo huts. The driver pulled out of the main street with its emptiness and aching light, and found the Amat's compound. There he put me down, shook hands and departed, refusing to accept a fare. Almost collapsing as my legs touched the ground, I waited a moment for circulation and strength to return before picking up the iron bar provided and striking the gong suspended by the gateway. Apart from the medieval grandiosity of this gesture there was nothing impressive about the circumstances of my arrival. The compound consisted of three sides of a square of mean huts, surrounded by a broken fence of the kind which sometimes encloses a suburban allotment. A wrecked two-pounder gun, with wheels askew, stood in the centre of this space. It was attended continually by a guard armed with a rifle. I was led in to the presence of a man with a mild, empty Kachin face, whom I felt instinctively to be a clerk. And a clerk he was. The Amat was away but, said the clerk, I could stay in his haw.

The haw proved to be the biggest of the huts. It was raised on piles, about five feet from the ground. I was installed in one of the two large bare rooms, which, when I arrived, was occupied by a circle of soldiers playing cards, and some children who were annoying them. The soldiers left, one by one, although the children returned later to watch me as I washed. Shortly afterwards four soldiers staggered in with a massive mahogany table and two chairs. When the table was put down, the bamboo floor sagged beneath it. The soldiers went away, and the clerk appeared in the doorway. He was carrying a bottle of shoum, or country spirit, as it is politely called by the Kachin bourgeoisie. This was not the ordinary market stuff, he assured me, but a bottle from the Amat's reserve, of special potency and flavour. He was right. A judicious sip roughened the lip membranes before passing in a scorching trickle down the throat. It tasted like vodka. Before withdrawing, the clerk asked me at what time he should arrange breakfast for the morning, adding that there would be various curries to order. I asked what was the usual time, and he said about eight o'clock. In Mu-Sé it had been eleven-thirty. It seemed that in the nineteen miles I had run into a new breakfast-time zone.

There was no way of closing the door except by tying it, which would have been churlish. It sagged perpetually eighteen inches open, a circumstance which gave endless pleasure to the clerk's children who lived in a kind of dependent hut, just across the bamboo landing outside. In this causeway they settled down, a sober, well-behaved group, to learn what they could of my way of life, absenting themselves only for an occasional bowl of rice. In the late afternoon a Kachin soldier arrived. He seemed to have been attached to me for some unknown duty, as he unstrapped a long, heavy-bladed dah, and propped it with an air of finality in a corner, before laying out his kit beneath it. To find out whether this incident involved supervision or control, I went out and ploughed through the dust down to the dismal main street, where, having discovered a Chinese eating-house, I employed my recently acquired knowledge to order a meal. I was waited on by the owner's Burmese wife, who carried a baby in a shawl upon her back. A dog lay curled in a shallow depression scraped in the earth under each table, and a huddle of Thibetans, wrapped in their togas, slept in a corner. Later, as a mild yellowness seeped into the waning sunlight they awoke and tried gently to arouse the interest of the customers in their dried lizards and coloured stones. All the Thibetans, here, as elsewhere in Burma, carried these treasures in British army haversacks. The senior member of the party, who wore a purple beret-shaped hat of plaited and lacquered osier, was the possessor of a jar of black unguent which caused some excitement. This I gathered was an extract of the organs of several rare animals. The restaurant owner licked it with connoisseurship, and made an offer, which was smilingly rejected. Someone bought a piece of glass which looked like a ruby for eight annas, one of which the vendor immediately gave to a beggar who was sipping a cup of free tea. The wares were then re-wrapped in their grimy rags and put back in the haversacks; after which the Thibetans settled down to sleep again.

Meanwhile the streets were astir in the cool of the evening and the eating-house was filling up. Customers lined up before the meat show-case where one of the proprietor's virgin daughters, acting as saleslady, was producing delicacies which passed from hand to hand, to be dangled and pinched, before being returned to their hooks. When a sale took place the sliver or collop was passed to another daughter whose headdress proclaimed her knowledge of the world, and, work-ing with a pair of scissors, she snipped the purchase into fragments manageable with chopsticks. These she arranged in neat piles to await free space in one of her father's frying pans. All this activity was abnormal and was due to the influx of visitors and merchants to the celebrated bazaar to be held next day. My arrival at Nam Hkam at just this moment was the only lucky piece of timing in all my travels in Burma. I had been warmly recommended in Rangoon to see the Nam Hkam bazaar, if at all possible; it was said to be one of the most important and colourful in the Far East, serving Western Yunnan as well as the Northern Shan States. Since it would be in full swing less than an hour after dawn, and I was tired, I went back to the haw as soon as it was dark. I found my bodyguard sitting at the table, looking into space; but when I got out the country spirit he soon cheered up.

I was up and about by seven, trying to prepare myself by a vigorous walk for the threatened ordeal of the breakfast table. Irregular, sporadic feeding and strange provender were beginning to take their toll, and I felt queasy at the thought of the 'various curries' the Amat's clerk had promised for the first meal of the day. At this hour Nam Hkam benefited from a background of mountains, cloaked in a mist which separated hill from hill and range from range. On these grew towering clumps of bamboo, pale, feathery eruptions in a landscape of smoking precipices and ravines. Below this ethereal panorama the town's profile seemed stunted and broken: this is a normal feature of provincial cities of the Far East and due to an ancient Mongolian prejudice — a racial memory perhaps of the nomadic tent — against the erection of buildings of more than one floor. Sumptuary laws, too, have operated against imposing architecture, except for religious ends. It was perhaps to be expected of the relatively democratic Mongolian order of society — democratic in that its rewards have always been attained in the main by merit and effort, rather than birth — that office and status when acquired should have been hedged about with so rigid a protocol. The position which a man had won was advertised by all the adjuncts of his existence, by the size and materials of his betel-box and spittoon, by his clothes, his animals, his house. It was all laid down. There was no question of living beyond one's means to impress the neighbours. If you had no official position you lived in a single-roomed shack with a palm-thatch. When you became a headman you were allowed something more solid, with teak pillars supporting a log roof. Myozas, or governors, were privileged to shelter beneath a roof of two storeys. Only the Sawbwa could aspire to the glory of a spire, to go with his gold umbrella, his velvet sandals and his peacock. Nam Hkam, then, was flat and straggling, with a few liquor and opium stores, tailors' establishments and inns, but very few shops to face the annihilating competition of the bazaar. There were a few small, uninteresting pagodas, one of which seemed to have been struck by a bomb. A heap of broken masonry in the courtyard contained several hundred Buddhas, some unusually well-carved and coloured, but although they seemed to have been abandoned there, I doubted the propriety of taking one away. By the wall a buffalo lay abandoned to die. Several sprightly crows were already pecking at the soft, accessible parts of the body; the anus, the nostrils and the lips. Occasionally a lid slid slowly back, disclosing a terrified eye, the head rolled sadly from side to side, and the crows hopped back. To have attempted to put the animal out of its misery in this consecrated spot, would have caused grave scandal, if not a riot.

Breakfast was all I had feared. It was preceded by a stiff aperitive of country spirit; then followed an inexorable succession of dishes, vegetable soup, red rice with spring onions, the promised curries, pickled vegetables, tea, poured from a great pot with a chain as handle — two cups at a time for each person. With forthright Kachin hospitality the Amat's clerk ladled out my portions, perplexed and disappointed at the size of my appetite. Feeling that only a twenty-four hours' fast could help, I staggered down the steps of the haw and made for the market. I could not have hoped for a more brilliant spectacle.

Beyond ranks of innumerable pack-animals, bullocks and ponies, tethered with the regimented discipline which characterizes the parking of cars at a sporting event in the West, the scene might have been taken from a lavish stage production of 'Prince Igor'. The first English administrator to reach Nam Hkam reported in 1889 that about six thousand people visited this market every five days, and this number had certainly not decreased. From Burma, I could identify various Shans, in their enormous hats; Kachins with their strings of coins and skirts woven in the colours and zigzag motifs of the Indians of Central America; Palaungs, and occasional Lishaws, who looked like untidy Cossacks in their belted tunics and shapeless trousers. But there were visitors from Yunnan who escaped identification; strapping maidens in voluminous white turbans; spirited groups which scattered and dispersed at the sight of a camera, flouncing away with flashing back-cast glances, and a swirl of long skirts, pigtails and sashes.

The Palaungs of Nam Hkam were particularly elegant in dashingly cut ankle-length coats of cotton-velvet panelled with light and dark blue and with purple inserts at the elbow. They wore made-up cylindrical turbans of dark blue material, from the back of which tumbled, in medieval European style, a veil or panel, reaching half way down the back. Jewellery was plain: a double or triple collar of silver beads. One patrician figure, who out-topped her neighbours' average of four-feet-nine by at least three inches, wore a turban that had developed into a kind of busby, its upper edge decorated with a looped chain of beads to match her necklace. Beside this majestic ensemble most European folk-costumes would have looked trivial and doll-like. It appears from the reports of the first administrators that such finery was previously restricted to the use of certain clans: it has now spread as one beneficial result, at least, of the degeneration of tribal organization. One can imagine the horror of the ladies of the senior clan, the Patorus – there was only a handful of them – when the whole of the female section of the Palaung nation took to wearing their exclusive model.

It is said that the Palaungs are the most peace-loving of the Burmese minorities. Peoples become in the first instance 'warrior peoples' by using up or outgrowing the resources of their habitat. As soon as the economic origin of their bellicosity is forgotten, it tends to be regarded as inherent martial virtue, to be secretly respected whether one approves of it or not. The Palaungs are an example of a people who through efficient adaptation to an environment do not need a regular fresh supply of *lebensraum*. They live in harmony with each other; crimes of violence are rare, and murder unknown. Clearly, they make bad soldiers and they were much despised as recruiting material in the British colonial army, whereas the turbulent and aggressive Kachins were the darlings of their British commanders and 'proved themselves magnificently' against the Turks in the 1914-18 war.

The Palaungs are terribly afflicted by goitre. I estimated that twenty-five per cent of the older women I saw were sufferers. Sometimes the head was no more than a promontory upon a mass of shapeless flesh, reaching as far as the breasts. One poor woman I saw had to go about supporting her goitre with her hands.

Like so many hill-peoples the Palaungs have a dislike of the plains which is strongly tinged with superstitious aversion, an attitude found in reverse among the plainsmen of the Far East, whose awe of heights causes them to locate their most sacred places on mountain tops.

The bazaar of Nam Hkam, where the first British administrator noticed that much Manchester cloth and haberdashery was sold, had not lost its enthusiasm for all the West had to offer. Local products included crudely carved and vilely coloured Burmese toys, bearing only a token resemblance to the owls and alligators they were supposed to represent, coarse pottery, exquisite Chinese crockery, stiff Mandalay silk used in the making of longyis, and artificial flowers. Indian influence showed itself in plastic models of the Taj Mahal. But two-thirds of the market space was allotted to the West — toothpastes, patent medicines, beauty products, cigarettes — even the well-known beverage claimed to possess extraordinary soporific qualities. There were tins of condensed milk too, valued as much for the container as the contents, empty tins having become a recognized Burmese measure. Thus two *let-kut* (the quantity which may be heaped upon the surface of two hands joined together) equals one condensed-milk tin — originally a *Kônsa*, or the amount of rice required by one person for a meal.

A demand had been produced for all these products by advertising in the Rangoon press; and the Rangoon agents would ship a proportion of what they received out to such markets as Nam Hkam, assuming that whatever the nature of the goods, their place of origin would sell them. Sometimes it was clear that the purpose of the product was not understood. A cheroot-seller, for instance, would on request, smear a little Vick Vapour-rub on the mouthpiece of a cheroot, before handing it to his customer.

There is no doubt that the East — such of it as remains open to occidental enterprise — is a certain and inexhaustible market for all that can be sent there. When one sees what Orientals can be induced to buy it is hard to believe that the East India Company had trouble in disposing of its broadcloths. Above all, the exporter cannot go wrong with patent medicines, to which people who have been brought up in an atmosphere of horoscopes and alchemy, surrender themselves naturally. All that is necessary is to find some way, by loans to be used in establishing industries or by the gift of agricultural machinery, of increasing purchasing power. The consumption of branded laxatives, stomach powders and cough cures would then be colossal. At the present time a Palaung has to put in a week's labour in his opium field before he can buy a packet of aspirins, or a fortnight before a tube of halitosis-averting toothpaste comes within his reach. If only science could find some way of increasing his production he might eventually become a consumer of shirts with non-shrinkable collars, ball-point pens, and electric shavers.

In the meantime the hill peoples will go on doing what they can to combat by the traditional methods the ninety-six diseases recognized by orthodox Burmans. These methods are most comprehensive, and include dosing with the remedies — most of them fearsome — contained in a vast *materia medica*, with arsenic, soot and excrement, and with the scrapings of meteoric stones. They include treatment by the exhibition of pictures of peacocks and hares, by semi-strangling, by probing with gold and silver needles, by beating with rods incised with cabalistic figures, by burning and scalding, by inhalation of perfumes and fetid stenches, by the playing of music, martial, strident or sympathetic, by the laying on of hands, the muttering of spells and prayer. Some of these methods have received belated praise from Western doctors, particularly that of acupuncture, which, dignified by a medico-scientific jargon, has something of a current vogue in France.

The contribution of the Shans to the science of healing is therapeutic shampooing. This is a form of massage, applied chiefly to the head, and here in Nam Hkam, between the tooth-pullers, a specialist was at work upon his victim, who writhed and groaned slightly under the manipulations of the iron fingers, while other patients, stripped to the waist, squatted in uneasy silence awaiting their turn. Shampooing, like all the other treatments, if given with proper regard to the patient's horoscope, is regarded as a panacea, except in the case of venereal ailments, which are thought to be of supernatural origin and produced by the nocturnal bites of nats. It is all very funny, in a way, and yet many Europeans living in these remote parts of the world go secretly for treatment to such practitioners, excusing themselves, if discovered, by saying that at least it can do no harm. When we remember the renowned and highly gifted English authoress who in recent years tried to arrest her fatal malady by inhaling the breath of cows, we realize that in medical matters, the more extravagant the treatment, the greater its appeal, even to the most intelligent of us.

Like all fairs, the bazaar of Nam Hkam had something special to offer in the way of holiday diet. This consisted of thin, buckled cakes, like large *chapaties*. Something similar in composition was produced in fancy shapes by squeezing maize-flour paste through machines into vats of boiling oil. Cooks were producing by a kind of legerdemain vast, swelling, edible creations, which developed on immersion in the boiling fat from the most insignificant beginnings of paste. Plunging a few thin white strings into the liquid they would slowly withdraw portentous, inflated shapes, which finally resembled the bare ribs of a mighty ox-carcass. The Palaungs, having sold their country spirit and their opium, bought great quantities of those unsubstantial fairings, departing to their eyries with panniers stuffed and ponies piled with fragile mountains of the Shan version of potato-crisps.

For the Shans themselves there were more solid refreshments in store. The killing of cows, which is illegal in Burma, and only carried on as a scandalous, black-market activity, is tolerated in the Shan States, where the brand of Buddhism is less strict, and does not prescribe a largely vegetarian diet. In a discreet corner of the market a buffalo was tethered by a rope round the horns, carried over a beam. A muscular and elaborately tattooed Shan, drawing his dah, advanced and struck the outstretched neck a practised blow that was more an accolade than a mortal wound. Going closer, he examined the gash laid open by the straining muscles; repeating the blow, almost as an afterthought. At this, the buffalo, which had remained passive, seemingly unconcerned, began to lash out with its hooves and a mighty flexing of the hindquarters, and then to slither, legs momentarily spread-eagled, assisting by its strainings the outgushing of its life. Finally it sank down, its rear legs sliding beneath it, and then gathering its strength and kicking out furiously, it half rose, before slipping back again. The butcher waited with patience, a long cheroot held in his teeth. Presently he produced and tried the edge of the short knife with which in a few minutes he would open up the belly, hack off the hooves, and skilfully release the tension of the hide at certain points, before stripping it off like an overcoat. Meanwhile the buffalo fought silently with huge muscles, against the lethargy that was dragging it down.

Picnicking Shan families began to gather, laughing happily. In the background, fires had been built, and braziers were already heating. Not a Burman was to be seen.

Thus the bazaar continued through the daylight hours, a good-natured and convivial assembly of half a dozen races, some of whose members could only speak with each other through the common medium of a few words of Shan. Such gatherings, every fifth day, are the mountain people's genial equivalent of the Sabbath, and even when feuds or warfare are in progress, the bazaars are recognized as neutral territory. There are no loud-mouthed disputes, scoldings or imprecations. The buying and selling, eating and drinking are all carried on with true oriental gentleness and forbearance. In the afternoon, when most of the serious business was over, the bottles of country spirit came out, and the shy, elusive beauties of the morning were to be seen taking unconcealed nips from their flasks — without, however, noticeable effect. Happy, slightly tipsy groups went wandering through the streets, while the mountains sank back into the haze, and a blue twilight settled on the town. The yellows and the greens drained out of the curving roofs so that it was no longer possible to distinguish the skilful metal counterfeit from the authentic original. A twinkling centipede twisted up the nearest hill-side — a Palaung family, with their lanterns, going home in Indian file. The traders who were staying the night retired into the opium and liquor stores, and light burst in a thousand spearpoints through the wide chinks of the bamboo constructions. The drivers of fifty worn-out three-ton lorries climbed up into their cabins, and went to sleep. And now the Kachin garrison issued from its barracks to guard the sleeping town.

A Kachin patrol was a cheerful affair, more social than warlike. Fires were lit in the streets in various parts of the town, then the main body of men split into small groups, who visited each fire in turn. Each group carried with it an elaborately carved rectangular frame in which were suspended five gongs of different sizes, all beaten simultaneously by clappers attached to a single bar operated by a lever. As soon as the party reached a fire the frame was set down, and one of the soldiers began to work the lever at an even, rapid tempo, producing a sweet, high-pitched and penetrating sound. When the beating of the gongs ceased, a member of the group would step out from the circle formed, sing a single verse and, taking two swords, while the gongs began again, break into a vigorous, posturing dance. This performance was repeated by each soldier in turn. One of them was old enough to have served under British officers, and remembered a few words of English. I asked him what the songs were about, imagining that they dealt with warlike exploits, but he said that they were 'funny stories about ladies'.

CHAPTER XV

CIRCUIT HOUSE, BHAMÓ

THE Amat's clerk said that he had reserved a place in a jeep bound for Bhamó at seven in the morning, so that when seven-thirty came and the jeep had not arrived, I became a little nervous. One after another, the merchants' lorries went thundering out of town, until only one was left, which was jacked-up to await the repair of a tyre. It seemed ungracious not to wait for the jeep, when an arrangement had been made, and yet if I allowed the last lorry to go and the jeep failed to appear, it would mean a five days' wait in Nam Hkam, until the next bazaar. Just as the wheel was being put back and I was about to begin negotiations with the driver, I heard the sound of a familiar burping acceleration, and the jeep arrived. The usual maximum of passengers was wedged in among the luggage and petrol cans, from which sprouted like exotic plants in a rock-garden an awkward bundle of umbrellas, as large as those to be found in continental cafés. In spite of my protests a polite re-arrangement took place for my benefit, so that I found myself seated in front, in relative comfort, with the one leg which could not be contained within the car supported on the front wing. We then set off through the fresh morning forest, alive with the movement of lizards and small birds, and strongly perfumed as if by unseen lilies. What was the origin of this fragrance, which in the imagination streamed from white, immaculate blossoms? In my jungle experiences I have never encountered flowers of the often repellent splendour described by tropical botanists, and here in the Shan uplands the flora, which was sparse and even trivial, bore a disappointing resemblance to that of Europe. In this area flowers a gigantic wild rose, and a species of honeysuckle, with corolla seven inches long, which is by far the largest known. But in these forest-clearings I saw nothing but a few shrinking primroses, violets and anemones; and further on, when we made a short stop and I could explore further, clematis, agrimony, convolvulus and willow-herb, none of which dispensed the mysterious bouquet, which now, as the sun rose higher, was swiftly fading.

At Man Wing my companions stopped to buy country spirit, which was better and cheaper here, they said, than anywhere in the country. This high-grade product was kept in motor-oil cans, while lesser distillations were supplied from ordinary jars. At Man Wing it was bazaar day, intelligently timed to catch traders returning from Nam Hkam. It was a much smaller affair than Nam Hkam had been, and conducted almost exclusively by Kachins, who appeared in a great variety of costumes, woven with the designs by which, in a stylized, dream-like and semi-conscious fashion, tribes sometimes record the few bare facts of their history — a serrated pattern of mountains crossed in their migrations; the yellow of the desert sands. Some of these Kachin motifs were indistinguishable from others I have photographed among the Maya Quiché Indians. I attribute no more to this than that such simple designs occur naturally to all primitive weavers. Their artistic value seemed great to me, and I should say that apart from occasional articles of silver jewellery, woven cloth is the only article of artistic interest produced in the mountains of the Indo-Chinese peninsula. Unfortunately such cloth, or the garments made from it, are not on sale in any of the bazaars, for at present every woman weaves the material for her own clothes. As soon as printed cottons come within her means, she will, as most Siamese girls have already done, renounce with contempt the gorgeous creations of her own hands, which are the result of the communal artistic imagination of her tribe throughout the centuries, delightedly substituting for them graceless, ready-made models. Art is sometimes protected by poverty, and civilization can be the destroyer of taste.

Soon after midday we arrived at Bhamó, which lay stifling and somnolent in the plains by the Irrawaddy. The jeep dropped me at the administrative buildings — a long, divided bamboo hut — and the driver accepted with a show of protest the modest ten rupees which is the recognized price for long distance de luxe travel in Burma.

Here, according to my instructions, I reported to the D.S.P. and the Deputy Commissioner, and was relieved to find that, although I was expected, no comment was made about my arrival from an unexpected direction. With the Commissioner's permission, it was arranged that I should put up at the Circuit House and, finding a decayed gharry, I drove there, at a cost of half that charged for a journey of a hundred miles.

The Circuit House was a forlorn structure in the English half-timbered mood, but of shell-like fragility. No sooner was I inside than in taking a kick at a hornet I put my foot through the wall. This bungalow was presided over by a functionary called the butler, an ancient and dignified survival, living in a kind of monastic seclusion with his memories of the Imperial days and the splendid personalities they had delivered into his charge. Almost before I could look round he produced, with the manner of one displaying an illuminated breviary, a visitors' book in which a number of the great had written their comments and testimonials. The last English one, dating from 1947, by a distinguished lady said, 'A dear old fellow — one of those old-fashioned Burmese servants who are so fast disappearing.' Subsequently there had been a few Burmese contributions, all of which had accorded genteel commendation on English models.

It was about two-thirty when I arrived at the Circuit House, and the butler, on his mettle, and anxious to show that none of the old traditions had been forgotten, said something like 'Ih — a — eh?' He repeated this several times before I realized that he was one of those Burmese who do not believe in the existence of English consonants, which are unemphatic compared with those in the Burmese language. Having discovered that I was being offered tea with eggs, I accepted with pleasure, settling down to the enjoyment of my room, for which, after about two weeks in bamboo huts, I felt quite an affection. By normal Burmese standards, it was choked with furniture. There was an iron bed, a chair and a table, on which stood a mirror and a toilet-roll. Hornets with long trailing stings sailed about the room, and when one came too close, I batted it away, using a book as a tennis-racket. Within ten minutes the tea arrived, formally arranged on a tray, with a bowlful of white sugar, real milk, and the two hard-boiled eggs rolling about and crashing heavily into each other with an appetite-provoking sound. When I thrust a spoon into the sugar, ants boiled out of it. I stirred among the crystals and still the ants came, till it seemed that hundreds had scrambled over the bowl's rim to swarm away to the edge of the table along the spokes of an invisible wheel. I ate and drank with enjoyment and relaxation. When I went to sugar the second cup of tea, the ants were back again. It was clear that they located the sugar by its smell, because wherever I perched the bowl, there would be ants in it within ten minutes. There were plenty of other insects about, particularly medium-sized spiders, that scuttled off in a panic if I moved in their direction and then hid under the table-legs or behind projections of the wall, leaving a hairy leg sticking out.

At about three-thirty, just as I was ready to take a siesta, I got a shock. There was a tap at the door, and the butler was there again, announcing with dignity, what, although shorn of its consonants, was unmistak-ably, 'Breakfast is served.' In came two trayfuls of honest, English food, more eggs — fried this time — fish with chips, bread and butter, jam and tea. Waving away this collation, I went into the cubicle attached to the room, threw jugfuls of water on the cockroaches crawling about the floor, and took a shower. The water splashed on the concrete floor, spread across it like a stain, and began to dry at the edges. Outside, the trees and the earth with its spears of whitened grass were glazed under the sun, and the gilded bell-shape of a pagoda, surmounted with a cap like a Burmese crown, glittered painfully. A barbet, known as the 'coppersmith', invisible adjunct to the Burmese landscape, hooted once every two seconds, and the brainfever bird added its hallucinatory shriek to this ensemble of heat and fatigue.

With the evening came slight relief, and I walked a dusty mile into the town. Turning into a street of shops I looked up and had a vision of a monumental shape, the mighty torso of a man standing at a first-floor window, his arms raised in the arrangement of a complex hair-style. It was the Sikh from Mandalay. I went into his shop, which was an ironmonger's, but which, with a certain elasticity in trading matters, also sold air-mail envelopes. I bought a packet, and his wife, a Burmese lady, gave me a cup of tea. The Sikh told me that he and his friends had finally managed to hire a jeep, and after a complicated and exhausting journey of four days they had reached Bhamó. They had met with no dacoits, although after what he had seen and heard, he had decided to stay quietly in Bhamó until the troubles were over. The Bhamó-Myitkyina areas were the only ones completely free from bandits or insurgent armies. Here, he said, if the heat would only let you, you could relax and be almost as happy as in a civilized country like India. Avoiding the direct and vulgar question why he didn't go back there, I inquired into his reason for remaining in trouble-torn Burma. India was the better place to live in, he said, there was no doubt about that — more civilized, more cosmopolitan. But Burma was the better place to make a living in — if I saw the difference.

The Chinese *restaurateur* of the evening's meal was more complimentary to the country of his adoption. He owned one of the half-dozen lugubrious eating-places along the Irrawaddy shore, and was busy, he said, four days in the week — the days when the two boats from Mandalay arrived, and when they left again. The cavern in which he conducted his business was distinguished from those of his competitors by a yard of fluorescent tubing, whose clammy light was an indication of enterprise in such a place. Although he had never formally learned English, he spoke it with the efficiency demonstrated by his race whenever a project is seriously undertaken. He came from Szechwan, he said, and one of his remote ancestors had been an Imperial cook. He delighted me by referring to his 'unworthy' restaurant and his 'humble' food — traditional self-deprecations which, until then, I had been convinced were to be found only in the speech of the Chinese of Ernest Bramah. His family had emigrated to Burma in his youth. He loved the country, had married a Burmese wife, and nothing would tempt him to return to China. In a few glowing words he summed up the Burmese character. The people were franker and more outspoken than his compatriots. 'If I am hungry in Burma, I will say so, and any man will give me food, without thinking anything about it. In China I must not ask. I must wait to be offered, or people will say, "This is an ill-mannered fellow".' My informant was also shrewd enough to suggest that in China conventions were stricter and hospitality more confined because the Chinese could not afford hospitality on the Burmese scale. In Yunnan if there were five members of a family, they could only live by all five working. In Burma, in a similar family, only one worked, and then, he said, not too hard. And how were things in China? I asked. It was evident that I had found at last a Chiang Kai-shek supporter. They were doing fine, he said, if only they hadn't gone just a little too far in the matter of squeeze. And now the Communists were carrying out a house-cleaning on a big scale. They were very strict, and people who couldn't believe that things had changed, were suffering. In Bhamó alone there were about a thousand refugees, poor people who had been chased out of their country over trifling matters which in the old days would have been beneath the Government's notice.

CHAPTER XVI

THE JADE COUNTRY

A T Bhamó there were other aids to civilization to go with that yard of glimmering fluorescence. I was able, for instance, for thirty rupees a day plus the cost of petrol, to hire a jeep with its driver; and next morning in the dawn and with the frantic whistling and shrilling of birds in our ears, we took the road north, to Myitkyina. It was a great luxury to be travelling at last with the power to stop whenever I wanted to, to linger as long as I liked over the most charming parts of the journey. By the time the heat of the sun could be felt we had reached the Tapeng river. A track from the main road, passing under a bower of orange flamboyants, followed the bank for a way, and up this we went in search of a clear stretch of river in which to swim. Down the narrow valley — most fateful of all the ways of entry into Burma — the water came, frothing among the white boulders, plunging in polished cascades of marbled green into profound pools, where a resistant bubble or a gyrating insect were the only indications of movement and direction.

Over the river hung a cold, sweet smell, carrying with it a sharp association of the shock and the delight of a plunge into opaque depths. Bamboos and tall blond grasses with feathered tops had decayed at their bases and fallen across the rocks, where, roasting in the sun, they gave off a concentrated scent of hay. Here river perfumes poured through and washed aside those of the forest. Small, dun birds — brown dippers — bobbed and flitted from rock to rock; and sometimes pied kingfishers passed, hanging for seconds in motionless contemplation above a pool, before darting away. Down by the water there was nothing flamboyant, mysterious or repellent. It was all familiar and nostalgic. There could have been no better place in Burma than this to study butterflies. They seemed attracted by the damp boulders, on which they alighted in infinite variety, wings spread and gently pulsating. There was no display here of garish colour, no exaggeration, but a rather subdued elegance and sombre good taste, like the *grande tenue* of a nobleman at the Court of Philip the Second.

During the rainy season the level of the water was much higher; now boulders had been left uncovered in which deep basins had been scooped by the action of the water. Some of these contained water, the colour of medium sherry, in which a few small, lethargic fish miraculously survived, a feat which only lost in stature when one remembered that this was the country of climbing perch and of lung fish, which, when their native pools dry up, undertake long overland treks in search of water.

Until 1769 all the area had been Chinese territory, and down this narrow, unimpressive valley the Mongol host had come riding, in 1284, to avenge the slaughter of their envoys by the Burmese king. Somewhere in the plain, within fifty miles of where I stood, at a spot which is now unknown because of the changing of the place-names, the spirits conjured up by the Mongol shamans — favoured perhaps by the reflex bow with its one hundred and sixty pounds pull — shot the Burmese guardian spirits full of arrows, and the Burmese army was annihilated. For full three months, according to the Burmese chronicle, they, the Burmese, slew the enemy and spared not even the feeders of elephants and horses, but when ten myriads were dead, the chief of the Mongols sent twenty myriads, and when the twenty myriads were dead, he sent forty myriads. The conflict seems to have made less impression on the Mongols, and Marco Polo speaks more of a punitive expedition carried out by a frontier force, a march of 'gleemen and jugglers' with a 'captain and a body of men-at-arms to help them' — a notable lack of agreement upon the fable of history.

Five hundred years later and, once again, at the mouth of this valley, the Burmese handsomely vindicated themselves. First of all there had been a dispute over a Chinese merchant who had wanted to build a bridge over the river for his ox-caravans. Just as in the case of the Mongol envoys, the Burmese found that disrespect had been shown, and they flung the merchant into prison. Shortly afterwards another Chinese merchant was killed in a brawl in Burma. In the comparatively primitive Burmese law manslaughter was a trivial offence, compoundable by the payment of compensation. The Chinese, however, had arrived at the eye-for-an-eye stage, and demanded the handing over of the killer, or a substitute, for execution by strangling. To their great credit, the Burmese, although menaced by a nation they knew to be infinitely more powerful than themselves, refused to give the man up — a resoluteness which shows up particularly well against the weak-kneed conduct of the British, in the next century, when, in similar circumstances, a British seaman was surrendered at Canton. However, the Chinese, under the Ch'ing emperor, were in the mood when wars like that of Jenkins' Ear are fought. The refusal by the Burmese to comply with their demands was thought outrageously unreasonable, particularly when, as it was pointed out, execution by strangling was not to be regarded as more than the just settlement of a debt, involving no stigma for the sufferer.

Several Chinese armies poured into Burma, the main force passing once again through this valley. In a war lasting four years they were completely out-generalled and finally defeated, and, by an act of magnanimity without parallel in Far Eastern annals, allowed to march back once more by the cool waters of this riverine Arcadia, to China. This time the disparity in armaments was reversed, because of the artillery which the Burmese had purchased or seized from the Europeans, with which, they shot the Chinese stockades to pieces. By allowing the defeated survivors to return to their country, the Burmese brilliantly avoided what would have become a war *à outrance* with all the resources of the Chinese Empire thrown into it. The Chinese were allowed to save their faces by conveniently forgetting the whole thing, without even a formal treaty of peace being negotiated between the two countries. After a few weeks, trade was silently resumed, and no further reference was made to the affair. No allusion is made in Chinese official histories to the Ch'ing invasion of Burma.

Seen from without, the jungle had more variety, more mystery, more charm, than the forests of the north. In the woodlands between Bhamó and Myitkyina there was none of the monotony to be observed elsewhere in the Indo-Chinese peninsula, where a particular tree had adapted itself so perfectly to its environment that no others could take root there, thus producing the regimented boredom of a plantation. Here there was infinite variety of shapes, of sizes, of colour, of degrees of luminosity, with each tree separated from its neighbours by a subtle variation of aerial perspective. There were some that raised themselves to impose upon the sky a symmetrical, trimly contained silhouette; others that exploded raggedly in anarchic confusion of branches; others which struggled up dripping with epiphytic plants, parasites and creepers, as if emerging weed-laden from the sea. There were trees that looked as if they were composed of moss, which soaked up the light in velvety absorption, and others that scattered the sun's rays in cascades from their metallic leaves. At the road's verge the trunks were screened by ferns, through which, as if in the arrangement of a gigantic bouquet, pale blue and lemon convolvulus flowers were threaded. Sometimes a scarlet carpet of let-pet, the edible blossoms of the cotton tree, had been laid across the road. The total effect was always one of brilliance, and freshness, and even gaiety.

Once, as we rumbled along, a school of gibbons dropped from the overhanging boughs, and avoided us with languid athleticism. We chased a baby wild boar that worked up such a speed that when it finally hurled itself into the jungle it left a noticeable hole in the screen of leaves. Here we saw many jungle fowl. They were almost as tame as the barnyard variety and just as stupid, running in demented zigzags in our path before taking to an easy, floating flight, their tails streaming out behind. Sometimes, in the rare clearings, we saw a most immaculate white harrier, with black wingtips, flapping low over the ferns. The most common bird along this forest road was the bee-eater, both the species which is almost indistinguishable from the European one, and the Burmese green variety, birds with an outright tropical panache. In flight the most streamlined of avian shapes; they were silhouetted like supersonic planes in the long, gliding interval following a few, quick wing-beats, as they swept from the branches after their prey. Green and golden-backed woodpeckers glinted at the mouths of flute-like rows of holes in the stumps of dead trees. Butterflies hovered in dark swarms over the buffaloes' droppings, and we were obliged to stop twice, when the engine boiled, to brush a blanket of them, an inch thick, from the radiator.

The Kachin villages we passed through had geometrical shapes in bamboo erected on posts at their outskirts, perhaps to mark the parish limits for the benefit of the tutelary spirit, whose shrine, or cage, was suspended near by. In one case a typical nat-shrine had been put up over a water-pipe which had been enterprisingly built to collect the water from a spring, and, perhaps, to imprison its presiding demon. The feathers of hoopoes and eagles — usually an arrangement of their tails and wings — were flown from masts. There were spirit-shrines too, built far from the villages in the jungle itself, wigwam-shaped constructions of leaves on a framework of branches, which looked as if they should have contained something, but which proved to be empty.

When we came out into open fields, buffaloes were wandering about, each with half a dozen tick-eating egrets perched on its back, and a retinue of others accompanying it on foot. On one occasion, when we had stopped to clean the butterflies out of the radiator, we happened to witness a buffalo fight. We had noticed, without paying any special attention, two bulls standing facing each other, about a hundred yards away, on the edge of a stream. In the background a few cows were grouped, and the bulls watched each other with the introspective air natural to these deliberate and lumbering creatures. I had looked away and then back again just at the moment when both animals moved towards one another, breaking, to my surprise, into a rapid, shambling run. The hollow crash as they met must have been audible a mile away; and startled by the sound a cloud of egrets, and several previously unseen cranes, launched themselves on the air. The fight developed into a pushing match, the buffaloes straining away, with front legs planted widely apart, and heads lowered until their muzzles almost touched the ground, the thick bosses of bone between the horns in continual, grinding contact. Unless one of the beasts could succeed in cracking the other's skull with the first impact, it seemed a harmless sort of conflict, as the horns were swept back in such a way

that their points could not be brought into use. In the end, after fifteen
minutes had passed, and neither animal had gained an inch, one
suddenly gave way, and allowed itself to be shoved into the river,
thus providing itself with the excuse to break off the battle by swim-
ming away. Having followed it into the water as far as honour demanded, the victor waded back to the unshared responsibility of the
waiting cows.

Myitkyina lay in a scorching plain across the Irrawaddy, to be
reached by ferry, a leisurely, time-wasting service run by the Burmese
Army. The ferry-boat, its shape blotted in the glare, was tied up under
the opposite bank, indifferent to the croakings of our horn, and a
yellow, half-mile wide flood ran between us. We pushed the nose of
the car into the speckled shade of some willows, and plucked the
heads off the yellow daisies that cut off our view of the river. There
was a hot, sweet smell of water that had baked in the sun on the mud-
flats all day.

We had discovered an Indian in a yoga pose by the track leading
down to the ferry, and now he unfolded his legs and joined us. He
was an engineer, working on a bridge-reconstruction job near by. He
had been marooned in the jungle for eighteen months and, after endless days of silence — he never troubled to learn more Burmese than
was necessary to give his instructions — his speech was beginning to
slow down, coming when it did in gushing releases, to be checked
again as if by a troublesome airlock in his throat. With despairing
tenacity he clung to such of the English rites as he could. It was Satur-
day evening, and he was going to Myitkyina, he said, 'to paint the
town red'. It was difficult to imagine this sad, earnest, fevered man,
giving himself, even in homage to tradition, to the debauchery he
hinted at. This strange, distorted echo of things English was renewed
when the ferry, having finally noticed us, dawdled over; a pair of
linked Viking boats, opening behind them a fan of glittering reflections
in the sallow water. 'Bad show to keep you waiting, old man,' said
the Burmese officer, slapping me sharply on the back. 'Why didn't
you blow your horn?'

The town of Myitkyina I saw only by night, as after an early-evening lunch at the Circuit House — a replica of that of Bhamó — I lay quietly awaiting the sunset before venturing out. Myitkyina was the last town of size before the Indian frontier, and there was a corresponding increase in Indian influence. Here there was an active and prosperous business community, and the long, single main street was radiant in the tropical night. Flickering myriads of winged insects filled the neon haze, and a man in flowing white robes went up and down playing on a pipe sweet, wild Pyrenean airs, of the kind you might have expected to hear in the Sierra del Cadi. I sat in a tea-shop and drank plain tea. There was a mosque across the way, a sort of two-dimensional Taj Mahal, the main structure and the flanking towers being cut out of flat metal, suitably painted, and supported on a framework. When viewed from the side, the whole construction vanished, as if subjected to enchantment, leaving only a minaret, like an ornamented oil-derrick. From its summit the muezzin was announcing at this moment, in a voice of exceptional quality, the truths of his religion, to the guitar players sitting in the rows of jeeps parked beneath. The radio in the tea-shop was tuned in to a Chinese station, which was broadcasting a slightly re-arranged oriental version of The Lambeth Walk, a current favourite in Chinese South-East Asia.

Myitkyina was the starting-point for the great and tragic trek of the refugees who fled from Burma through the Hukawng Valley, before the Japanese advance, in the summer of 1942. Why should this mass flight have turned into a disaster, in which it is estimated that 20,000 persons lost their lives? On the map the distance from Myitkyina to Margherita, the first town over the Indian border, does not look great. It cannot be over three hundred miles, and the first hundred of them — to Sumprabum — were covered in many cases in motor vehicles. No hostility was shown to the refugees by the tribesmen inhabiting the thinly populated hills through which they passed. How was it, then, that so few escaped? A few extracts from the diary of my friend Lee, who was caught up in this exodus, may help to explain.

His original party of eight — which was later swollen to twenty —

consisted of his wife, Ma Pyo, a Burmese girl, their eighteen-months-old son, their servants, a junior officer, and his batman. They arrived at Myitkyina on May 4th, 'organized' and hid vehicles on the west bank of the river and spent the next three days ferrying civilians and a few wounded soldiers across, using the ferry-boat which had been deserted by its regular crew. On May 7th the Burmese steersman ran off, Japanese fighters strafed the last of the transport planes on the Myitkyina airfield, and the Japanese ground troops were reported very near the town, coming up the Bhamó road. The last party of refugees was therefore ferried across, and Lee and his people set off in their three cars and reached Sumprabum — where the motor road comes to an end — next day. A great multitude of bewildered refugees were encamped here, trying to find coolies before setting out on foot. No one had any idea of what lay ahead, and a usual estimate of the distance to be covered was ninety miles. Lee notes that thirty-eight schoolgirls from the Baptist school in Moulmein had got thus far. A few months later, in hospital in India, he met one of the two survivors.

At this moment, things did not look too bad — at least, to an old mining prospector. Lee knew that they had a long walk in front of them, but he had no doubt that by keeping good discipline, and by covering reasonable daily stages, they would get to India in two weeks at the most. The chief drawback was Ma Pyo's condition. She was six months pregnant, and Lee was furious when she turned down the offer of a female missionary to take her and their baby son, and to keep them safe with her in the Kachin hills, where the missionary had great influence, and proposed to hide out. With an outburst of wrath which establishes the Old Testament mood of their expedition, he assured her that she would be shot if she held the party up by going sick. 'But,' he says, 'I should have known better than to doubt the stamina of a Burmese girl. They are small and dainty, but mighty tough. At one time or another every man in my party lost heart and gave trouble, so that I had to drive them like animals; but Pyo calmly carried on. She did more than her share.' There are further references in the diary to the superior resistance of the womenfolk. 'We met a huge Sikh woman with her six children, the eldest about ten years and the youngest a few weeks old. She had no one else with her, no food, spare clothing or bedding. She was worried about her milk lasting out for the baby, but was otherwise cheerful, and too proud to ask for assistance. We did what we could, and left her plugging steadily along, carrying two kids, with the other four helping each other.'

So they had started out confidently enough, with Lee, the professional backwoodsman, at their head. But that night the Wet Monsoon broke, and without their knowing it, twenty thousand had been condemned to death. With the first showers, the mosquitoes came out, and it rained without stopping for ten days. Ten days happens to be the incubation period of malaria, and by the end of that time most of the refugees had it. A few who were taken with cerebral accesses died within a few hours. Others lay down in the wet jungle, and shivered and starved. A few, like Lee and his party, kept staggering on through the rain, fever or no fever. Lee, who had it worse than the others, became half-blind. When his head cleared a little he remarked that they were passing the first of the dead bodies, and learned, to his surprise, from the others, that they had passed many dead during the previous two days. It was particularly bad in the outskirts of the villages, where the semi-domesticated pigs hung about to feed on the dead — and on the dying. After that Lee gave up trying to shoot pigs for food, finding that his people would no longer touch their meat.

From this time until they crossed the frontier of India, a month later, they were never out of the sight and smell of death; and at this point the refugees dropped, as if with loathing, their civilized poses and pretences. Civilization provides a whalebone corseting, and when this is unfastened, the individual either turns to jelly or begins to flex unsuspected muscles. From now on Lee found something exaggerated in people's conduct, including his own. They had turned into ham actors in an old-fashioned movie, either heroes or villains. It was a study in black and white, with no half-tones.

The gregarious instinct survived these apocalyptic conditions. 'The godowns were crammed full of refugees; with smallpox, cholera, dysentery and malaria rampant,' but decency was the first casualty, '. . . they would not even leave the camp and go into the jungle to answer the call of nature.' And colour prejudice persisted to the bitter end. 'We found an Anglo-Burmese boy of about thirteen years, calling "Aunty, Aunty". When we asked him what he was doing there all alone, he replied, "My legs will not work, so my Daddy and Mummy have gone on with my sister, who is very white and not dark like me."'

They kept on coming upon camps which the Tea Planters' Association had been operating, but which had been abandoned, and were like water-logged graveyards, with unburied corpses everywhere. Lee, as something of a connoisseur of death on battlefields, was offended by the incorrectness of these civilian postures. They were all undignified. People had died while defecating, or drinking, and had polluted the water supply with the corruption of their bodies. 'The only person I saw who died in a dignified manner was an elderly Mohammedan gentleman. He was a wealthy man, as he had a number of servants with him. When he could travel no further and knew his end was near, he had his servants spread rugs of good quality under a shelter, and then had them stretch him out on them. He crossed his arms and told his people to spread the last rug over him. They did so.'

As for himself, Lee noticed the rapid growth of a protective shell of callousness. To illustrate this, he mentions that on May 24th — the second day of his recovery from malaria — they found a Chinese, unable to walk, but sitting with a happy grin on a pile of rice he had found in a shed. A mile further on they came upon another, lying face downwards, in the last stages of hunger and exhaustion. Lee rolled him over, and sacrificed a little of his precious store of brandy to bring him round. After a while they got him on his feet, cut two walking sticks for him to pull himself along with, and told him how to join his countryman on the rice heap. 'At that time I felt sentimental,' Lee says. 'Had this incident happened three weeks later, I would have passed the man, and left him to die without a second thought.'

On June 8th, after floundering for a fortnight along tracks that were knee-deep in mud in places, they reached the Nam Yung river. It had been converted by the rains into a roaring torrent. Within an hour and a half of their arrival, they saw nine men in succession who tried to cross it torn from the guide rope and drowned. One Gurkha woman, on seeing her husband carried away, gave birth to a premature child. It was born dead, and thrown into the river. That night the guide rope gave way and they were stranded. There were four hundred and fifty demoralized refugees at the crossing and several thousand on the way. Lee found a place up-stream where the river split into two arms, the nearest of which was only sixty feet wide. All they had to do was to drop one of the large trees growing on the bank across it, use it as a bridge, and repeat the manœuvre on the further bank. But of the four hundred and fifty waiting to cross only twenty-two would volunteer to help cut down the tree. They were all so weak that they could only peck at it with their dahs for a few minutes at a time. 'We nibbled at that tree like so many woodpeckers.' In the end it fell in the wrong direction, lengthways along the stream. Then when another day had been spent in felling a second tree, which had dropped into the correct position, it was suddenly noticed that the water was falling, for it had stopped raining in the upper reaches of the river. At this moment a party of Oorias turned up, ex-fishermen from the Puri coast of India. They were all expert swimmers. It was then decided to repair the guide rope, which the Oorias agreed to swim across with, and to re-attempt a crossing of the main stream. Six or seven orderly batches, five at a time, made the crossing, with Lee covering the rope with his pistol from the northern shore. Then the crowd panicked. About thirty at once rushed the rope. It broke under the strain, and they were all swept away. Lee and his party went on without looking back.

Immediately after this came what were for Lee the two worst moments of the whole journey. His old Chinese servant was in a very bad state. He could not keep down any food, and had lost the use of his legs. They were obliged to leave him to die, an action for which he assures me he has never been able to forgive himself. About this time it seemed clear that his baby son also would not survive. He had carried the child on his back for the whole journey, and now it seemed to be in the last stages of dysentery; it was in a state of coma, and constantly oozing blood and pus. As there appeared to be no hope, Lee decided to put him out of his suffering and administered a lethal dose of morphia tablets, 'enough,' he says, 'to kill ten men. To our astonishment he immediately recovered; and later on, when he had dysentery again, I repeated the morphia treatment on a minor scale, again with success.'

And so, at the end of June, they came finally into India. Most of the males in the party collapsed utterly as soon as they reached safety, and several nearly died. Lee's normal weight of one hundred and fifty-five pounds had been reduced to ninety pounds. Ma Pyo was the only one who had not lost weight; but she was covered with sores. About eighteen thousand refugees coming this way had got through before them, but most of these, by starting earlier, had avoided the worst rains. There were very few to follow.

The centre of the Burmese jade industry was at Mogaung, near Myitkyina, and next morning I asked the driver to take me there. But it soon appeared that the direct road marked on my map no longer existed, and as Mogaung could only be reached by an enormous detour, the driver said that he would take me to a small jade mine which was more easily reached. We drove perhaps ten miles out of Myitkyina, walked for half an hour up a valley, and there was the mine, a series of small caverns in the hill-side, only one of which looked as if it might have been excavated in recent times. The driver assured me that these, as well as some pits to be seen in the half-dry bed of the river, were being worked. To a question as to the miners' whereabouts, I received the astonishing reply that they had gone to chapel. Judging perhaps from the tone of my voice that an affirmative answer was expected, he also assured me in answer to a further question that the traditional method of 'fishing' for jade by paddling bare-footed in the stream was still followed here. It is one of the many picturesque fallacies with which the jade industry is beset, that the best pieces are always found, by touch, in this way. Outside the caverns, a few dirty pieces of rock were strewn about. These, the driver said, were jade of inferior quality, and having observed that precious stones are usually without attraction in their unprepared state, I was prepared to believe that this was so.

The history of jade provides an interesting illustration of the creation by a refined and luxurious society of its symbol of wealth. The white nephrite chosen possessed all the qualifications required. It was beautiful and rare; it could be obtained only with immense trouble – the original Jade Mountain was at K'un Lun in South-East Turkestan – and its fashioning into jewellery, owing to its extreme hardness, called for the expenditure of infinite labour and much technical skill. In the original quarries in Turkestan a certain small amount of green jadeite was also found. By virtue of its rarity this green stone became practically priceless. With a kind of dim recognition of the influence of metallic oxides in establishing the jade's colour, many attempts were made to fake this valuable green by such ingenious methods as burying copper in contact with blocks of white nephrite. With the adoption of jade symbols for the State worship of the Heaven, Earth and the 'Four Quarters', jade assumed for the Chinese the prestige associated with gold in the West; and it is safe to say that had one of the Biblical Three Wise Men of the East come from China, jade would have been his gift.

The discovery by a thirteenth-century Chinese prospector, at a moment when the K'un Lun mines had reached exhaustion, of great quantities of jadeite in the Kachin States of Burma, caused a sensation in the Celestial Empire, and Mogaung became the El Dorado of many Chinese expeditions, the members of which mostly perished, after horrible privations of the type suffered by their Spanish counterparts in their search for gold. Finally the trade was established, and it was found that, most happily, although jadeite of pure translucent green existed, it was rare, compared to the colours produced by the action of metallic oxides, other than copper, upon the silicate. There was plenty of green jadeite at Mogaung, but most of it was the wrong green, or it was too opaque, or was variable in colour, and thus succeeded in one way or another in defeating the demands of finicky connoisseurship. The undermining of Chinese values was averted. Otherwise, one suspects, it would have been necessary to combat the threatened devaluation in some way, perhaps by the disappearance, for reasons of State, of all those concerned in the mine's discovery.

As things were, Chinese economy remained unshaken. Some sort of a jade-rush took place. Laden caravans set out for China, and were regularly ambushed and looted by jade-thirsty freebooters, although the majority got through safely, to swell what was believed to be the wealth of the nation. Remembering that in their war with Burma, the Chinese forces made a bee-line for Mogaung, which they occupied, it may be surmised that the ends in view by those who provoked the conflict were less pure than those of justice.

Prices were kept inflated and production restricted by the fact that all the jade mines were located in the Kachin tribal area. The Kachins insisted on working the mines in their own way, steadfastly declining all offers involving leases or contracts. In their search for the stone, the Kachins relied upon divination. Quarries were opened with elaborate sacrifices and feasting, and then only after the omens had been consulted to decide whether or not the stone was to be allowed to 'mature', it being a Kachin opinion that the colour improved with keeping. Even so the workings might be held up over some dispute about the sharing of the proceeds, a punctilious matter in which every member of the clan, whether present or absent, was taken into consideration. Work was carried on only in March and April. After that the mines became flooded by the rains, and took the rest of the year to dry out. Meanwhile the Chinese buyers sat by, twiddling their thumbs in impotent exasperation, unconscious of the fact that by great good fortune the incompetence of the Kachins worked in their favour and cancelled out the disadvantage that Burma was nearer the cities of China than were the mines of South-East Turkestan. In the last century prices were much enhanced when King Mindon, an enthusiastic monopolist, tried to set himself up as middleman of the industry, and the Kachins retorted by discovering only inferior jade.

The Chinese have never been able to consider jade as mere 'dead' substance; they have always had a rather modern view of the nature of matter. From the earliest times, it was associated with the five cardinal virtues: charity, modesty, courage, justice and wisdom (one notes in passing the omission from this category of the peculiarly Christian faith and hope). It was also quite inevitable that it should be believed that jade could be taken internally with beneficial results. Once a year, therefore, the Emperor fasted ceremonially, consuming nothing but powdered jade of the most exquisite colour. This was for the good of the Empire; but, in the individual, the liver as well as all the organs in mystical association with it, according to the Chinese medical philosophy, were benefited by homoeopathic doses. The Chinese in their refined, almost tortured aestheticism, recognize 126 colours of jade, some of them baffling to Western amateurs, who find difficulty in differentiating between such shades as sky-blue and the blue of the sky 'after it has been washed by a shower'. Nor can many Western experts claim, as do the Chinese, to distinguish one variety of jade from another by the touch.

At the present time it seems likely that the jade mania may have come to an abrupt end. Production at Mogaung was entirely for the Chinese market, the stone being otherwise valueless. It is difficult to imagine that China's present rulers would sanction this type of import, or that they would approve of so many Chinese man-hours being employed on the production of trinkets, whatever their artistic merit — unless for export. Perhaps, as the driver said so confidently, the open-cast miners in this valley had indeed gone to chapel; or perhaps they had given up waiting for the Chinese merchants to come to the auctions, and had gone back to cultivate their opium, the market for which — if less spectacular — has always been dependable.

CHAPTER XVII

DOWN THE IRRAWADDY

HAVING learned that in the dry season only rare military boats went down the river from Myitkyina to Bhamó, I decided to return to Bhamó by road and to take a river steamer thence to Mandalay. This stretch of the river was covered by a twice-weekly boat service, and the trip took three days. When I had made some preliminary inquiries about this part of the journey, at the offices of the Irrawaddy Water Transport Board in Rangoon, the information to be had was surprisingly vague. It was known that the boats passed through areas held by both types of Communists, as well as P.V.O.s, and that although they were usually attacked, an escort of soldiers was carried and no boat had so far been lost. What they were not sure about was the nature of the accommodation. The executive I saw thought I would have to sleep on deck and take my own food with me.

At the company's Bhamó office the picture painted was a brighter one, to the extent at least that there was a regular food supply. A butler attended to the needs of first-class passengers, and there was even a choice of Burmese or Chinese food.

At seven in the morning I walked a plank over the shining Irrawaddy mud separating the solid bank from a shallow-draught lighter, one of a number which were hastening with passengers and goods to the steamer anchored in mid-stream. Like most river-steamers it had a romantic and anachronistic air; a flat-bottomed and skeletal construction of open-sided decks, terribly vulnerable, it seemed in its flimsiness, to assault of any kind. The *Pauktan*, of 106 tons displacement and licensed to carry 228 deck-passengers on 2053 square feet of deck-space (when not occupied by cattle, cargo or other encumbrances) proved, to my surprise, not to be a survival of the last century, but a postwar production.

The show-boat illusion was dissipated as soon as I put my foot on the iron deck, after boarding the ship close by a central redoubt covered by steel plating, from behind which came a cushioned thumping of powerful engines. On one side of this was the deck-passengers' kitchen in which, as I passed, a cook was hacking through a piece of dried fish held on a block. It took two blows of his heavy dah to cut off each segment. Early arrivals had already staked out their claims to deck space. As soon as they arrived they spread out mats or carpets, made tea and prepared bowls of rice and fish which they ate with ready holiday appetite. Before and after doing so they made a constant procession up to a row of sinister iron prison-cells mounted in the stern, labelled in English, Women and Men Wash Place.

After half an hour, an army launch came alongside with an escort of fifty soldiers, each man carrying, besides his rifle and normal kit, an embroidered pillow. A few minutes later there was a second influx of the military, twenty soldiers who were escorting forty-seven Chinese Nationalist internees and five dacoits. The escort party had started out with fifty Chinese, but three had already escaped. They were being taken to an internment camp at Meiktila. The dacoits were going to a prison two days' journey away. Two of them — one a Chinese soldier — had committed murders, and all five, although, as was to be expected, they looked exceedingly depressed, seemed from their appearance incapable of desperate deeds. The Chinese murderer in particular had a gentle and sensitive face.

The military took over the whole of the upper deck, laying out their kit, army-fashion, in neat rows, the embroidered pillows — some with lace fringes — perched squarely on haversacks. Sentries were posted at the tops of the companion-ways. The dacoits, now chained hand and foot, were seated in a melancholy row. To reduce the chafing of their gyves, they had been allowed to wrap rags round the metal. The Chinese formed squatting circles and began to play a game with engraved ivory counters, while their guards looked on with keen interest. A group of pongyis had formed round one of their number who had produced a snapshot album. To my surprise, most of the pictures were of girls, including one combing her hair in front of a mirror. On the deck below barge-load after barge-load of passengers continued to come aboard, alternating with hundreds of bales of dried fish, the odour of which slowly filled every corner of the ship. Most of the passengers, too, had brought with them tough, grey, salt-powdered hunks of fish, and, nervous at first of the promiscuous contacts of voyages, carried them everywhere they went, so that for some hours the decks and approaches of the *Pauktan* were heavy with the inter-twining of ammoniacal stenches.

Much to my surprise, in view of the ship's semi-transparent silhouette, there were cabins on the *Pauktan*, containing besides the bed, an electric fan, a wash-basin which emptied out into a bowl placed below, and a placard recommending the Asia Chop-Chop Shop at Katha. A minute triangular saloon was fitted into the bows, where you could sit with an excellent view of the river; and first-class passengers, Burmese and Chinese, who had retired here kicked off their sandals and looked up beamingly at the approach of footsteps, ready to ask politely, 'May I know your destination, sir?' In this room meals were served, presided over by the butler, the Burmese counterpart in dignity and con-servatism of attire of the impressive domestic who in England survives chiefly in advertisement descriptions of gracious living.

A good hour after the advertised sailing-time passengers were still arriving. Even when the last of the lighters had cast off, small boats came racing up, with much excited hailing and waving, disgorging fares who for the most part appeared to have come along on the spur of the moment, as they were without luggage. This, in fact, was the case. On making inquiries I learned that these late-comers were mem-bers of parties who had been seeing friends off, and then had suddenly felt an urge to join them. On the boat there were many happy and unforeseen reunions. In the end, the captain got tired of this kind of thing; a bell rang and up came the anchor. Leaving in the lurch a couple of boat-loads of impulsive Burmans, we began to slide down the river, accompanied by a dipping, slowly-flapping escort of Indian river terns.

All the world's great waterways are scenically uninteresting except in places where the river narrows in its passage through mountains or a gorge. Otherwise, the expanse of water is too great, the banks too far away. Here the Irrawaddy was half a mile to a mile wide, and the monotony of clouded water and the close vegetation of the distant shores was broken only when the pilot, steering a course that wound in great sweeping curves through an unseen channel of deep water, sometimes came close to the banks. The water opened in folds at the bows, carrying a broken, dusty sparkle, and although the sun was high the water had a cold, breath-catching smell of stagnant pools. The banks had been undermined, laying bare the roots of trees in a pale tracery, like some coral growth exposed by the recession of the sea. We soon passed one of the hundreds of ships that had been sunk or scuttled during the war. It had become an extension of the jungle, a boat-shaped peninsula, from which, surprisingly, a smoke-stack and one paddle protruded. The deck-rail embraced a variety of luxuriant grasses, bushes and one small tree — a vantage point selected by a bittern to survey the waters.

Within a few hours we entered the second or middle defile, where the river, narrowing perhaps to 150 yards, was shut in by hills covered by the most luxuriant forest, a multiple volcanic eruption of foliage, beneath which a wall of green lava toppled over upon a foreshore of glistening mud. As we nosed forward, silently cleaving the surface of clouded jade, the channel ahead closed in as if we had reached the end of a dark lake, barred by a cliff rising a sheer 800 feet out of the water. Then, as we turned a tree-crowded headland, the water could be seen, going on in glossy patches beyond the black boulders. Most travellers have recorded that they saw elephants here, but there were no elephants when the *Pauktan* passed through, although at a blast on the ship's siren a flight of parakeets broke from the treetops and came low overhead, a brief green glitter in the blue.

The defiles of the Irrawaddy are said to be of extreme depth, and I have read that a steamer which dropped anchor here failed to reach bottom when 630 feet of chain had run out, and, getting out of control, was lost. The butler told me that Burmese Loch Ness monsters are seen with fair regularity, undulant creatures with the inoffensive heads of asses or sheep, which show themselves at times of national crisis, or when comets are seen. Their appearance has no more than a monitory significance, and without harming passing boatmen, they are content to belch a little smoke before disappearing below the surface. It is an accepted fact that river-sharks haunt some of the bays.

We stopped at the village of Shwegu, where most of the population seemed to have gathered on the sloping bank to sell crude earthenware pots, vilely decorated by the moulded addition of glossy, ceramic peacocks. The art of Shwegu in particular and Burma in general is a disaster, ranking in the scale of debasement, with the honourable exception of its lacquer-ware, as about level with that of modern Egypt. But the little saleswomen, most of them in sparrow's-egg blue longyis and big Shan hats, were charming, and their pots — however deplorable separately — were arranged in the most effective mass compositions. The passengers were delighted with them, and scrambled ashore as soon as the gangplank was let down, to buy great quantities of these depressing souvenirs.

Beyond Shwegu a few barren islands appeared, fringed with sand-spits bearing ranks of motionless cormorants, some sunning themselves with wings heraldically opened. Once we saw an eagle wading majestically in the shadows, thus revealing itself as a surprisingly long-limbed bird. Pied kingfishers hung motionless in the air, their long beaks hanging down like hornets' stings, and sometimes dropped, as if an unseen thread had snapped, upon their insect quarry. In its fishing this bird employed a different technique, involving an extraordinary aerobatic feat — a trick which I had never seen practised before. While travelling at full speed, at perhaps seventy miles an hour, parallel to, and just above the water's surface, it would suddenly — at least, so it appeared to me — spot a fish, and then, unable to turn quickly, would at once lose speed and reverse its direction by purposely striking the water. It did so with wings partially opened, in such a way that the impact actually caused it to bounce back, at the same time allowing it to change direction and then go into a shallow dive after its prey. The whole operation, which I was never tired of watching, took about a second, and I wondered when and how the first kingfisher had discovered the possibilities of this manœuvre, and whether it was generally practised throughout the pied-kingfisher clan, or only by the Burmese birds.

Towards the evening, while the sun was still fairly high in the sky, the landscape suddenly lost its colours. The creamy-yellows of the water, the gilding of the sand-spits, the infinitely varied greens of the jungle trees, the banks, which were sometimes the bluish-white of water seeping through chalk, sometimes brick red, all relapsed into a leaden uniformity, a flat, photographic monochrome; it was more like a brightly moonlit scene than one viewed by the light of day. As the line of the distant mountains was erased from the sky and a tide of mist began to rise up the jungle tree-trunks, the ship was turned into the shore to join a dark cluster of junks.

This was Katha, where we were to stay the night, but although the town was said to be in Government hands, the Chop-Chop Shop, alas, was out of bounds, and a trip ashore was not thought desirable. Bren guns had been set up on both decks, and on the bridge — which was also armoured — and their muzzles thrust shorewards in the gathering gloom, which was suddenly violated by the brusque glare of the ship's searchlight. Extra guards had been posted over the prisoners who, with the failing light, had stopped gambling for match-sticks and were singing those rather tuneless European-type marching songs which are believed in the Far East to instil martial virtue. The opium-smokers among the Chinese had been humanely issued with an opium-ration, and had been sent away into a corner to smoke it. The officer who pointed this out was very proud of the fact that there was no opium-smoking in the Burmese army. Even the dacoits — two of whom it was whispered would be executed next day — had not been forgotten. Earlier in the day, after some self-examination as to the propriety of the action, and with the officer's permission, I had given them cheroots. Now there was an official issue.

CHAPTER XVIII

A MILD ALARM

MORNING came, accompanied by soft fluvial sounds, the light slap of water on the hull, the creaking of the junks' timbers, the splash of leaping fish. Night evaporated along the western horizon and, with it, a rippling veil of egrets was drawn back from the water. A little red had seeped into the leaden landscape, and presently where sky and water met without division, the sun raised itself on a long, clean-cut shaft of reflection. It was a polar spectacle, an arctic night in midsummer. Soon the ship quickened with the engine's subdued convulsion. Nosing out into the stream, it dragged in its wake ropes of unearthly blue through water the colour of tin. Wherever the water was stirred up, it leaped to life as if brilliant lamps had suddenly been lit below the surface. The sun, which had now broken away from its shaft of reflection, climbed swiftly into the sky, and as it did so the mists passed up out of the jungle, like the plumes of smoke from a railway station where many expresses are about to depart.

Here the river was shallow, and our course wound through a hidden channel. Speed was reduced, with the clanging of bells, and one of the Malabar crew stood in the bows taking soundings with ritual cries and the flourishes of a temple dancer. Whenever a satisfactory depth was reached he gave a triumphant shout of 'Allah akbar!' a pious equivalent of 'All's well'.

Tigyaing was in insurgent hands — what brand of insurgents was not clear — but by virtue of some kind of live-and-let-live arrangement, we were allowed to anchor there, a little off-shore, to discharge and take on cargo. The river-barges here were the most handsome boats I had seen in the country — in fact, in any country. They were built of rich, red teak, providentially left unpainted. By keeping the deck free of any encumbrances but a single, elegant deckhouse, placed well back, and with the curved line of its roof exactly repeating that of the high, carved stern, an extraordinary purity of outline had been achieved. There was an element of what is now known as stream-lining in these flowing curves, which undoubtedly reflected the tastes of Burmese boat-builders of bygone centuries. I hoped to have the opportunity to study one of these boats at leisure in Rangoon, but later found that they were a speciality of Upper Burma, and not to be found on the lower reaches of the river.

A few miles below Tigyaing there was some excitement. The river's course was divided here by a large island, and the right-hand channel we took was a narrow one, obliging us to approach sometimes very close to the bank, which was thickly wooded. We passed a village in a clearing, which might have been the objective, previously, of a Government landing party, because only the framework of the houses remained. The place had not been burned. The people had just moved elsewhere and taken their portable sections of bamboo walls with them. A red flag still flew from one of the roofs.

Further down we passed the sister steamer, making the journey up-stream to Bhamó. She signalled that she had just been attacked. This news was received with the utmost phlegm, and was passed on to me, without sign of emotion, by the butler. The soldiers of the Kachin Rifles set about organizing the defence, settling themselves comfortably in a row of chairs along the lower deck, with muzzles of rifles and Bren guns supported by the deck rail. A few others lay down behind the funnel, on the corrugated-iron covering to the top deck. From this position they were soon driven out by the escape of smoke and fumes produced when the engines were driven at full-speed. The passengers' behaviour was equally restrained. The young people took refuge, without excitement, behind a flimsy barricade of bales of fish. The Chinese prisoners showed amused interest. The old people and the convicts were indifferent. Only the pongyis paraded in the open, secure in the armour of righteousness, and peered and pointed into the green tangle, which sometimes came so near that we passed almost beneath the branches of the largest jungle trees.

But no signs of aggression were forthcoming at the spot where the other ship had been fired upon, and soon the soldiers put their guns down: the Chinese, who had gathered at their backs with professional interest, went back to their gambling, and the ordinary well-behaved tumult of the shipboard life started again. There had been no official declaration of a state of alarm, and now no responsible person decreed that the emergency had passed. The passengers just got tired of waiting for something to happen and decided to go on playing cards, or cooking their food.

I had just gone down for a shower, when there was a sound, muffled, yet amplified in the iron sounding-box of the bathroom, like the rattle of a distant anchor-chain going down. Immediately the room began to jar and vibrate under the hammering of the Bren guns above. I ran up on deck, but there was nothing left of the action but a smell of cordite. The gunners, lolling back in their chairs, were slapping fresh magazines into the breeches, and taking leisurely aim again, and as they did so the crowded cloisters of the jungle suddenly slipped away as our course took us into mid-stream again. There were no casualties, a fact which convinced me that such attacks are without terroristic intention, and aim only at compelling the Burmese Government to divert the maximum number of troops to escort duties. It would have been impossible to empty a machine-gun magazine into such a crowded ship, at twenty yards — even at random — without killing and wounding a number of people.

We had been delayed, so that the sun set while we were still some way from our destination for the night — Kyaukmyaung. At the approach of dusk, the terns, absent since the morning, returned, drifting past us up the river in groups, flapping languidly just above their reflections in the water. All round us dark smoke rose up where the Shans were firing the jungle before sowing their rice, and when the dark came the mountains were ringwormed with fire. The ship's searchlights stabbed out, and swung from side to side, illuminating stark boulders fringing the water's edge as we neared the third cataract, and patches of floating weed streamed past like silver plaques, stars and medallions. Soon brilliant motes appeared in the beam. These thickened until, with speed reduced, we appeared to be pushing forward into a blizzard. The flakes composing this singular storm proved to be winged insects, half fly and half moth, which soon filled the ship, flapping softly in the face and hair, churned by the electric fans into glittering whirlpools, deadening the footfalls in the carpet of their fallen bodies. There was no way of escaping them. When the cabin's windows were shut they spurted, as if under pressure, beneath the door, toasted themselves on the electric light bulb and fell into the wash-basin and drinking glasses. Had they possessed the power to sting, we should all have died, but they were quite harmless, though evidently suffering from some mass dementia. Curiously enough, they were all at the point of death, because after whirring round the room for a few moments they dropped to the floor, and lay still. Within twenty minutes it was all over, the air cleared and the ship's decks, passages and companion-ways were covered with a layer, half an inch thick, of small, feebly moving shapes.

The Kyaukmyaung shore, as we came in, twinkled with a dancing, firefly illumination. This was produced by a night market, held on the deep, sloping bank, to coincide with the boat's arrival. The water's edge and a path leading up to the village were lined with stalls, each lit by a wick standing in a cup of oil. Villagers coming down to meet the boat swung torches as they walked; hence the flickering effect. Most of the passengers went ashore to stretch their legs, and to buy the soup, rice, eggs, or members of chicken offered by the stall-holders. A speciality of this place was yardlong tubes of bamboo, filled with a much sought-after variety of sticky rice. These cost six annas each. All these edibles were sold by the village beauties, silk-clad and be-flowered. It is not considered demeaning in Burma to keep a market stall, and in this way marriageable girls present themselves discreetly for the inspection of prospective husbands. The market at Kyauk-myaung performed, in fact, a double function.

Kyaukmyaung, too, was for the dacoits the end of the road. Here the irons of each man were joined to a long chain, and thus they were marched away with the clinking anklets of earthbound dancers, up the bank and into the darkness.

Dawn again showed us a landscape engraved in steel, ragged ardent clouds stirred into the sky, a river coldly ensanguined.

Immediately below Kyaukmyaung, we entered the third and lowest defile of the Irrawaddy. It was less impressive than the second, but still sufficiently a wonder of nature to be surrounded with its magic aura. Here there was an island, and it was quite inevitable that a monastery should have been built upon it. The monastery of Thihadaw, now seemingly ruined, long possessed an engaging reputation because of the monks' skill in taming fish. In Burma, fish suffer from their position on the fringe of animal creation, and are victimized by the cunning sophistry which sees no harm in eating them if they happen to have died when taken out of the water. For this reason they have always evoked a special compassion in the breasts of the gentle Buddhist brotherhood, and many monasteries have tanks where fish, saved from the nets by these holy men, lead a pampered existence, sharing with their protectors the alms of the pious. At Thihadaw the monks had tamed the resident population of the Irrawaddy for half a mile around, and it was a favourite tourist spectacle to see them calling up five-feet dog-fish, to feed them and stick honorific patches of gold-leaf on the backs of their heads. These fish were intelligent enough never to wander far from their sanctuary. It is said that the arrival of the English had a deplorable effect on such pleasant customs. Unhappily, the fish which were most readily tamed were also the most appreciated for the table by the barbarous newcomers, and the prices offered tempted the cupidity of the fishermen. To combat the slaughter, the monks adopted many extraordinary measures. Once, at the mouth of the Irrawaddy, a canal was dug at immense labour, joining the river to a monastery tank, and the fish were trained upon a danger signal given vocally or by the beating of the banks, to swim up into the monastery enclosure, where the good men stood guard over them, cudgel in hand.

Below the defile the river spread out, its surface broken by wooded islands and rippling with shallows, where groups of fishing adjutants and herons waded. The banks were steep but shallow, and as the boat's wash reached them, parched earth showered down, and floated like powdered chocolate on the water's surface. Here there were more villages, the grey of their low bamboo shacks pierced by the fierce green of the river's edge grass. There was also more traffic; in particular, barges going upstream, poled forward smoothly and swiftly by teams of men — usually three on each side — who, laying their weight on their poles, marched with languid precision from stem to stern, returning endlessly to repeat the manœuvre. Small steamers also began to appear on the river. They were flying white flags.

Just above Mandalay the skyline was sharply broken by what looked like one of those freak hills which are a feature of the Moulmein area. For several miles I had watched the growth of this small, isolated mountain, which, as we approached, loomed from the tall trees surrounding it, to overtop a low range of distant hills. Noticing my interest, the butler told me that this was an unfinished pagoda, and only then I remembered the notorious Mengun, which, however, I had not expected to find by half so huge.

The Mengun Pagoda was the work of King Bodawpaya, one of the many oriental princes who at one time or another set out to put up the greatest building in the world. The work was started in 1790, and occupied most of the labour force of the country, which was conscribed and organized on military lines for seven years. At the end of that time a prophecy became current — it had been heard before during the pagoda-building mania which preceded the Mongol invasion: 'The great pagoda is finished, and the country is ruined.' There was something in this, because in a roundabout way this lunatic enterprise certainly accelerated the downfall of the Burmese kingdom. When Burmese manpower seemed insufficient, Bodawpaya recruited thousands of Arakanese, none of whom returned home. The Arakanese belief that the king considered their nation expendable brought about a revolt followed by mass emigration across the border into Assam. When the Burmese went after them, they clashed with the British and thus, eventually, the first Anglo-Burmese war came about. The Mengun Pagoda, when work on it ceased, had reached 165 feet of the proposed height of 500 feet.

Bodawpaya, a kind of Burmese Ivan the Terrible who never slept twice in the same bed, affected a monkishness commonly found in a certain type of tyrant, and it must have made him all the more sinister to his people. He was much concerned with works of merit, of which the Mengun Pagoda was to be his greatest. Believing that it would ensure his apotheosis, he went so far as to anticipate the work's completion in announcing his divinity. In much the same way a modern Burman will adopt the title *paya*, pagoda builder (one entitled to enter Nirvana without further incarnation) as soon as the first instalment-payment on the building has been made. To their eternal credit — since the king thought nothing of burning a few pongyis to death in wicker cages — this claim was immediately contested by the Buddhist priesthood, whose particular glory it is, like the prophets of old, and unlike many of the spiritual leaders of our times, that they have never been ready to sell their religion for the State's support, nor afraid to stand up to a tyrant. From the time when Narathihapate, fleeing before the Mongols, gave the order for his concubines to be drowned, and his chaplain warned him that their murder would entail as a consequence the king's reincarnation as an animal, Burmese history is full of such instances.

By all accounts the ferocity of this king startled even the Burmese, accustomed as they were to ruthlessness in the affairs of state. At his accession, when surplus members of the royal family were eliminated in the usual way, they were burned alive, including the previous king's four principal queens, who were accorded the privilege, however, of dying with their babies in their arms. This monster was diabolically efficient in most of his undertakings and led a charmed life. He built enormous public works, including reservoirs, destroyed his enemies, forbade drinking alcohol on pain of death, captured a perfect specimen of a white elephant, and was the first Burmese monarch to obtain a Buddha tooth from China. He died full of years and honour, and was survived by 122 children.

Into the relic chamber of the Mengun Pagoda — the first of its kind to be lead-lined — went, in addition to the Buddha tooth, all the most exquisite things produced in his day, Buddha-images, models of pagodas and monasteries in gold and silver, European clocks, clock-work toys, and the very latest child of European inventive genius—a machine for making soda-water.

This was the last attempt but one of a Burmese king to storm the Kingdom of Heaven by pagoda-building. The final fiasco was left to King Mindon, who, determined to outclass even the Mengun, had a whole hill cut into blocks to furnish stone, and dug canals several miles long for the huge lighters which were to carry the materials to the selected site. After four years of mass labour the pagoda had only risen four feet, and a French engineer who told the king that it would take eighty-four years to complete nar-rowly escaped crucifixion. Then the king died, and the thing was immediately abandoned.

We tied up on the Mandalay shore in the middle of a sweltering, dust-laden afternoon. A line of gharries, as bizarre in their ornament as properties from the Russian ballet, waited at the top of the slimy bank. I got into one of these and went off in it to see my friend U Tok Galé, and within half an hour was back in my old room over the cinema, suddenly realizing, as I heard them again through the mecha-nical blare and racket, that in the country of the Shans and Kachins I had missed the mild, sweet sound of the triangular pagoda-gongs of Burma.

Having reached Mandalay after hearing no more than a few shots fired, as a matter of routine exercise rather than in anger, I was now ambitious to continue the journey to Rangoon otherwise than by air. The Burman rarely raises obstacles to such a project on the score of mere danger. At the police headquarters, the D.S.P. said that naturally no one ever travelled by train, unless it was to reach a town not served by air; but the fact remained that the Mandalay-Rangoon line — the only one operating in the country — was open, more or less. The train service was, in fact, a fairly regular one, only held up from time to time to repair bridges, or remove wreckage from the line. As far as he was concerned there was no objection. He didn't see that there was any point in running the trains if people were forbidden to travel on them. He suggested that I should apply to the station master for more details.

The station master was most helpful. The Rangoon express would be running next morning at 6.15. He had just received news that the previous train, that of March 15th, had been dynamited at a place called Yeni, but as the dynamiting had taken place several hours ago, the wreckage should have been cleared in time to let tomorrow's train through. It would be a piece of unheard-of bad luck, he added, if they lost two trains in succession. And at what time would it get to Rangoon? . . . Get to Rangoon? The station master was slightly surprised. Naturally, it wouldn't. It was called the Rangoon express because it went in the direction of Rangoon, and it might travel five, ten or fifty miles before the line was dynamited, or a bridge blown up, or with good luck it might even reach Tatkón, which was about 150 miles away. After that it would turn round and come back, because between Tatkón and Pyinmana, sixty miles or so, much of the permanent way had been removed. The railway, said the station master — incorrectly as it turned out — furnished transport to get travellers across this gap; it might be lorries or it might even be bullock-carts. These were held up pretty regularly by dacoits, but even if passengers were robbed — and it was very stupid to carry more than a few rupees — they usually got to Pyinmana safely enough in the end. At Pyinmana, with reasonable luck, a train would be found waiting to leave for Rangoon. The D.S.P., he said, had been misinformed in the matter of the military escort. There was none. In fact, the only hope of the trains getting through was to run them without military escorts.

He promised to keep me a good second class seat — not over the wheels.

On our way back, Tok Galé asked me if I believed in ghosts. 'I ask you,' he said, 'because they say that this is the worst thing about travelling by train.' He kept an open mind on the matter himself, mentioning that although he had been passing a well-known haunted banyan tree every day for a number of years, he had never seen anything unusual. However, the fact was that travellers by train complained that they suffered from supernatural molestation. The ghosts came crowding up at night, headless and handless, and all the grislier and more menacing for this deprivation. Tatkón was the worst place for them; and Tok Galé thought that a possible reason for this might be the large number of unburied corpses left lying in the jungle near by, after the insurgent troubles. It was on this warning note that we said goodbye.

CHAPTER XIX

RANGOON EXPRESS

THE long train was made up of converted cattle-trucks, marked second or third class. In the second class there were two benches running the length of the ex-truck, but in the third class the space was divided up into sections, so that twice the number of people could be squeezed in. Until 6.15 the phlegmatic crowd on the departure platform was split up into nearly motionless social groups, as if before the performance of a première which nobody particularly wanted to attend. Then a man called the platform superintendent took a handbell from under his arm and shook it, and the train gave a lurch. The passengers who were already in their seats fell on top of each other, and picked themselves up, smiling with dazed pleasure. Those on the platform dashed for the doors. The platform superintendent pushed me into a second class compartment which he had insisted on keeping empty for me, and which was not over the wheels. 'Remember,' he said, 'in Burma there are no Communists, only people who want a change of government.' The train then moved away from him, and he turned and sank back from sight among the drifting groups of those who had come to see friends off, and in a moment the melancholy ringing of his bell was swallowed up in the clashing steel concussion of the wheels.

I found myself confined in a compartment measuring about nine feet by seven. There were glassless windows which could be covered by pulling down wooden shutters. The door, which had no handle, was fastened by an inside bolt. Passengers were asked to pull the chain in case of emergency, and in the lavatory, which smelt very badly, a notice invited them to depress the handle. But there was no chain and no handle. The electric light came on when two wires were twisted together. Mosquitoes lived in the dark places under the benches and streamed out in such numbers that they seemed to move in rough formation. A few large cockroaches crawled aimlessly about the floor.

Outside, the suburbs of Mandalay, caught in the sallow light of the rising sun filtered through strips of indigo mist, went lurching past. And then, almost immediately, the bungalows and the African huts merged with the mouldering pagodas of Amarapura, with mighty, broken walls, brick-choked moats, headless Buddhas, and a zooful of fabulous monsters, all strangled with cactus and scrub and flowering weeds. Here, with the city's abandonment at a monarch's whim, had been squandered the labours of 10,000 lives. Among the nearest pagodas lay the twisted and charred wreckage of rolling-stock where it had been thrown clear of the line, and left.

I was about to change carriages at the first station at which we stopped, when a smart, bespectacled young Burmese put his hand through the open top of the door, even before the train had come to a standstill, and unbolted it. He then jumped in, looked round the compartment, smiled quickly in my direction, took out a clean hand-kerchief, unfolded it, and wiped the opposite bench. After that, he jumped out again, and held the door open for another man to enter. The second-comer was an elderly man, tall and dignified, with a stubble of grey hair, and an extremely dark complexion. He came in, walking with some difficulty as if at the head of a procession, and sat down facing me. He wore a longyi, and a white sports shirt, neatly repaired in several places at the neck; two fountain-pens protruded from the breast pocket. Having seated himself he made a slight gesture to the young man who had come in first, and he, in response, trotted over to a group of women and children gathered in the background. From them he obtained a garland of flowers, which he came in and placed round the old man's neck. He was backing respectfully away when an uplifted hand halted him. 'Have you got your notebook?' the elderly man asked. The young Burman said he had. 'Good,' said the other. 'Make a note of these requirements.' And in an old, precise and rather harsh voice, he dictated a memorandum. The Burman, whom I now supposed to be his secretary, shut the notebook, put it away, and was dismissed.

Now two children entered the carriage, a boy of, I supposed, twelve, followed by a girl of about ten. They were handsome and grave, and dressed in Indian style. Falling to their knees, one after the other, they placed their hands together as if in prayer, and touched the floor of the compartment three times with their foreheads. While this ceremony was going on, the old man looked out of the window. As soon as the boy and girl had gone, he opened a suitcase, producing a small pile of *Reader's Digests* and a biscuit tin commemorating the Coronation of Edward VII, upon which had been screwed a plaque, with the inscription, in English, 'God is Light, Life and Infinite Magnet.' Turning his attention now to me, he suddenly smiled with a charm for which I had been unprepared, displaying in his dark face fine white teeth and the tip of an extremely pink tongue. 'I am Mr. Pereira,' he said. 'I am usually known as Uncle.'

Mr. Pereira, despite the patriarchal aloofness of his manner towards his staff and his children, proved to be a genial travelling companion. I judged him to be an Indian, with possible Burmese, and even – as his name suggested – Portuguese blood. Within a few minutes of the train's starting off again, he told me that he was a Buddhist monk, on a kind of sick-leave from his monastery. I gathered that his intense interest in religion had been a recent development and, owing to certain qualms and doubts he had experienced over the Buddhist non-recognition of the eternal soul, he had voluntarily accepted a year's penitential discipline, called tapas, which involved meditation and strict fasting. He had just been released from hospital, where he had spent six weeks recovering from the effects, and was now on his way to Rangoon for further treatment. Fortunately his intellectual capacity had been strengthened along with the depletion of his physical reserves, and now he found no difficulty in the calm acceptance of the personality's extinction in Nirvana. So much, indeed, had he come to crave this release that he had ordered the building of a pagoda on the Sagaing hills. It was to cost 50,000 rupees, of which sum he had been able to raise a half, thus exhausting the family's capital. But the sacrifice was well worth it, he was convinced; he added suddenly, with the kind of smile that usually goes with a wink, 'I have assuredly purchased a ticket to a higher plane of existence.'

He opened the biscuit tin and took out a photograph of his unfinished work of merit, in the relic chamber of which, he mentioned, had been placed a quantity of earth from the spot where Buddha preached his first sermon. There were other photographs — some of religious objects, such as the Buddha-tooth of Kandy — but mostly of railway disasters. Mr. Pereira was an old railwayman, and his affection for his former career had not been obliterated by his subsequent religious pre-occupations. At the next station several railway officials joined us, and he entered with vivacity into the technicalities of their shop-talk, while the snapshots of derailed engines and smashed carriages passed, with cries of admiration, from hand to hand. English was the chosen language of these men, who were Burmans and Anglo-Burmans, and they spoke it with pleasure and exuberance. Sometimes they lapsed for a few sentences into Burmese, but even then it was a Burmese studded with English words like 'emergency', 'reconstruction', 'insurgents', 'those sods'. And then the Burmese sentences would fill up with English technical jargon, the Burmese words become rarer and rarer, and once again they would be speaking English.

The indifference displayed by the generality of the passengers towards the hazards of the journey was replaced here by a positive zest for danger. The railwaymen were eager to display inside information about such alarming topics as the sorry state of the bridges we were passing over, most of which had been blown up several times. It was clear that from their familiarity with the structural weaknesses, of which no layman could have a knowledge, had been bred a kind of possessive affection. Some bridges had been patched up in makeshift ways which flouted engineering theory, and they were proud and happy about it, waiting impatiently for the bridge to come, trying to make me understand why a repaired main-girder could not be expected to withstand the strain we were about to impose, claiming heatedly to feel the bridge — when we had reached it — sway under the train's weight. 'But don't worry,' said a merry little Burmese Deputy-Inspector of Wagons, 'trains don't fall into the river. They blow into the air.' He threw up his hands, made an explosive noise with his lips, and laughed gaily.

In the insurgent areas, as they were called, he also explained, it was usual to economize on materials whenever possible. For instance, as they were always having to replace rails, they used only two bolts to secure them to the sleepers, instead of the regulation four. A colleague now chimed in with the information that the telegraph wires had been cut on the previous night, which always meant an attack; so the engine driver had been given a red ticket — 'to proceed with caution'. But what was the use? The guard, a Mr. Brunnings, was bound to bring bad luck. He was a regular Jonah, and some drivers refused to have him on the train, although the drivers themselves were no better. They fancied themselves as speed-kings and went so fast that they didn't notice a small gap in the rail. The speaker mentioned that he had jumped a twenty-inch gap in his 'petrol-special' the other day. They were like infantrymen who derive a perverse comfort from exaggerating their sorrows, and it was almost with satisfaction that they acclaimed, just after we had passed Myittha, the violent application of the brakes.

We all got out and walked up to the front. About twenty-five yards from the engine, a small charge had exploded under a rail. The rail had been torn by the explosion, and one of the jagged ends thrust up into the air. Round this the passengers gathered reverently, under their bright display of sunshades. The dull journey had been leavened with incident, and although unexcited they were appreciative. Left to themselves they would have settled down here, as at a pagoda outing, to a picnic. But the engine's imperious whistle called them away, and the train began to back slowly towards the station we had just left, jolting to a halt after covering about a hundred yards, as another mine exploded in its rear.

We were stranded in a dead-flat sun-wasted landscape. The paddies held a few yellow pools, and buffaloes emerged, as if seen at the moment of creation, from their hidden wallows. About a mile from the line an untidy village broke into the pattern of the fields. You could just make out the point of red where a flag hung from the Mogul turret of a house which had once belonged to an Indian landlord. A senior official, going on leave somewhere, had his contribution of pessimism to make. He knew this village from past experience. It was the headquarters of about 300 Communists. The Government was going to have to burn it, he said. And what might the Communists be expected to do now? Nothing much, the official said, with perhaps a trace of regret — at least, judging by previous experiences. At the most they might send a squad of men to look over the passengers, in case there were any political hostages worth taking. With the diffidence which I felt was expected in such unemotional company, I asked what was their attitude to Europeans. The official said he didn't know, because Europeans didn't travel by train. In any case, he would have taken me for a merchant from some vaguely Middle-Eastern country, an Iranian perhaps.

The suggestion gave me an idea. My sun-tan had reached a depth which made me darker than some of the Asiatic passengers, and I had got into the habit on journeys like this of wearing a longyi and sandals. Sandals were really essential, because you were always having to kick off your footwear when entering a habitation of any kind — and this included a second class railway carriage made out of a railway truck. The longyi would have looked like a ridiculous affectation and have been out of the question had there been any Europeans about, but there were none, and in this heat and dirt it had great hygienic advantages. I had two, keeping a clean one in reserve. They could be washed out and dried very quickly, and in this way I managed a change almost every day. It was now agreed among my travelling companions that should insurgents search the train, it would be safer — in view of the Red-Flag Communists' attitude towards imperialist exploiters — for me to be an Iranian. But, said the senior official, nothing whatever would happen — we should see.

His conviction seemed to lack solidity after the account of a similar incident I had just been reading in a copy of *The Burman*, bought at the last station. 'It was 10 o'clock in the morning,' stated the account in the consciously literary style favoured by Burmese reporting, 'that the Special left Shwebo. Twenty-five minutes later it reached milestone 439 3-4 and struck the mine. With the detonation the ill-fated train was subjected to heavy rifle fire. Insurgents then came forwards towards the train to loot ... The exchange of fire quickly drew Township Officer Wetlet, and a squad of U.M.P. (Union of Burma Military Police) on the scene. After a brief engagement the insurgents were routed.' Mr. Pereira was quite convinced of his ability to defeat any such assault by the sheer weight of moral authority. At all events, if the insurgents attempted to approach our compartment, he would throw them into utter confusion by the preaching of the Law. For himself, he was quite imperturbable, for besides the other advantages of being a pagoda-builder, he was assured of release from the earthly effects of the Three Calamities: Starvation, Plague and Warfare.

But there were no signs of life from the village. Time passed slowly, and the old man entertained the company with the resumé of a paper he had read to the Rotary Club of Rangoon. The subject was Charity, and it was illustrated by many instances, some of which were difficult to appreciate in the grotesqueness of the guise the virtue had assumed. There was the story of King Mindon, which I heard for the first time. In a previous existence the king had been a female demon, inhabiting Mandalay Hill, who had sheltered the Buddha, and, cutting off her breasts, had presented them — 'in a devotional ardour', as Mr. Pereira put it. This act of merit was rewarded in the next incarnation by a change of sex, as well as the dignity of the Dragon Throne. He also recounted two familiar instances of the Buddha's all-embracing compassion, in his previous existences. On one occasion, when as a human being he had come across a starving tigress with two cubs, he had surrendered himself to be eaten. In the other instance happening to be incarnated as a jungle-fowl at a time of famine, he had sought out a pilgrim and saved the holy man from death from starvation by the supreme sacrifice. There was nothing in these stories which his hearers would have found difficult to believe. They were not even particularly amazed when the Deputy Inspector of Wagons described a camera he had seen. Persons when photographed with this in their normal attire, came out in the nude.

Two hours passed in this way, and a gloominess began to infect the company. The way things were going, it looked as though we should be four days in getting to Rangoon. The train was not allowed to travel at night, and we should be stranded in some God-forsaken spot, with nothing to eat. The exhilaration of escaping a major danger having passed, the smaller inconveniences and imponderables now loomed disproportionately. Mr. Pereira began to fret, and to plot alternative courses of action. He had important friends at Thazi, which we might reach in an hour after we started off again, and he wondered whether they could be persuaded to hire us a car to go as far as Yamethin. Or we could leave the train at Thazi, spend the night there in comfort, and then look round for some way of carrying on next day. But supposing we took this chance, and then found that his friends were away? That meant that we might be stranded high and dry for days. No, Mr. Pereira finally decided, this was not a good idea. It was too risky. But what were the chances, he wondered, of persuading the station master at Thazi to put a 'petrol special' at the disposition of four distinguished travellers? We could then dash ahead, full speed, in front of the train, and be sure of getting to Yamethin that night. There might be something in that. Once at Yamethin, he could pull strings in all directions to get transport to Pyinmana — even Toungoo. Thus it appeared that even his year's meditation on such themes as futility and evanescence had not entirely cured Mr. Pereira of a habit of vain hopes and vain illusions.

Somebody then told him that there was a gang of workmen on the train, going on leave to their homes, and Mr. Pereira emitted a scandalized cry. Why had he not been told before? We were carrying spare rails; so let the foreman or senior workman be called into his presence and he would exhort them, with all the weight of his moral influence, to replace the torn rail. Mr. Pereira's suitcase was opened in the middle of the carriage floor, and there displayed on the top, were his neatly folded yellow robes.

Someone had just gone off for the men, when a distant rattling was heard, and all the passengers were suddenly looking in the same direction. It was a 'petrol special' from Myittha, and it carried not only a breakdown gang, but vendors of samusa (fried mincemeat and onion patties), fried chicken and Vimto — a non-alcoholic beverage which sometimes takes the place of Coca-Cola in soft-currency areas. Immediately the picnic atmosphere revived. Ladies fluttered from the carriages like unsuspected butterflies from the shadows of a wood; someone began to pluck at the strings of a guitar, and a conjurer gave a free show by the side of the track. Mr. Pereira ate heartily, although restricting himself to putto rice, baked in a length of bamboo. Afterwards he spotted my bottle of mepacrine. 'What are those tablets? Pray give me two to try.' I assured him that they did not contain the vitamins by which he was mildly obsessed; but there was no way of dissuading him from taking the tablets, which he put in his mouth, and sucked with contentment and appreciation.

Soon after we were on our way again. At the next station we collected another permanent addition to our party. This was a junior station master, an Anglo-Burman who was inoffensively drunk for the whole journey. He carried with him a bottle of country spirit, retiring with it to the lavatory from time to time, to avoid Mr. Pereira's censorious eye. His Burmese wife and his children were travelling third class, and whenever the train stopped, the numerous family was re-united in our compartment. The degree of this man's befuddlement was uneven, following the curve of an irregular graph which rose and fell gently, dependent upon the maintenance of fresh supplies of country spirit in the villages we stopped at. When he was in a semi-sober condition, he seemed, like most Anglo-Burmans – although they swarm in official positions – to be unhappy with his lot; but soon after the bottle had been refilled he became expansive, in a quite unBurmese way. As this was happening, his opinion of me steadily increased, till by the time he reached the top of the manic curve he believed I was the American Ambassador, and presented me as such to various friends travelling on the train.

At Thazi we met the up-train, returning – six hours late – from Yamethin. It reported the impossibility of reaching Tatkón, as three bridges had been demolished on this side of the town. Bridge-guards had been mortared, and a railway repair-staff kidnapped on the outskirts. Hearing of this, the junior station master, who had promoted himself, in a happy fantasy, to an executive position, decided to go and confer with the engine driver. But by this time we were already on our way again, doing thirty miles an hour, and escaping the restraining hands, he got the door open, swung out into space and back again, collapsed on the floor, and went to sleep.

For a short time we had a companion who was not a railwayman but an officer of the Military Police, a thickset fellow with an unusually brutal face. From him I learned a sinister fact which explained the insurgents' war to the death with the U.M.P., and also, perhaps, threw some light on Tok Galé's ghost story. 'When we take insurgents,' said this man, with a ferocious leer, 'we cut them.' Cut them? — I did not follow. 'We cut them with our dahs,' the fellow said, bringing down his arm in a ferocious swipe. 'In our country there is a belief that the spirits of dead men will guard the bridges.' So that was it, and I wondered how many misguided peasants had been sacrificed to the river spirits in this way.

The bridges were without number. All the important ones were guarded by slit trenches and machine-gun nests, and we stopped to give water to their defenders. Near one was a recent wreck with what looked like a brand-new American locomotive, still shining and well-oiled, lying on its side so that we could study its complicated internals. The guards had comfortably installed themselves in 'basha' huts, put together quickly with branches and palm-leaves in a couple of the trucks which had landed upright. The record number of bridges to be blown up in one night in any one administrative area, was five, said a member of the repair staff. It was raining 'like the dickens' at the time, and he had to issue fourteen quarts of country spirit to the men, to keep them on their feet and to get the work done. 'By the morning, the trains were speeding on their way. Then my chief sends for me, intending, as I suppose, to bestow a compliment. But this is not so, and all he wants to know is, who is going to pay for the country spirit?' And the man, fat and cheerful, roared with laughter at the memory of his disillusionment.

Listening to such stories I could not help feeling that the keeping open of the Mandalay-Rangoon line must be almost the outstanding example of tenacity in the face of appalling obstacles in the annals of railway history, and that it illuminated a side of the Burmese character which had received little recognition in Colonial days. The speaker had often run up against insurgents, but found them easy enough to get on with if you didn't make the fatal mistake of associating with soldiers. 'They observe us at our labours without hindrance. Sometimes a warning shot rings out and we get to hell. That, my dear colleagues, is the set-up. From running continuously I am rejuvenated. All appetites and sleeping much improved.' Only the other day his 'petrol special' had refused to start after he had been out to inspect a sabotaged bridge, and while he was cleaning out the carburettor a couple of White-Flag Communists had come along and taken him to their headquarters. They took his watch and pocket-book and, after questioning him about the number of government troops in Toungoo, told him that he could go. They expected him to walk home seven miles, although it was after dark. Naturally, he refused, saw to it that he got breakfast next morning, and then asked to see an officer, told him about the watch and pocket-book, and got them back.

CHAPTER XX

RIVAL PARTIES

CONFOUNDING all the pessimistic prophecies, we got into Yamethin at nightfall. It was announced that the train would stay there for the night, and return to Mandalay next day, and that passengers might sleep in the train. While Mr. Pereira stayed on guard, the junior station master, or J.S.M. as he had better be known, a young Indian wagon-inspector called Nair, and myself, went out to buy our evening meal. There was actually a shop licensed to sell beer. It was tucked away in a side-street, and customers went in under the eye of two or three of the kind of people who gather when an accident has happened, and drank with furtive bravado, standing at an ordinary store-counter. Ice was sent out for and charged separately. We ate curried chicken in an Indian shack where the dust settled so quickly that we covered our plates with palm leaves in the pauses between eating. Afterwards we chewed betel – in my case for the first time. The taste was at first sweet and sharp, and afterwards slightly soapy, with a faint childhood recollection of the taste of bath water on a sponge. At this point the J.S.M. announced that he was going in search of 'the fancy' which was to be found on the edge of the jungle, and with a cry of 'cheery-bye' reeled happily away into the night. We found out later that he was driven back, without having achieved his purpose, by a government patrol. There was a great deal of military activity in the Yamethin area. The Communists had a stronghold ten miles away at Aingto, and penetrated to the outskirts of the town, where, as I learned from a newspaper when we reached Rangoon, they had held a people's court on the night we were in Yamethin, and executed a prisoner.

A curfew was imposed at nine o'clock, but this did not seem to apply to the precincts of the station where the town's nocturnal activities were concentrated. The water-supply, turned on for a few

240

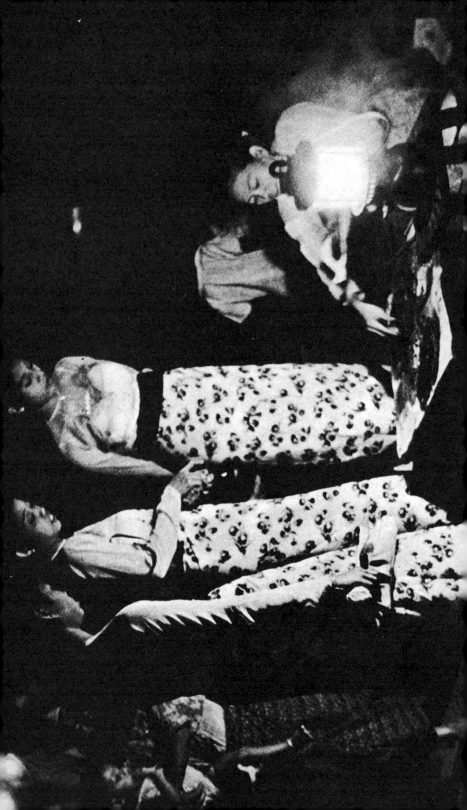

minutes daily, had been cornered by the enterprising and re-issued here
in the form of slabs of ice-cream on sticks. It was also possible to buy a
cup of tea, the sale being conditional on the consumption of pyagyo —
a fried ball of ground peas and curry. With traditional magnificence a
burgher of the town had chosen to celebrate some windfall by offering
a free theatrical show — also in the station yard. It was a well-known
piece with a plot about a queen's love for a legless dwarf, that Anouilh
himself might have been proud to have invented. For several hours I
watched the leisurely unfolding of the story, with its numerous inter-
ruptions by slap-stick and dancing. About a third of the way through
the play I gave up and went back to the carriage.

The others were already there and Mr. Pereira, who had just decided
to get up and go for a stroll, was told of the curfew. 'Curfew,' he said
dreamily, a little later, 'a curious word. Have you ever thought of its
origin? I read something about it in a *Reader's Digest*.' He lay stretched
out along one of the lower benches, and above him a plank had been
let down on a chain to form an upper bunk. Upon this Nair reposed,
uncomfortable at the thought of the disrespect involved in sleeping
above a venerable pagoda-builder. An argument had raged for some
time before the sleeping arrangements had finally been settled and
anyone could be induced to occupy this position, left vacant by the
fact that Mr. Pereira was incapable of the physical effort involved in
climbing into the upper bunk.

As it was, he was wakeful and restless. 'I am unable to sleep, Mr.
Nair,' he moaned. 'Lacking my glass of Wincarnis, I cannot relax.
The heat, too, is unseasonable.' Then I found myself waiting for something, a further development of Mr. Pereira's discourse, which, as I
seemed to have stumbled on a key to his thought-processes, I knew
must follow. I had only a few moments to wait. 'Psychology has
shown us, Mr. Nair,' the harsh, pedagogic voice began, 'that there are
different levels of sleep . . .' The J.S.M. woke up with a groan, sat up
in his bunk and said, 'From the jungle's edge, ravishingly she came out
to me, like the actress of the screen — Joan, is it? — I do not know her
name. But we were restricted by impediment, and — ah . . .' he fell
back, and his voice trailed off into snores. Out in the yard, the orchestra

banged and squealed in endless, zestful improvisation. The wall of the carriage held the heat where the sun had struck it, and an invisible sheet of cellophane across the window prevented any air from entering. Passengers still clung to the platform in unhappy groups, and from the grumbling of their voices an uneasy pattern of dream was forming. A voice murmured, far back in the brain, it seemed, 'Forty-two degrees. Multiply forty-two by nine, and divide by five. Now add thirty-two. Yamethin is the hottest place in Burma. But it is opinion that next month it will be hotter.'

With every morning, at the hour of setting out, came an unfailing exhilaration, when the perfume flowed steadily from the invisible flowering bushes in the forest, which — itself unseen — was there somewhere, beyond the low hills, or as in Yamethin, crowding at the threshold of the town.

In the early hours Mr. Pereira had got up, switched on the light and gone into the lavatory for the scrupulous and lengthy ritual of his toilet. The best time to concentrate, he explained later, was between the hours of four and six, before the bustle of the world destroys the emanations of the higher sphere. 'The brain, Mr. Nair, may be likened to a radio machine, of highly-tuned receptivity.' And so we lay and struggled weakly on the edge of consciousness, while Mr. Pereira splashed about, recited his mantras, and acquired spiritual strength to face the day.

By 6.30, when we stood in the station yard, waiting for lorries, some of this intake of magnetic power had already been expended, and there were even signs of nervous irritability. Besides a following of temporary associates — occupants of other carriages, with whom we were on terms of only slight familiarity — our party consisted of the four of the night before, plus the J.S.M.'s wife and three children. Contrary to assurances, no arrangements had been made by the railway company to get passengers to Pyinmana. This was left entirely to their own ingenuity. And although Mr. Pereira had several times mentioned powerful friends in Yamethin, who could be relied upon, if the occasion arose, to put transport at our disposal, they were no longer alluded to. Instead, having found that among my many documents was a letter of introduction to the D.S.P. of the town, he urged me to call on this official and endeavour, on the strength of this letter, to have a lorry placed at the disposal of our party. There were several objections to this proposition; the chief being that I saw no reason to appeal to the official unless in a case of genuine emergency. In any case — and this was the argument that carried the weight with Mr. Pereira — it was to be supposed that the D.S.P. would not be available before eight, or nine, and by that time any lorry going southwards would most likely have left.

His hopes in this direction having been shattered, Mr. Pereira now ordered Nair into action. Within a few minutes Nair was back to say that he had found a lorry that would shortly be leaving for Pyinmana. It was a three-tonner, engaged at that moment in taking on a load of five tons of lead, a few hundred yards from where we stood, down the railway line. It would complete its load with a ton of potatoes, and fifteen passengers, and their luggage. Shortly afterwards it appeared, but Mr. Pereira shook his head. He had produced a small handbook on numerology, by an author with the pen-name of Cheerio; it was a best-seller in Burma, although this was the first time I had seen it put to practical use. The number of the truck he said flatly, was not propitious, and he would not travel by it. His disfavour quickly spread, and the other members of the group also turned away. Happily, another lorry arrived a few minutes later, and its number, 7101, was judged acceptable. It also stopped to take on an immense load of potatoes, upon the towering summit of which we perched, with a splendid but swaying view of the country.

For some reason — probably connected with its supposed vulnerability in case of attack — Mr. Pereira refused to accept a seat of honour in the driver's cabin, and had to be lifted, by a kind of Alpine rescue feat, to a resting place among the peaks. At intervals of almost precisely five minutes our lorry stopped, while a member of the crew got down, partially dismantled the petrol supply-system, and blew air through it with a foot-pump. Mr. Pereira, who had brought out a sheaf of notes dealing with a lecture he had given on the comparison of

Buddhism with Christianity, and was about to hold forth, became exasperated with this and even rapped sharply with his stick on the roof of the driver's cabin, whenever the tell-tale spluttering started.

It took us two hours to cover the twenty miles to Tatkón, and here we stopped for lengthy repairs, since, besides the trouble with the petrol supply, the front brakes had seized and had had to be disconnected. I went over to the station and raised the matter of the ghosts with an unemployed ticket collector. He roared with laughter at the absurdity of the rumour. 'Why, anybody knows that it's not everyone who can see a ghost. It's a matter of psychology; therefore they can't frighten *all* the passengers.'

After Tatkón my friends were able, with relish, to renew their pessimism. The stretch of road between Tatkón and Pyinmana, they assured me, was the most dangerous in all Burma. The conversation turned naturally on descriptions of atrocious events that had taken place in these hilly and pleasantly wooded surroundings. We were passing through what might have been the Wye Valley, in the exhaustion of late autumn, yet lashed by a strange sun, with a river meandering among the rocks, and eagles flapping overhead. The woods had been patchily and inefficiently burned back from the road, so that there was cover for an ambush only at intervals of about a hundred yards. All the many small bridges had been blown up, and replaced by temporary structures of wood or metal. Sometimes these secondary bridges had been demolished too, so that we were obliged after all to ford the stream in a lurching, swaying rush. Battles had been fought along this main north-south axis. It was a graveyard of 'soft' military vehicles, and there were a few burned-out tanks lying about. Some of these wrecks, bowered in ferns, probably dated from Japanese days, and small dun-coloured birds had taken possession of them and were popping in and out of the shell holes. This drive was a memorable torture. The craters of shells and mines had only been loosely filled in, and the surface had been deeply rutted and macerated by armoured traffic. Sprawled out like fakirs across the protuberances of our potato sacks, we were tossed from side to side and shot into the air as the lorry's wheels crashed into the holes in the road. A few square feet of tarpaulin had been rigged up on a crude frame over our heads, and the sun struck at us through its many openings. Groaningly Mr. Pereira implored me for more mepacrine to help him to endure the ordeal.

We reached Pyinmana by the early afternoon, entering the town by streets where dentists, as if in celebration of a great victory, had hung out many banners, upon which fleshless jaws grinned in ecstasy. The lorry dropped us at the Hwa Sein Store, a wooden-framed building from a Wild-Western film, where we fell into chairs round a table, while Mr. Pereira, on the verge of collapse, refreshed himself with an Ovaltine. We sat there for half an hour, afraid of what the effort to move might cost us. Sweat glistened like powdered mica on our skins. A Thibetan, vaguely outlined against the sun as if seen in a floodlit aquarium, floated up out of the street. His eyes glowed through the strands of hair hanging down over his face. Untying the yak's-hair knots that secured a paper packet, he showered gems on the table top. The J.S.M. bought an emerald for eight annas, and tenderly presented it to his wife.

A gharry took us to the station, where we found the train that would leave for Rangoon next day already standing at a platform. Here Mr. Pereira came into his own at last. Formally presenting himself to the station master, he had a second class carriage reserved for our party, and a notice was hung on the door to say that it was occupied by railway officials. At the same time, he learned an important piece of news. At Pyinmana, the senior railway staff occupied a small block of flats near the station, and this possessed the splendid amenity of a communal bathroom. The station master recommended us to present ourselves there, precisely at four o'clock, when the water would be turned on for half an hour. He gave us a chit of introduction for the man in charge of the bath.

We went there and found a small group of railwaymen waiting in reverent silence as if for the performance of some fairly dependable miracle, such as the liquefaction of the blood of St. Januarius. The man in charge of the bath stood with his back to the door, of which he held the key. A few years before, the bathroom must have been a showpiece, and even now it was luxurious and sybaritic in the desolation of Pyinmana, which, as an important marshalling-yard, must have been bombed on numerous occasions. A few tiles survived on the floor, like a broken Roman mosaic, in an amorphous surface of cement. The bath had a huge, chromium-plated tap, which someone still went to the trouble of polishing, although it had been swivelled round until it hung over the floor, and the daily blessing of water was delivered, not through this, which had become no more than a symbol, but from a cruelly naked pipe, which jutted directly from a hole in the wall. Just as the hour of four clanged somewhere in the town, moisture gathered at the rim of the pipe, and the first drops began to splash in the stagnant lake at the bottom of the bath. Any natural desire a Burman might have felt to be the first to assuage his skin's prickly heat, was easily outweighed by considerations of the merit to be earned by deferring to a stranger. I was merely asked not to splash on the floor any of the precious fluid more than I could help. The water was amber-coloured, but, as the man in charge of the bath had proudly claimed, clear. Although quite warm by ordinary standards, it was indescribably refreshing after two scorching, waterless days.

Over the top of the broken door could be seen the remains of a baronial folly in the Oriental style, a gabled, red-brick house, of which only the façade remained, flanked by two machicolated towers. In the other corner of the view was a pseudo-Renaissance building in the Portuguese style, to which had been added four Mogul turrets, and two towers terminating in onion-shaped cupolas. This, too, had been burned out.

As I stood at the door of the bathroom, while the water evaporated like alcohol from the skin, the whole panorama of the marshalling-yards came into view. There was a background of palms partially screening the ruined gothic and Asiatic fantasies, and a few trees with lacquered foliage, from which hung down black beans. Beneath the trees were long lines of goods-trucks, most of which would never run on their own wheels again; and distributed about the yards were step-pyramids of railway sleepers, which were in constant demand to prop up temporary bridges. Along the tracks, and round these obstacles, sauntered parading crowds, the girls in longyis of bright silk, and carrying parasols, the men wearing sun-helmets which, being enamelled green and blue, looked like chamber-pots. A dozen Indian labourers were cooking their food, each, for fear of contamination, at a separate fire. There were two sounds, the occasional deep purring of a pagoda gong of rare quality, and the shrieking of kites in the sky. In this scene there were no clear, sharp colours. It was overlaid by yellow light, as if seen through a shop-window over which a sheet of yellow cellophane had been stretched to prevent the goods from fading. To me, coming out of the damp coolness of the bathroom, it was like plunging into warm milk.

Pyinmana had previously been the headquarters of Thakin Than Tun, leader of the White-Flag Communists. Three months after I left they re-entered the town and fought a battle with Government troops in its streets). From this stronghold, which was later stormed by Government troops, he directed the insurrection which broke out on March 6th, 1948; it was the first of a series of revolts directed against the Socialist Government by a number of racial and political minorities. Of all the insurgent movements, that of the White-Flag Communists in combination with the Karen National Defence Organization, was the most serious. It started off with a succession of victories. Towns were captured all over Burma, until finally, a year after the outbreak, Mandalay itself fell; and Rangoon, and the Government's survival, were threatened. After this the tide slowly turned. The insurgents were beaten by shortage of ammunition, their internal divisions, and by the tenacity of the Government forces. Mandalay was recaptured shortly after its fall, and all the large towns in insurgent hands occupied one by one. The Karens withdrew into the mountainous area known as Karenni, lying between the towns of Loi Kaw, Papun and Thaton, while the Communists, the P.V.O., and the army mutineers took refuge in the small villages and the jungles, where they still carry on their fight. The Communists appear slowly to be absorbing their competitors, with a consequent accretion of strength.

The Burmese insurrections have a formless and bewildering complexity that make them almost incomprehensible to the Westerner who has not studied their history on the spot. To an outsider the programmes of all the insurgent groups seem identical. They are all apparently of the extreme Left, and resolved to extirpate landlords and capitalists, permit freedom of worship, distribute the land to the peasants, and smash fascism. Each body accuses all the others of failing to respect these ideals, and all accuse the A.F.P.F.L. (Anti-Fascist People's Freedom League) Government of being no more than a sham behind which the brutal exploitation of the country by foreign interests is permitted to continue.

Behind the façade of anti-Government 'democratic-fronts', and the barrage of allegation, one suspects on examining the facts a clash of power-hungry personalities, from which some have emerged defeated to become the relentless opponents of those who have reached the top. The departure of the British from Burma left a yawning vacuum of Governmental office to be filled, and offered in the army the prospect of immediate promotion for thousands of officers and men. Many were hurt in the scramble. As an illustration of the attitude of the disappointed place-hunter — and of the real motive behind a political coup — a better example could not be found than the two leaders of the army mutiny who, after announcing their intention of abolishing feudal landlordism, offered to surrender if they were guaranteed the portfolios of Defence and Home Affairs.

The P.V.O.s (Peoples Voluntary Organization) were originally the Burmese equivalent of the Maquis, formed after the war into this body in an attempt to keep its members under disciplined control while the process of post-war resettlement went on. The resettlement of the rank and file of peasants was a simple matter, but the officer-class, having tasted power, refused to return to the banality of its pre-war existence, and quietly refilled the ranks as fast as they were emptied with any restless spirits who cared to join, irrespective of military or resistance services. They then drew up their political programme, but since it had to be Leftist, and there was nothing they could think of to add to that of the Communists, or of the Government, they amalgamated these pro-

grammes, but dropped from one the expropriation of foreign con-
cerns, and from the other, the land reforms. The P.V.O.s revolted in
July 1948, when the Communist insurrection was well under way, and
for a time joined forces with them. Later they fought each other with
particular ferocity, and the P.V.O.s split into two groups, white and
yellow, the whites remaining underground and the yellows joining the
Government to fight their erstwhile comrades.

The formation of the Red-Flag Communist organization, as an off-
shoot of the original Burma Communist Party, appears likewise to
have been a matter of internal politics and of political rivalry between
the two principal figures in the movement. Thakin Than Tun, who
headed the party before the split occurred, served as a minister during
the Japanese occupation, while Thakin Soe, leader of those who broke
away, spent most of the war as an underground fighter. It was his
contention that as the Communist Party was a party of struggle, only
those fashioned by struggle could give correct leadership. He also
accused Thakin Than Tun of misappropriation of party funds, and the
latter retaliated by an attack on Thakin Soe's morals, which were said
to be lax even by the easiest of Burmese polygamistic standards. After
the break each side gave priority over the other political tasks in hand to
the other's extermination. Thakin Soe, however, by the severity and
ruthlessness of his methods has continually lost the support of the
Burmese peasantry, while his White-Flag rivals by their relative mildness and strict discipline have extended their influence, and have even
attracted middle-class cultivators — whom Thakin Soe would be
inclined to extirpate as Kulaks — into their fold.

It is interesting to study the phrasing of the manifestos produced by
these various parties. The language of political censure, monotonous
and repetitive as it is at any time, is further enfeebled here by a very
special Burmese problem. It seems that at some time, perhaps at the
turn of the century, when the Fathers of the Western Left were relaxing
with their families at the Berlin Tiergarten, they were much impressed
by the appearance, and by what they read of the habits, of certain
animals; and on the basis of this composed a short lexicon of execra-
tion, which unfortunately their political inheritors in all parts of the

world have taken over. In a Buddhist environment, however, such animals as hyenas, jackals and vultures, eaters of carrion-flesh, and not killers in their own right, occupy a highly honourable position. Much strain is therefore put upon the remaining clichés of political abuse. The Karens, who would probably be reactionary enough if ever they could seize power, call the present Government 'collaborators and stooges'; the Burmese army is ineptly described as the 'handmaid of the imperialists'; while the system is 'dominated by adulterers, thieves, dacoits, self-seekers, and those who are extremely vicious'. The P.V.O.s propose to wipe out 'such opportunists as bad-hats, landlords, counter-revolutionaries and deviationists' — deviationist having become here a meaningless term of abuse, since the P.V.O.s subscribe to no Party-line. They themselves, in fact, are described as deviationists by the Communists, who accuse them in their manifesto entitled 'Why we are fighting the P.V.O.' of 'sucking deliciously' the freshly spilt blood of fighters for freedom and democracy. Each party and movement reviles the others and the Government in power, as 'fascists' — another word from which the meaning has drained. All speak of the activities of their own side as an expression of that mystic entity, 'the people' — the people's Government, or the people's will.

To have completed this almost utter chaos, it would have been necessary only to introduce the warring religious factions, now endemic in Indo-China, but in Burma excluded by the universality of Buddhism. In the situation of this unfortunate country there is an element of grim Wellsian prediction come to fulfilment.

CHAPTER XXI

THE BUFFALO DANCE

STANDING on a high place in Pyinmana — the balcony of the railwaymen's flats — and looking out across the derelict rolling-stock, the scorched brick and twisted girders, one saw a glitter of fire, an encrusted brilliance of towers and turrets, that arose shining over at the edge of the town. Even at a mile's distance there was no doubt that this was some gaudy pretence, but of such a magnitude that a visit, even in this murderous sunshine, was not to be avoided.

Mr. Nair agreed to come with me and, cautiously picking our way through the pools of shadow, we made towards this lustrous illusion, through mean lanes scavenged by dogs which disease had clipped into grotesque, poodle shapes. We found a field full of Chinese pavilions with streaming banners, joss-houses, pagodas with many-tiered roofs, Tartar tents, huge kiosks with façades of peacocks and dog-faced lions. It was a city that might have been built by an Imperial army encamped for a lengthy siege, and in it had been assembled all the glorious beginnings of fair-ground architecture and carnival floats. It was extraordinary what opulence had been achieved merely by the endless variegation of colours — mostly metallic — and decorative shapes with which every surface had been closely covered. In their erection of this dreamland of wood and paper, the people of Pyinmana seemed to have reacted in an understandable way to the drabness of civic reality. There was something defiant in its spurning of the realities. At night-time there would be theatrical shows, and boxers would dance in their corners before butting and clawing each other behind the peacock façades; but in the meantime, the place was deserted with the exception of a small crowd gathered at a booth in a corner to watch a nat-pwè.

The booth was roughly built of woven bamboo, its floor covered with matting. There was a shelf running round three sides, and on this the images of the thirty-seven nats squatted moodily. They were a poor collection of idols. Reflecting the fall in dramatic pitch of Burmese life, such god-like attributes as a dozen arms, each raised to flourish a sword, had disappeared, discarded in the nat evolution as something now as useless as the tail in humans. The convincing malevolence of some of the images to be seen in collections, carved in the days when the nats presided at human sacrifices, inspired spectacular dacoities and bullied kings, was missing here. These were the mean faces of black-marketeers, of usurers calculating percentages and premeditating fore-closure. Among the images was a gilded buffalo mask, also unimpressive as a work of art. The horns were entwined with leaves and sprigs of herbs.

At the moment of my arrival two stout, middle-aged Burmese women were weaving about in a dance in the cleared space before the images. The dance had no particular form; there were none of the symbolical hand or head movements imported from India into the South-East Asian dance, and none of the painfully learned acrobatics of the Burmese. These were the spontaneous gyrations of the devotees of a West-Indian revivalist cult, preceding, perhaps, an orgy of testifying. The shapeless robes went with the dance. There was an orchestra of drums, gongs, and a squealing hné; and its members, playing with a zest bordering on fury, kept the dancers in a continuous whirl. Before the dancers had set themselves in motion helpers had bustled round them carefully adjusting their turbans, but these immediately became untied, allowing their hair to stream from them like black comet tails. With eyes closed they collided with each other and went spinning away in new directions. Cheek-bones and foreheads took on a polish of sweat; foam bespattered their chins. The women helpers dashed after them with bottles of beer, which the dancers sucked at sightlessly and showered back through mouths and nostrils. The audience remained strangely untouched by this frenzy. They laughed and chatted sociably, and gave the breast to their young babies. Although all were drably and poorly dressed by Burmese standards, there must have been some who were socially important, because acolytes kept coming and presenting them with sprigs of greenery. Suddenly there was a stir of interest. The dancers, colliding once again, had fallen to the ground. Now they writhed on their stomachs towards the nat images, and having reached them remained to pray convulsively.

The priest was tall for a Burman, and I could not help fancying that he bore a facial resemblance to certain of the nats. There was an impudent self-possession about him. He was quite clearly a powerful person, a stork among the frogs. I was struck once again by the extraordinary similarity between professional counterparts of different races. I had seen this face, this confident and slightly contemptuous manner, in Haiti; but that time it had been a voodoo houngan. Before beginning his part of the ceremony the priest sent one of his assistants, who was importantly dressed in a threadbare British officer's uniform, to tell me to remove my sandals, and not to take photographs when he danced. Although I was not actually inside the booth, and therefore technically showing no disrespect, I decided to acquiesce in the first demand, and to ignore the second, although with discretion.

Taking up a spray of leaves in each hand the priest went into an easy, swinging dance. He waved the leaves about as a Jamaican obeahman might have waved a pair of maracas. After a time he stopped and signalled gropingly, eyes closed, for the buffalo mask to be brought. At this the crowd stiffened. The amiable gossip died away. Spitting out their cheroots, the members of the orchestra struck out in a new, purposeful rhythm. The mask was handed to the priest by one of the fat dancers. She held it at arm's length, and he took it from her, and keeping it about a foot from his face, began another stage of the dance. This consisted in mimicking the actions of a buffalo charging, turning away, charging again; directed at first one section, then another of the shrinking crowd. He then stopped, put on the mask, and immediately fell down. The drama of the moment was much heightened by the crash of drums and gongs. These barbaric and wonderfully timed musical effects jarred one for a hair-raising fraction of a second into a sensation of the reality in the performance.

The buffalo-priest lay writhing on the ground. At the end of the convulsion he raised himself painfully to his knees, and then charged, head down — with remarkable speed in view of his posture — into a group of children who fled screaming from the booth. He was restrained from following them, and from charging in other directions by the prayers, the entreaties, the strokings, of several of his female followers. Finally, quietened down, he was led, still on hands and knees, to a large enamelled basin, in which floated bananas and green herbs. Thus the ceremony culminated in the man's making a ritual meal — of buffalo food. Pushing his face beneath the mask down into the bowl, he caught a banana in his teeth, and emerging, ate half of it complete with skin. After that, the buffalo mask was untied and put back on the shelf, and while the priest was led away into the background to recover, the female dancers prepared themselves once more to go into action.

What was the meaning of this ritual? Clearly the women were nat-ka-daws — spirit wives, and professional prophetesses, whom I had read all about in a little booklet on the subject, published in Burma. Nat-ka-daws prophesy publicly on such occasions, and by private arrangement on the payment of a small fee. It is a regular and recognized profession, of which there are so many members that it has been seriously suggested that they should be classified under their own occupational heading in the forthcoming census of Burma. They differ from spirit mediums in most other parts of the world in that they are considered as married to the insatiably polygamistic nats who possess them, and who through them convey their wishes and decisions to animistic Burmese humanity. Such a relationship usually begins with the nat falling in love with the woman. According to my Burmese authority, he visits her at night, well-perfumed and 'dressed in up-to-date clothes' (and one quails before the vision of a Mongolian folk-hero in an American-style, flowered sports-shirt and a plastic belt). When actually in possession of his lady-love, he can be expelled by a saya — an expert in white magic — or (in the Colonial days) by an officer of the Crown in full uniform. Nothing is said in the booklet about a nat's reaction to Burmese republican officials. Normally, however, a woman's relations or friends would not interfere, because, just as possession by a lwa carries social prestige among the Haitian adherents of the voodoo cult, it is a paying proposition in the lower strata of Burmese society for a woman to become the bride of a nat.

The union is regularized at the bridegroom's expense, with mystical entertainments on a lavish scale, the nat usually being represented by another wife, to whom the bride is solemnly given away by her parents or guardians. The occasion is one for rejoicing. The girl has been recognized by the powerful guild of nat-ka-daws as one of themselves. From that time on she earns an easy living by fortune-telling, or, if she decides to go into business, the capital is put up 'by the nat', that is to say by the wealthy and powerful association of his wives. Nat-ka-daws, owing to their prestige and power among their neighbours, prosper in all their enterprises. The principal drawback to this arrangement appears to be that a girl who has married a nat cannot re-marry without his permission, which is rarely given. But a most fortunate aspect of the matter lies in the fact that the nats are said to prefer spiritual to physical charm, and that women whose lack of attractions has kept them single are often married off in this way. The union is supposed to be far from platonic, and the nat's visits, in incubus shape, are said to be more frequent than those of a normal husband.

Here as elsewhere the phenomenon of possession is accompanied, according to medical evidence, by some physical change; the heart's action is increased, cheeks are flushed, respiration is shallow and of the thoracic type; the subject sweats profusely, reaches a kind of cataleptic state with complete insensibility to pain, and, when questions are answered, often replies in a masculine voice. These and other signs are closely observed by experts, who decide whether possession has taken place, and who are also able to decide by variations of manner and expression which nat is involved. It is particularly interesting that a nat-ka-daw when possessed by Shwe-Na-be, the dragon nat, writhes and wriggles in snake-like fashion, in exactly the same way as do devotees of the voodoo cult when possessed by dumballa, the West African serpent-god. After learning something of the nat-ka-daws, I now realized for the first time what the Jesuit Borri had meant when he had said, writing in the seventeenth century, that it was considered highly honourable in Indo-China to become the wife of the devil, and that such unions were much indulged in by upper-class Annamese women, who sometimes produced eggs as a result. It now seemed clear to me that at one time formal matches with the spirits were arranged by other Mongolian peoples than the Burmese, and that it might have been — and might still be in remote parts of the Indo-Chinese peninsula — a fairly wide-spread custom, linked up with the legendary oviparous kings.

It remains to offer a possible explanation of the buffalo dance, to hazard a guess at the legendary or even historical occasion that had inspired it — since other animistic ceremonies, and in particular the one at Taungbyon, re-enact in dramatic form some tragic story that has become ineradicably fixed in folk-memory. I had never heard of a buffalo-nat before, and it is certainly not included in the exclusive original circle of the Thirty-seven. The only explanation, therefore, that I can offer is based upon the remark of an onlooker, who said that the ceremony commemorated the ravaging of the country in ancient times by a buffalo.

In my superficial studies of Burmese history, limited to what has been translated into English, I have been able to find only one note-worthy mention of a buffalo. This occurs in the description of the great King Anawhrata's death. Although the Burmese kings in their lifetimes conformed sometimes to the prosaic pattern of history, as we understand it, the manner of their deaths — particularly that of Anawhrata — was often Arthurian. The king had been returning from a profitable expedition, during which he had built monasteries, dams, channels, reservoirs and canals, and was just entering the city gates of Pagan when a hunter approached to report that a wild buffalo called Çakkhupala was ravaging the countryside. On hearing this the king turned back, with the pious intention of ridding his people of this menace. He was surrounded by seven thousand ministers, and at the head of four armies, but, says the chronicle, 'the moral karma of the king's former acts was exhausted'. The buffalo, which had been an enemy in a previous life, charged and reached over the back of the royal elephant, and gored the king to death. So the king's ministers and his hosts, his queens, the fifty hump-backed women and the fifty bandy-legged women who served him wearing livery of gold, the

[facing: NAT-KA-DAWS — WIVES OF THE SPIRITS

women to sound tabors, the women-drummers, harpists and trumpeters, all broke up and scattered in confusion.

What are the facts that have been transmuted here into a dream? Did the nation, symbolized in the person of the king, undergo a tragic experience, suffering perhaps at ·this time — or even centuries earlier, since the annals are very confused — defeat at the hands of invaders whose totem was the buffalo? An interesting speculation. Burmese written history which speaks of a succession of 587,000 kings, and omitted from the records events which failed to conform to sacred predictions, is not necessarily more reliable than the legends of the people. But, at all events, it seemed likely that here was all that remained in the popular memory of an ancient tragedy, whatever it was: a piece of self-hypnotic mumbo-jumbo, and two fat women who believed themselves to be the brides of a demon.

Night, which lay like a stifling cloak upon Pyinmana, brought no relief from the heat. In the station precincts, there was a curious gathering of passengers, and of those who used the station-yard for their social promenadings, in a long line on each side of the train which would leave next morning for Rangoon. The J.S.M. came teetering up to explain. He was sucking an American Cream Soda through a straw in the belief that it was country spirit, and his expression, as the beads of perspiration formed and followed regular channels down his face, was of a man bravely enduring torture. The people, the J.S.M. explained, were waiting for the water-truck. At any moment an engine would draw it along the rails past our train, stopping at each carriage to fill up the small cistern carried in the roof. Usually there was an overflow from each cistern, and those who were waiting would catch the surplus, or as much as they could of it, in their cups, or just wet their clothes with it.

Shortly afterwards the water-tanker came along, with an entourage of well-dressed citizens, who, as the water streamed down the coaches, pressed themselves tightly against the woodwork, or even got down on the track and crouched by the wheels to allow the water to trickle on their upturned faces, their chests, their backs. Some of

facing: POSSESSED BY THE BUFFALO-SPIRIT]

the men stripped off their shirts, soaked them and put them on again.

Finding that while the passengers luxuriated in momentary damp-
ness our compartment had been left empty, I went in to begin the
stealthy massacre of the mosquitoes and cockroaches, a task which I
had carried out in several furtive instalments on the journey from
Mandalay to Yamethin. This time I was less successful. All the cockroaches, which were as tame and trusting, and as fat in their way as
monastery catfish, were disposed of in a few seconds, and I was quite
absorbed with the mosquitoes, which could be caught in the air, sometimes two at a time, and squashed by closing the fist, when I heard a
sound like a slight groan. Mr. Pereira had hoisted himself silently into
the carriage, and was standing behind me, his eye fixed on the corpse
of a cockroach, lying feet uppermost in the middle of the floor. Did
I realize, he asked me, as soon as he could get command of his voice,
that this poor, assassinated creature might quite well be my grandfather
in another incarnation? The obvious answer to this was that had my
grandfather indeed been reincarnated as a Burmese cockroach, I should
have regarded it as an act of kindness to release him from what seemed
to me — and would probably, from what I remembered of him, have
seemed to him — an unsatisfactory existence. This only produced a
sermon on Kan and Karma, on cause and effect, into which the matter
of merit-acquisition, and thence, pagoda-building inevitably entered.
Rebellious at last, I asked him if he didn't think that in his own case,
it would have been equally, or even more, meritorious to have given
his money to the Mandalay leper asylum. The classic answer would
have been, not at all, because the lepers were working off in their
present unfortunate condition the adverse balance of their karma,
created through misdeeds in previous existences, and there was therefore nothing much to be done about it. But by this time Mr. Pereira
had recovered himself completely and, remembering the need for
Absolute Tolerance, however mistaken a point of view, mildly agreed
that it might have been a good thing — the soft answer that turneth
away wrath, which, in his case, meant one more mark on the credit
side of the balance.

Thus the dreadful night wore on. Since the departure platform of the Rangoon train had become also the town's social centre, there was an enduring babel, in which the keynote was sounded by a mad woman who stood in a clear place for many hours, haranguing the crowd. She was well dressed and cared for, and whenever her hair, which was crowned with cornflowers, escaped its bounds, someone would re-arrange it for her. Because of the dry quality of the heat, the tempta-tions and pleasures of life had been simplified, and reduced to the alleviation of thirst. The devil presiding over the delights involved was a dreaming, white-bearded Hindu, who kept a stall with bottles of Vimto and American Cream Soda. His stock, besides these, con-sisted of a block of ice, and an ordinary carpenter's plane. When a drink was ordered, he would get the cap off the bottle after a long struggle, take a glass out of a slop-pail full of dirty water, and pour in the contents of the bottle. Then he would unwrap the block of ice from its grimy sacking, plane off a sliver, crumple it and put it in the glass, when it would instantly vanish, as if plunged into boiling water. He was agonizingly slow, and as these bottles of branded mineral waters are supposed in any case to contain a quantity nicely calculated not quite to quench the thirst, the only thing to do was to keep a standing order. Once the ice ran out, and there was a long delay while another block was dragged by means of a pair of clamps and a chain along the platform.

About midnight, I carried away what remained of the old man's bottles, went back to the carriage and climbed into my bunk. Mr. Pereira, although not asleep, seemed pleasantly relaxed. 'This evening, Mr. Nair, I was able to obtain my customary Wincarnis. I believe that I shall pass a good night.'

The J.S.M. by ransacking the town had found a supply of country spirit and was occupied by delusions of grandeur. A rumbling John-sonian undertone had entered his speech.

'Yesterday was it? — No, of course, it could not have been yester-day — but no matter — I encountered at the residence of a friend of mine, where I was taking food, the A.D.P.W. (Assistant Director of Permanent Ways). After saluting him, I broached the matter of pro-motion.'

'And what response did he vouchsafe?'

'My dear colleague — ' (the voice faltered, with a sudden alcoholic change in the wind's direction) 'he invited me to get to hell.'

'The dickens he did! These buggers are all the same.'

The next day was passed among the parched greys and yellows of harvested paddy-fields, which now awaited the rains. From this dun wilderness arose nothing but a skyline serration of pagodas, and the low formless silhouettes of towns which had once been dynastic capitals, the greatest and most glorious of South-East Asia in their day. '... The streetes thereof are the fayrest that I have seene ... the lodgings within are made of wood all over gilded, with fine pinacles, and very costly worke, covered with plates of golde.' Thus wrote Caesar Fredericke of the capital of the kingdom of Pegu, now dissolved in anarchy. The names of these towns were now, as we passed through them, the motive of a melancholy commentary. Ela. 'That was a nice place. It was a coaling station, but it has been burned several times, also recently. Steel Brothers' saw-mill, also burned down.' Toungoo. 'These are territories dominated by the Karens. Much damage has been done. I do not think they can rebuild. It is stated that the leaders have offered ceremonial food to the monks who will present a petition for amnesty. Also these men's leader Saw Tapu Lay is observing daily Sabbath. I do not know. But still shooting continues with all modern weapons, and the dropping of bombs.' Pegu. 'Mostly there are Communists who will not agree that food shall come into this town. Therefore all the paddy remains in the villages, and the farmers cannot eat so much rice. They would like to sell this paddy to the Government who will pay rupees 285 per hundred bags. But this rice they may not sell and they cannot eat it. In this town the people do not eat. It is very ruined.'

CHAPTER XXII

THE SHWEDAGON

IN Rangoon the great annual pagoda festival was being held, that of the full moon of Tabaung, which coincides with Easter in the West. The Shwedagon Pagoda is the heart and soul of Rangoon, the chief place of pilgrimage in the Buddhist world, the Buddhist equivalent of the Kaaba at Mecca, and, in sum, a great and glorious monument. 'The fairest place, as I suppose,' thought Ralph Fitch, 'that is in the world.' Fitch had seen the splendours of the Mogul Empire, and it is a consolation to think that as the Shwedagon has been, if anything, improved since Elizabethan days, there still exists one tiny oasis, in a desert of pinchbeck modernity, where the prodigious glamour of the ancient Orient endures.

The special sanctity of the Shwedagon arises from the fact that it is the only pagoda recognized as enshrining relics not only of Gautama, but of the three Buddhas preceding him. Those of the Master consist of eight hairs, four of them original, given in his lifetime, and four others, miraculous reproductions generated from them in the course of their journey from India. These, according to the account in the official guidebook, flew up, when the casket containing them was opened, to a height of seven palm trees. They emitted rays of variegated hues, which caused the dumb to speak, the deaf to hear, and the lame to walk. Later, a rain of jewels fell, covering the earth to knee's depth. The treasure buried with these relics was of such value that, centuries later, the report of it reached the ears of the King of China, who made a magic figure in human form, and sent it to rob the shrine. This creature, says the chronicle, was so dazzled by the pagoda's appearance, that it hesitated, and while in this bemused state was attacked and cut to pieces by the Shwedagon's spirit-guardians. It was the habit of the Burmese kings to make extravagant gifts for the embellishment of the Shwedagon, diamond vanes, jewel-encrusted finial umbrellas, or at least their weight in gold, to be used in re-gilding the spire. The wealth that other Oriental princes kept in vaults and coffers was here spread out under the sun to astound humanity. Two of the three greatest bells in the world were cast and hung here. Both were seized by foreigners — one by the Portuguese, and one by the British — and both, causing the capsizal of the ships that carried them away, were sunk in the river. Shinsawbu, Queen of the Talaungs, won so much respect by building the great terrace and the walls, that the most flattering thing the Burmese could think of to say about Queen Victoria was that she was a reincarnation of this queen.

Early on the morning of Good Friday, when the festival was at its height, I took a car out to the pagoda to gather a few last-minute impressions of the Burmese *en fête*. The Shwedagon lies three or four miles to the north of the town. The last quarter of a mile I covered on foot, while ahead a volcano of gold rose slowly up from among the trees, into the dusty blue of the sky. Pilgrims, when afar off, prostrate themselves in the direction of this cone as it comes first into sight. The road was lined with shrines and monsters. Streams of jeeps went past, taking early-morning worshippers. A few of them were disguised with a carnival decoration of cardboard peacocks, and were carrying boys, about to enter the novitiate, to pray at the pagoda before the ceremony began. The boys wore expensive imitations of the old Burmese court dress, with gilt helmets and epaulets like sprouting wings, and their attendants struggled to hold golden umbrellas over their heads.

I left my shoes with a flower-seller at the entrance to the covered stairway, bought some flowers from her, and began to climb the steps. There were two or three hundreds of them, left purposely rough and uneven — like the *pavé* in a French village — to ensure a slow and respectful approach. All the way up, there were stalls selling flowers, gongs, votive offerings, and ugly toys. Barefooted crowds were climbing and descending the steps with the murmuring of hushed voices, and the rustle of harsh, new silks. The air was full of the odour of flowers standing in vases. From somewhere above, light was spreading down the dark shaft, and from its source, too, the sound — like a deep, melodious breathing — of gongs.

Coming out of the cavernous approach on to the wide, glistening expanse of terrace, I plunged suddenly into the most brilliant spectacle I had ever seen. Fitch, a merchant adventurer, who had surveyed without comment the splendours of the Venice, the Ormuz, the Goa and the East Indies of his day, had stood here in admiration, although unable to refrain from a sour aside on the vanity of consuming gold in such a way. The terrace is flanked by shrines, with a press of guardian ogres, fabulous beasts, and mild-faced, winged gorgons squeezed in between and behind them; and then, in the immediate background, rises a golden escarpment, a featureless cliff of precious metal, spreading a misty dazzlement, in which the crawling shapes of pilgrims, sticking on their gold-leaf, are black, vaguely seen insects.

The innumerable foreground shrines were banked with flowers, and decked with the votive parasols which usefully protect an image from the sun in a tropical country, and often replace the candles necessary to light its cavern in the north. Round the glittering pyramid went Rangoon's Easter-parade of the gay and the devout. When they wanted to pray — which they did most poetically, with offerings of flowers held between the clasped palms — there were hundreds of images to choose from, of gold, of silver, of marble or wood. (Like most peoples who incline themselves before images, Buddhists insist with the gravest emphasis that they are not worshipping the material object, but the great principle it represents.) People worshipped individually, or in groups, in the large shrines or out in the hot sunshine of the terrace, prostrating themselves vaguely towards the spire of the pagoda. Year old babies were lowered tenderly into the ritual position, where, often unable to straighten themselves, they sprawled in adoration, until recovered. On this day there were many ways to acquire merit: by buying water (in petrol cans) from the sellers and pouring it over the images that sat in the hot sun; by re-lighting candles that had gone out, and re-placing parasols that had fallen down; by taking up the deer's antlers provided, and striking a gong, and then the ground beneath it, to call the attention of the nats of the earth and sky to the worshipper's prayers.

Until the recent troublous times Buddhists from all over the East,

journeying as freely as did European pilgrims to Santiago de Com-
postela and Monte Sant' Angelo, visited the Shwedagon for this
festival. Now, apart from the Burmese, there were only Thibetans,
whose tenacious piety nothing could daunt.

A few hundred yards from the foot of the pagoda, the Government
had organized a secular festival, a combination of a pwè and industrial
samples-fair, that was not quite successfully one thing or the other. At
night it came to vociferous life beneath the golden symbol of renunciation shining in the moonlit sky above it.

There was an open-air theatre with an actress and two clowns, but
it was not very good. Perhaps the atmosphere was wrong. The
formal organization seemed to have stripped the thing of its spon-
taneity. Although the loudspeakers poured out a tremendous babel of
noise, and the lights hurt the eyes, this could not compare for authentic
quality with the pwès got up by the neighbours of the various districts
of Kemmendine.

I spent half an hour watching the boxing, noticing that pongyis
were allowed in to see this ungodly spectacle without charge. Half
the audience were members of the yellow robe. The boxers came out
and prostrated themselves, foreheads touching the ground, to their
corners; the obeisance was returned by their seconds. The challenger
then executed a very slow war-dance to the music of drums and
flutes, stopping occasionally to beat himself on the chest in the Tarzan
manner. After that the opponents advanced towards each other with
ballet steps, like *Ramayana* champions about to hurl fiery javelins.
Suddenly they went into action, leaping into the air like fighting-cocks.
There was much initial flurry, an exciting spectacle lasting a few
seconds, when both men tried to floor each other with flying kicks.
But this exuberance soon died down, as it does in fighting-cocks too.
A clinch followed with unrestricted use of knees, fists and elbows.
The winner is decided when, as a spectator explained, 'the first blood
oozes out'. With typical regard for foreign susceptibilities this man
was kindly doing his best to outline the rules governing the contest,
when he was roughly interrupted by a forthright Westernized fellow

who said, 'Nothing is debarred to them. They may even kick each other in the sensitive parts.'

At midnight a straight theatrical show started in one of the tents, and I sampled an hour of a performance that would go on all night. The first scene showed a young Burman engaged in the hopeless courtship of a girl who, it was made clear, led him on, only to spurn him cruelly. At first she smiled, but the moment he approached, her smile turned to a grimace of contempt. These tactics were repeated several times. It was most baffling. But then the scene changed and we were whisked back in time a hundred years or so, to be present at a function of the court, with our hero in a previous existence as a prince, and the lady who had first been treating him with such unexplained malice, in the role of a minor lady of the palace. By their gestures it was evident that the prince had trifled with her affections, and was now casting her off in favour of one more suited to his station. The scene changed again . . . and so did the epoch. What an aid to a flagging plot, to be able to extend the device of the flash-back, not only to the characters' pasts, but to their previous incarnations! But also, alas, how it holds up the action!

Much of the industrial section of the festival could not have been more boring. As most native Burmese industries are still in the planning stage, there was little to see. One booth gave a soap-making demonstration; another tried to extract drama from the workings of an automatic self-photographing machine; a third displayed a revolting collection of Kewpie dolls, under a banner which said, 'Burma makes fine rubber toys'. But there was one exhibit — and it was the main one — which amply compensated for the dullness of the rest. This was the pavilion the Government had taken for its anti-corruption campaign. The Burmese have no objection at all to the washing of dirty linen in public, and at this time Burmese newspapers were full of stories of the various rackets practised by Government officials. The current scandal was over import-licences, in which, it seemed, a great trade was going on. They were usually obtained by persons who had no experience whatever, and no capital, but who happened to have a friend or relative in the Government. Sometimes such shadow-firms, with accommodation addresses, turned out, upon investigation, to be conducted by the wives of the high officials themselves. In any case, the licence when granted was sold to a firm of established reputation, usually at a price equal to the landed value of the goods — ninety per cent of which, however, was paid by the intermediary, or shadow firm, as a bribe to the official granting the licence. As an immediate result of this system, the prices of the imported goods affected were enormously increased, usually to double the normal figure, or more. What was more pernicious in the long run, from the national point of view, was that although in a desperate financial condition, Burma found itself importing all kinds of useless luxuries upon which this toll could be levied. One of the letters published in the press instanced the licences granted to import silk from Japan, which Burma, as a silk producer, does not require. The importers turned out to be a timber-cutting company and a flour mill.

In the Anti-Corruption Pavilion, these manipulators were dealt with, with a hint of defeatism, perhaps, as far as this life went. Seeming to resign themselves to the wicked man's prosperity in this world, the Burmese Government had set themselves to show what awaited him in the next. For their illustrated fable they had chosen a mild fellow of average virtue and weakness, lifted from a comic-strip or toothpaste advertisement, and his downfall was ascribed to the promptings of an ambitious wife, a fact which drew much protest in the Rangoon press from feminists.

In the first of a series of pictures he is shown relaxing from departmental cares in the surroundings of a modest home, listening thoughtfully to the pleadings of his wife, who, seated on the arm of the sofa, bends over him to pour the poison of covetousness into his ear. In Picture Two, he has already sold his soul to the devil. The furniture has been modernized, and there is a big radio-set on the table. The honest mediocrity of his appearance has been rectified. He wears a made-up turban. His wife — since the dress of Burmese women has reached an apex of taste which no mere access of ill-gotten wealth can assail — is as before; but there is a twinkle of gems at her throat. Picture Three. Having over-eaten, the husband dies of an acute attack of indigestion. His soul is seen leaving his body. In a vertical position, and respectably clothed, it floats upwards, and is about to pass through a modernistic candelabra. Four. A judge of hell receives him, in appropriately Dantesque surroundings; a rocky area, where huge vultures perch at intervals. The judge is dressed, with the solid conservatism of the last generation, in the Burmese equivalent of a morning suit and top-hat. Picture Five. It now comes to light that the young man has only once accepted a bribe and, most fortunately, it is also discovered that the link connecting soul and body is not quite severed. He is to be given another chance. But to make sure the warning has not been lost, the judge first takes him on a brief, conducted tour of hell, which is organized, on Gilbert and Sullivan lines, to make the punishment fit the crime. Thus arms-traffickers are chased by ravening hounds across a landscape set with bayonets. Corrupt Public Works Department officials are run over by ghostly replicas of their steamrollers. Excise men who have succumbed stagger blindly through a ravine seething with the fumes of noxious liquors. Co-operative officials who misappropriate rations queue up, ration card in hand, for molten silver to be poured down their throats. Railway executives who sell privilege tickets and take bribes for freight priorities are flogged by demons with lengths of rail. Meanwhile, as the final vision reveals, the unfortunate young man's wife has already re-married, and is busily engaged in spending his loot with her new husband.

First reaction to this morality: if a Burmese evil-doer could really be deterred by such propaganda — and the Government evidently thought he could — it showed that heaven and hell were nearer to a Buddhist than I had ever suspected. Secondly, I found it hard to think of the Burmese woman, outwardly so tranquil and so demure, in the role of a Lady Macbeth.

The organization of such a show struck me as a praiseworthy and heartening attitude on the part of the government of Burma, which, whatever its failings, possesses in full measure the politically saving grace of self-criticism. They knew that their administration was riddled with corruption, and instead of trying to hush it up, they gave it all the publicity they could. And that, it seemed to me, was the quickest way to mend matters.

No one could have been more cheerfully frank about their short-comings and their failures than the Burmese. Were things better in the British times? Nine out of ten of them laughed out loud at the absurdity of such a question. 'Better? . . . Why even bring it up? Everyone was well off then. We didn't know how well off we were.' The Burmese seem to be above nursing old scores, and they either forget or pretend to forget the other side of the picture — the disdains and exclusions by which it was made clear to them that they were regarded, in their own country, as an inferior people. The Burmese never bitterly remind the British visitor of this, and he is freely welcomed by them within the portals of those institutions from which they were debarred.

But in any case these were the minor irritations of the skin, which did not amount to much, except as symptoms of a deep-seated ailment. What was really wrong was that under colonial tutelage the Burmese or any other people lost — or as in this case were in the process of losing — their national character. The only culture they could rebuild for themselves was never much more than a poor, provincial imitation of that of the occupying power. Colonies — and Burma was an example — were sometimes prosperous, but colonial prosperity is a wretched substitute for lost nationhood. Before they could be real Burmese again, and not — at least, so far as the upper classes went — imitation Englishmen, the Burmese had to stand on their own feet, and left to fend for themselves. Whatever the temporary material consequences, I regard it as the greatest possible good fortune for them that this has happened.

And now on the eve of my departure from Burma, I re-gathered my impressions in an attempt to form some kind of personal estimate of this fascinating country's prospects. From my record of the present-day somewhat chaotic travelling conditions, the reader may have deduced a pessimism which would not be altogether justified. The

Burmese nation stands upon foundations, both economic and psychological, of peculiar solidity. These provide a resilience which has pulled it safely through several historic crises of the gravest kind.

To deal with the psychological aspect; Burma has, in the first place, the extreme fortune to be entirely free from the damaging myths of colour, race and caste, that bedevil the internal relationships of so many nations. Secondly, it has freed itself from Western domination almost with the ease of removing an unwanted garment. As a result, no trace of bitterness remains, and a Westerner can travel with at least as much safety as a Burmese from one end of the country to the other, meeting, as I did, with nothing but the most genial and touching hospitality. Then, once again, owing to the nation's background of Buddhist indoctrination it is free from the delusion — the bane of the West, and much of the East — of the supreme value of material accumulation. There is some corruption and money-grubbing in high places, but real prestige in Burma — and it is very real — lies not with the millionaire, but with the penniless monk. On the national scale this means that there is no reason why the Burmese should not avoid or by-pass that grim interlude in human development heralded in the West by the Industrial Revolution, and rest content to live within their present very adequate means, leaving Tennessee Valley Projects and their like to those who believe that the kingdom of heaven on earth will be here when every family has its refrigerator, as well as two cars in the garage. I state here my sincere belief that the average Burmese peasant working his own land, lives a fuller and happier life, and is a more successful human being than the average Western factory hand or office worker. His work is creative, free of clock-punching and deadly routine, and allows him an enormous amount of leisure, which he consumes with expertness and relish. From the leisure aspect only, it is the difference between filling in coupons, and keeping one's own fighting-cocks; between standing in the four and sixes on Sunday afternoon, and the full-blooded pleasures of a three-day pwè.

As for the material basis for Burma's future, it is excellent. The country is wonderfully fertile, and reasonably populated. That is to say that without much effort enough food can be grown for everyone.

Even in the present state of tragic disorder the Burmese can still export annually several million tons of rice. All that is necessary, then, is to cure the people of their infantile craving for manufactured trash from overseas that fills their markets, and to import only essential medicines, hospital equipment, means of transport and agricultural machinery. If necessary a little teak could be cut, and oil pumped to help pay for this. While the population stays at its present level the Burmese need neither kolhozes nor Boulder Dams (nor, since they cannot afford an atomic pile, do they need armaments); and there is no mysterious natural law which compels a country to produce a greater population than its own soil can support. Above all, they do not need the glittering baubles described in the advertisement sections of American magazines. The Burmese way of life has never been based on unnecessary consumption, and there is no reason why it ever should. It is as good as any, as it is.

It now remains for the Burmese to compose their differences, to cease to be intoxicated by reach-me-down political formulae and to split doctrinal hairs while the dismemberment of their country goes unheeded. If this can be done (and as yet there is not the slightest sign of it), all that remains is to avoid as the plague all alliances that may lead to their country's being crushed between the millstones of the East and West, and to settle down to the carrying out of those just agrarian reforms upon which all political parties seem to be agreed. Herein lies a simple blueprint for Utopia.

INDEX

TRAVELS
WITH MYSELF
AND
ANOTHER

MARTHA GELLHORN

'I was seized by the idea of this book while sitting on a rotten little beach at the western tip of Crete, flanked by a waterlogged shoe and a rusted potty ... This is not a proper travel book: it is an account of my best horror journeys, chosen from a wide range, recollected with tenderness now that they are past.'

Must surely be ranked as one of the funniest travel books of our time – second only to *A Short Walk in the Hindu Kush* ... It doesn't matter whether this author is experiencing marrow-freezing misadventures in war-ravaged China, or driving a landrover through East African game-parks, or conversing with hippies in Israel, or spending a week in a Moscow Intourist Hotel. Martha Gellhorn's reactions are what count and one enjoys equally her blistering scorn of humbug, her hilarious eccentricities, her unsentimental compassion.
Dervla Murphy, The Irish Times

Spun with a fine blend of irony and epigram. She is incapable of writing a dull sentence.
The Times

Miss Gellhorn has a novelist's eye, a flair for black comedy and a short fuse ... There is not a boring word in her humane and often funny book.
The New York Times

THREE CAME HOME

A woman's ordeal in a Japanese prison camp

AGNES KEITH

When the Japanese swept through Borneo in 1942, Agnes Keith was captured with her two-year-old son. Even though keeping notes was a capital offence, she wrote a diary on the backs of labels and in the margins of old newspapers, which she buried in tins or sewed inside her son's home-made toys. Unlike many other narrators of camp life, Agnes Keith gives an honest and rounded description of her Japanese captors. The camp commander, Colonel Suga, was responsible for a forced march which killed all but three out of 2,970 prisoners; yet he regularly took children for joy-rides in his car, stuffing them with sweets, and sending them back to camp with armfuls of flowers from his garden.

This is one of the most remarkable books you will every read.
John Carey, The Sunday Times

No one who reads her unforgettable narrative of the years she passed in Borneo during the war can fail to share her emotions with something very like the intensity of personal experience.
The Times Literary Supplement

Three Came Home should rank with the great imprisonment stories of all times.
The New York Herald Tribune

SCUM
OF THE
EARTH

ARTHUR KOESTLER

At the beginning of the Second World War, Koestler was living in the South of France working on *Darkness at Noon*. After retreating to Paris he was imprisoned as an undesirable alien, even though he had been a crusader against fascism. He was brutally treated, and it was typical that, when he had to empty the latrine bins, a sadistic guard wouldn't allow him to wear gloves. He was, though, luckier than the many other innocent refugees who were handed over to the Nazis for torture or execution. *Scum of the Earth* is more than the story of Koestler's survival among these horrors: it is also a description of what happpens when a nation loses its honour and its pride.

A memorable story, vivid, powerful and deeply searching.
The Times Literary Supplement

This is a book in a thousand, by far the best book to come out of the collapse of France.
The Guardian

Koestler's personal history of France at War. It is, I think, the finest book that has come out of that cauldron.
New York Herald Tribune.

THE HONOURED SOCIETY

The Sicilian Mafia observed

NORMAN LEWIS

Epilogue by Marcello Cimino

Norman Lewis describes how, after Mussolini came close to destroying the Mafia, the U.S. army returned them to power in 1944. Henceforth they infiltrated every aspect of Sicilian life, corrupting landowners, the police, the judiciary, and even the church. In one of the most astonishing chapters, the author tells the story of how an eighty-year-old priest, Padre Camelo, led his monks on escapades of murder and extortion, frequently using the confessional box for transmitting threats.

One of the great travel writers of our time.
Eric Newby, The Observer

This book has not a dull moment in it; it is indeed imbued with that quality of terribilita which Giuliano himself was said to possess.
The Spectator

It is deftly written, and every page is horribly absorbing.
The Times

The Honoured Society is the most penetrating book ever written on the Mafia.
Time Out

NAPLES '44

An Intelligence Officer in the Italian labyrinth

NORMAN LEWIS

Norman Lewis arrived in Naples as an Intelligence Officer attached to the American Fifth Army. By 1944 the city's inhabitants were so destitute that all the tropical fish in the aquarium had been devoured, and even respectable women had been driven to prostitution. The mafia gradually became so indispensable to the occupying forces that it succeeded in regaining its former power. Despite the cruelty and suffering he encountered, Norman Lewis writes in this diary, 'A year among the Italians has converted me to such an admiration for their humanity and culture that were I given the chance to be born again, Italy would be the country of my choice'.

A wonderful book.
Richard West, The Spectator

As unique an experience for the reader as it must have been a unique experience for the writer.
Graham Greene

Here is a book of gripping fascination in its flow of bizarre anecdote and character sketch; and it is much more than that.
J.W. Lambert, The Sunday Times

One goes on reading page after page as if eating cherries.
Luigi Barzini, New York Review of Books

A VIEW OF
THE WORLD

Selected writings

NORMAN LEWIS

These twenty articles, written over a period of thirty years,
include an interview with Castro's executioner; a meeting
with a tragic Ernest Hemingway; a farcical trip to the Chocos of
Panama; a description of a fishing community in an unspoilt
Ibiza; an extraordinary story of bandits in the highlands of
Sardinia, and Lewis's famous report on the genocide of South
America's Indians.

I have no hesitation in calling Norman Lewis one of the best writers,
not of any particular decade, but of our century.
Graham Greene, reviewing The Missionaries in The Daily Telegraph

A View of the World will carry Norman Lewis's reputation even higher
than it already is. It is a triumph.
Patrick Marnham, The Literary Review

Everything is portrayed with a brilliance which makes all other
travel-writing read like the blurb on a brochure.
Time Out

Norman Lewis is outstandingly the best travel writer of our age, if not
the best since Marco Polo.
Auberon Waugh

PORTRAIT OF A TURKISH FAMILY

IRFAN ORGA

Afterword by Ateş Orga

Irfan Orga was born into a prosperous family of the old Turkey under the Sultans. His mother was a beauty, married at thirteen, and lived in the total seclusion befitting her class. His grandmother, who also lived in their home, was an eccentric autocrat, determined at all costs to maintain her traditional habits. The 1914 War, however, brought ruin to the family and a transformation to Turkey. The red fez was ousted by the cloth cap, and the family was forced to adapt to an unimaginably impoverished life. In 1941 Irfan Orga arrived in London where, seven years later, he wrote this extraordinary story of his family's survival.

This book is a little masterpiece.
Robert Fox, The Daily Telegraph

An unusually convincing autobiographical sketch. The entire portrait is good.
Peter Quennell, The Daily Mail

I hope that many people will read this book. As a story, it is intimate, original and moving, As a historical document, it gives a rare insight into the psychological transformation which has come over the unchanging East...A wholly delightful book.
Harold Nicolson, The Observer

It is just as though someone had opened a door marked 'Private' and showed you what was inside . . . A most interesting and affectionate book.
Sir John Betjeman

RITES

A childhood in Guatemala

VICTOR PERERA

Victor Perera's father, a talmudic scholar, was a first-generation immigrant who began as an itinerant pedlar, selling bolts of cloth to Indians. After arranging by post his marriage to a third-cousin from Jerusalem, he gradually became one of the capital's leading merchants. His son moved with a child's adaptability between the sheltered life of his bourgeois family and the catholic, anti-semitic, and sex-dominated world outside. While his Indian nurse, his white classmates, and his mestizo best friend were all destroyed by the violent character of life in Guatemala, Victor Perera managed to survive.

Rites is an important book for anyone who wants a fuller understanding of the reality of Central America... it alters our perception at a fundamental level.
San Francisco Chronicle

Perera writes with a constant sparkle.
Catholic Herald

One closes this short book with a sharpened perception not only of life in mid-twentieth century Guatemala, but of life in Latin America as a whole ... Perera demonstrates a lively wit on almost every page.
Times Literary Supplement

THE GINGER TREE

A novel

OSWALD WYND

In 1903 a 20-year-old Scots girl sailed to the Far East in order to marry a British military attaché in Peking. She soon horrifies the British community by having an affair with a Japanese soldier, Count Kurihama. As a result she is rejected by her husband and ostracised by her family. The Ginger Tree is the story of her survival in an alien culture.

What is so wonderful about the book is Oswald Wynd's ability to chart the mind of a completely unspoilt innocent Scottish girl, from her first chaperoned voyage to meet her fiancé in China, through the traumatic scandals that followed, and through her growing understanding of the Japanese mentality.
The New York Times

Highly enjoyable and has an almost documentary fascination.
The Times

Sensitively written, beautifully understated . . . this honest book is one of the few contemporary novels to show Japan as it was and is.
The Japan Times

I've read it twice, once because it swept me along on a wave of pure enjoyment, and a second time to pinpoint why this had been so. It is a quite extraordinary achievement.
Sue Earle, South China Morning Post

ELAND

53 Eland Road
London SW11 5JX
Fax 071–924 2229

All our books are printed on fine, pliable, cream-coloured
paper. Since 1984 they have been sewn as well as glued.
This gives larger margins in the gutter, as well as making
the books stronger.
We take immense trouble to select only the most readable
books. If you do not enjoy an Eland title, please send it
back to us, and we will refund the purchase price.

If you would like to be sent our catalogue, or to be
included in future mailing lists, write to us at the above
address.